Documents and Debates
General Editor: John Wroughton, M.A., F.R.Hist.S.

Politics, Religion and Society in Revolutionary England, 1640–1660

Howard Tomlinson
Headmaster,
Hereford Cathedral School

and

David Gregg
Head of Economics and Politics,
Bradfield College

MACMILLAN

First published 1989

Published by
MACMILLAN EDUCATION LTD
Houndmills, Basingstoke, Hampshire RG21 2XS
and London
Companies and representatives
throughout the world

Typeset by Wessex Typesetters
(Division of The Eastern Press Ltd)
Frome, Somerset

Printed in Hong Kong

British Library Cataloguing in Publication Data
Tomlinson, Howard
Politics, religion and society in
revolutionary England 1640–1660.—
(Documents and debates).
1. England, 1625–1660
I. Title   II. Gregg, David   III. Series
942.06'2
ISBN 0–333–39261–2

Contents

Acknowledgements

Any book of this type is necessarily a collective effort to a greater or lesser degree, and production of a manuscript would be impossible without both the forbearance and encouragement of family, colleagues, friends and sympathetic librarians. This general rule is particularly apposite in this case. Although both authors have now moved on to pastures new, most of the work was undertaken at Wellington College, Berkshire, and any merit that the book possesses owes much to the congenial and stimulating historical atmosphere of that institution. Particular thanks are due to the Master, D. H. Newsome, and to 'early modern' specialists at Wellington: Kenneth Fincham, Robert Sopwith and Peter White. Mark Lovett and Richard Smyth also contributed much, as did those former pupils who provided valuable criticism of early drafts of the manuscript.

The greatest debt is to Heather Tomlinson who not only read and commented on the early chapters, but also relinquished precious leisure time with her husband without complaint. David Gwyn provided invaluable assistance with proof reading at a later stage. For any errors of style or substance which remain, however, the authors are entirely culpable.

Many libraries and institutions provided research facilities which were of incalculable benefit. Chief among these were the British Library, the Bodleian Library, the library of the University of Reading and the History Faculty library at Oxford. St John's College, Oxford, generously granted places for vacation study to schoolmasters and Linacre College, Oxford, provided rooms periodically to assist this project. For all of the above we are extremely grateful.

Howard Tomlinson
David Gregg

General Editor's Preface

This book forms part of a series entitled *Documents and Debates*, which is aimed primarily at sixth formers. The earlier volumes in the series each covered approximately one century of history, using material both from original documents and from modern historians. The more recent volumes, however, are designed in response to the changing trends in history examinations at 18 plus, most of which now demand the study of documentary sources and the testing of historical skills. Each volume therefore concentrates on a particular topic within a narrower span of time. It consists of eight sections, each dealing with a major theme in depth, illustrated by extracts drawn from primary sources. The series intends partly to provide experience for those pupils who are required to answer questions on documentary material at A-level, and partly to provide pupils of all abilities with a digestible and interesting collection of source material, which will extend the normal textbook approach.

The book is designed essentially for the pupil's own personal use. The author's introduction will put the period as a whole into perspective, highlighting the central issues, main controversies, available source material and recent developments. Although it is clearly not our intention to replace the traditional textbook, each section will carry its own brief introduction, which will set the documents into context. A wide variety of source material has been used in order to give the pupils the maximum amount of experience – letters, speeches, newspapers, memoirs, diaries, official papers, Acts of Parliament, Minute Books, accounts, local documents, family papers, etc. The questions vary in difficulty, but aim throughout to compel the pupil to think in depth by the use of unfamiliar material. Historical knowledge and understanding will be tested, as well as basic comprehension. Pupils will also be encouraged by the questions to assess the reliability of evidence, to recognise bias and emotional prejudice, to reconcile conflicting accounts and to extract the essential from the irrelevant. Some questions require knowledge outside the immediate extract and are intended for further research or discussion, based on the pupil's general knowledge of the period. Finally, we hope that students using this material will learn something of the nature of historical inquiry and the role of the historian.   John Wroughton

To Heather and Brenda

Introduction

Periods of revolutionary upheaval exercise a compelling attraction for historians, and the English civil war is no exception to this general rule. At such moments, dramatic social, constitutional and economic changes are compressed into brief years – even months – and the breakdown of censorship and expansion of political consciousness produces a veritable ferment of radical suggestions for social reconstruction. Historians profit from a wealth of information describing the real or supposed intentions of principal actors in the historical drama, and can postulate causal links in the origins of revolution. Differing analyses of economic, political, religious and cultural factors emerge: leading to historical dispute and academic controversy. Broad sociological accounts are refuted by individual biographers; the relative merits of long- and short-term causes are debated; connections between economic and religious interests are proposed. Every historical study is itself the result of a sophisticated interplay between the personal evaluation of source material by the historian, and the social environment in which the historian lives and operates – as a consequence each generation is required, to large extent, to rewrite history in its own image. For this reason, much historical writing is not only a commentary upon past events but, on another level, an insight into present circumstances. The historiography of the English civil war reflects this pattern. As the most radical experiment in constitutional reform and political practice, the period naturally attracts historians as bees to a honeycomb. Since primary sources became more readily accessible in the late eighteenth century few epochs in English history have been the subject of such sustained academic interest. Likewise, few periods have generated such profound controversy among historians or such a wealth of conflicting interpretations. Many of these matters still remain unresolved today.

The nature of historical debate over a particular event or period can often best be understood by reference to a chronological historiography. Much of the most instructive writing is located in contemporary accounts of the 1640s rebellion – and arguably the most significant are those of Thomas Hobbes, James Harrington and Edward Hyde, Earl of Clarendon. None of these authors were entirely neutral in the 1640s and all were to greater or lesser degree Royalist associates; yet they produced three fundamentally dissimilar analyses of the revolution. Hobbes revealed a remarkable propensity for altering his allegiance over this period. His major political work *Leviathan* was regarded by Royalist exiles as a *de facto* vindication of revolution. His intentions, however, were to indicate the centrality of order as a political principle and to avoid the potential anarchy of revolutionary situations by providing for a novel form of authority. Order and stability demanded the establishment of an unchallengeable and indivisible sovereign. Royalists naturally viewed this proposal with suspicion, perceiving in *Leviathan* a legitimation of the Commonwealth and an implicit repudiation of the traditional buttresses of monarchy found in patriarchalism and the divine right of kings.

Harrington produced an alternative account in *The Commonwealth of Oceana* (1656), designed to show that republicanism was the natural outcome of English historical development, and exploring the role of land tenure in the origins of conflict. According to Harrington, civil war occurred through a disfunction in the relationship between economic and political power. He held that the financial problems of the aristocracy led to an increasing 'equality of estates' which in turn prompted demands for greater access to political influence. However, an 'equality of power' was incompatible with a monarchical system stressing royal prerogatives and claiming divine sanction for absolutism. This fracture led to war as the king came to rely upon the inappropriate advice of a self-serving clergy and upon military force to quell opposition.

The Earl of Clarendon disagreed profoundly with these interpretations. Both Hobbes and Harrington were political philosophers, providing accounts of the civil war and Interregnum in such a way as to lend credibility to their own prescriptions. By contrast, Clarendon was the historian *par excellence* of the period. His concern was to reveal to posterity the dangers of political presumption – this was accomplished by providing a chronicle of the disruptions and maladies contingent upon popular rebellion, parliamentary usurpation and Cromwellian government.

From the outset, therefore, it is evident that the causes and consequences of the events of 1640–60 were open to conflicting interpretations. Disagreement has remained a consistent feature of later work on the period – twentieth-century scholars, for example, have sought dramatically to revise views associated with the great nineteenth-century civil war historians such as Macauley, S. R. Gardiner, Firth and so on. Their work has been subject to revisionist and Marxist criticism from divergent perspectives. Some historians study the nature of parliamentary opposition to the personal rule of Charles i; others debate the role of the Anglican hierarchy and popular fears of Catholicism in the origins of conflict; while others emphasise the differing local perspectives in the 1640s and the desire for neutrality. Marxists consider evidence of nascent capitalism in the growth of commerce and the correlation between puritanism and a peculiarly 'bourgeois' perception of the economy – identifying examples of premature social and political radicalism among artisans and soldiers in the New Model Army. Later reinterpretations stress the 'possessive individualism' of many such reformers.

The intention of this short book is not to present the conflicting arguments in detail – this function is adequately fulfilled elsewhere (notably in R. C. Richardson, *The Debate on the English Revolution* and in Christopher Daniels and John Morrill (eds), *Charles I*). Moreover, it is to be hoped that students will examine the works of major civil war historians as they become increasingly familiar with the details of the period. By contrast, this volume seeks to present the accounts, opinions and interpretations of those who actively participated in the events of the war and Interregnum. Early chapters consider the divisions between the king and sections within Parliament leading up to the outbreak of hostilities. Later chapters deal with disputes over military objectives between parliamentarians, and with the frustrations of radical political and religious reformers during the civil wars. Final sections discuss the establishment and ultimate demise of the Protectorate, as well as the neglected subject of European reaction to regicide and the foreign policy of Oliver Cromwell. In all cases, the intention has been to allow contemporary actors to speak for themselves and to permit students to assess this material in the light of their existing knowledge of the 1640s and 1650s. With more obscure sources, however, it has been necessary to place material within an appropriate context in order to facilitate comprehension. Each chapter consists, therefore, primarily of original sources from the civil war – many reprinted here for the first time – but also of short introductory sections designed to assist the reader's own reflection and interpretation.

The book is intended to act as a guide for those who are familiar, or are becoming familiar, with the broad outlines of the so-called English 'revolution' of the mid-seventeenth century, and who would like to discover more of the ideas and contentions current among the 'revolutionaries'. As such, it is designed not to replace conventional textbooks, but rather to complement them by making additional sources available to the student. The objective has been to elucidate rather than confuse, but to conclude on a cautionary note – the subject remains a controversial one, and it is always wise to consider why an author is motivated to present a particular argument. We hope that this brief book may encourage some to seek out for themselves more of the extensive original sources which make this such a fertile and fascinating period for historical analysis.

David Gregg
Howard Tomlinson

I   The Long Parliament, 1640–1641

1   The Dismantling of Prerogative Government

The extent of hostility to the king's personal rule is revealed by the passion of the speeches made on 7 November 1640, the fifth day of the new Parliament (documents A,a–b). John Pym himself, in response to the speeches of Rudyerd, Bagshaw and the rest, declared on that day that there was a design 'to alter the Kingdom both in religion and government' and moved that a settled committee should be formed 'to find out the danger the King and Kingdom is in'. All were agreed with Pym on the need 'for a reformation . . . finding out authors and punishment of them'. But it was clear that at this stage these authors were other than the king for it was admitted 'the King can do no wrong; the law casts all miscarriages upon the ministers'.

One of the major preoccupations of the following months was to bring these ministers to 'justice'. Strafford, Laud and Finch, three of the principal servants during the personal rule, were prime targets (documents B,a–c) but by no means the only ones. It was resolved that the Lords Hamilton and Cottington should be brought to account; Sir Robert Berkeley, a justice of the King's Bench, notorious for his extravagant defence of ship money, was impeached of high treason for 'traitorously and wickedly' endeavouring 'to subvert the fundamental law' and 'introduce an arbitrary and tyrannical government'; and five of the other judges who had voted against Hampden were impeached for misdemeanour.

The Commons also 'received informations of a very high nature against Matthew Wren, Lord Bishop of Ely, for setting up idolatry and superstition in divers places and exercising and acting some things of that nature in his own person' and drew up articles of impeachment against him. Many of these procedures were supported by those who were later to become Royalists. Edward Hyde, for example, was as vigorous as Lord Falkland (document B,c) in his prosecution of the judges, whom he denounced as having 'shamefully forfeited that reputation, awe and reverence which the wisdom, courage and gravity of their venerable predecessors had contracted and fastened to the places they now hold'.

Equally, there were few defenders of either the institutions or the financial methods of prerogative government. In a spate of restrictive legislation, statutes swept away the prerogative courts and royal financial expedients of the 1630s (documents C, a–f). It was not quite a comprehensive programme. The moribund Court of Requests and, more surprising, the Court of Wards escaped censure and all that remained of the attacks on monopolies (the holders of which were described by Culpepper as 'the frogs of Egypt') and purveyance was an Act 'for the better ordering and regulating of the office of Clerk of the Market . . . and for the reformation of false weights and measures' (17 Car. I, c. 19). Nevertheless the measures that did reach the statute book were breathtaking in their audacity. The speed with which the legislation passed (the last major measures were passed in August 1641) moreover, testifies to the unity of opinion amongst parliamentarians in favour of abolition.

More important even than these statutes were those underpinning the life of Parliament. The Triennial Act passed on 15 February 1641 and the Act against Dissolution of 10 May (documents D, a–b) were attempts to ensure that a long personal rule could never happen again. These Acts, in the words of Professor Russell, 'gave the parliament a permanent institutional existence and, for the first time, make it accurate to speak of "parliament" and not of "parliaments"'. For all that, neither they nor the Acts against other aspects of the king's prerogative brought a settlement any nearer. Charles I gave his assent to these statutes reluctantly and under duress, as a price of gaining a settlement with the Scots. Once the danger was over there was, of course, no guarantee that he would keep his word. The constitutional gains of 1641 could only be made permanent if the parliamentary leaders were to be brought into the king's confidence and given a share of executive power.

A Zeal for Reform: Speeches by Rudyerd and Bagshaw, 7 November 1640

(*a*)
I have often thought and said, that it must be some great extremity, that would recover and rectify this state; and when that extremity did come, it would be a great hazard whether it might prove a remedy or ruin. We are now, Mr. Speaker, upon that vertical
5   turning point, and therefore it is no time to palliate, to foment our own undoing.

Let us set upon the remedy. We must first know the disease . . . His Majesty is wiser than they that have advised him, and therefore he cannot but see and feel their subverting, destructive councils,
10   which speak louder than I can speak of them for they ring a doleful

deadly knell over the whole kingdom. His Majesty best knows who they are. For us, let the matters bolt out the men; their actions discover them. They are men that talk loudly of the king's service, and yet have done none but their own, and that's too evident.

15 They speak highly of the king's power, but they have made it a miserable power that produceth nothing but weakness both to the king and kingdom. They have exhausted the king's revenue to the bottom; nay through the bottom, and beyond. They have spent vast sums of money wastefully, fruitlessly, dangerously so that

20 more money, without other counsels, will be but a swift undoing. They have always peremptorily pursued one obstinate pernicious course: first they bring things to an extremity; then they make that extremity of their own making, the reason of their next action, seven times worse than the former, and there we are at this instant.

25 They have almost spoiled the best instituted government in the world; for sovereignty in a king, liberty to the subject, the proportionable temper of both which makes the happiest state for power, for riches, for duration. They have unmannerly and slubberingly cast all their projects, all their machinations upon the

30 king, which no wise or good minister of the state ever did, but would still take all harsh, distasteful things upon themselves, to clear, to sweeten their master. They have not suffered his Majesty to appear unto his people, in his own native goodness. They have eclipsed him by their interposition. But although gross, condense

35 bodies, may obscure and hinder the sun from shining out, yet he is still the same in his own splendour. And when they are removed, all creatures under him are directed by his light, comforted by his beams. But they have framed a superstitious seeming maxim of state for their own turn: that, if a king suffer men to be torn from

40 him, he shall never have any good service done him. When the plain truth is, that this is the surest way to preserve a king from having ill servants about him. And the divine truth likewise is: take away the wicked from the king, and his throne shall be established. . . .

(*b*)

45 The law saith, that all justice is in the king . . . and he commits it to his judges for the execution, wherein he trusts them with two of the chiefest flowers which belong to his Crown: the administration of his justice, and the exposition of his laws. But he will not trust them without an oath . . . But when I cast my

50 eyes upon the inferior courts of justice, wherein no such oath is required – I mean the High Commission, and other ecclesiastical courts – my soul hath bled for the wrong and pressures which I have observed to have been done and committed in these courts, against the king's good people; especially for the most monstrous

55 abuse of the oath *ex officio*. . . . I have some reason to know this,

that have been an attendant to the court these five years for my self, and a dear friend of mine, sometimes knight of our shire, for a mere trivial business; that the most that could be proved against him, was the putting on his hat in the time of sermon. Of which
60 court I shall say more, and make good what I say, when those ulcers come to be opened.

Mr. Speaker, I say, these worthies that spake before me, have told you of our miseries, but I cannot tell you of the remedies . . . for no laws will now do us good. Better laws could not have been
65 made, than the Statute of Monopolies against Projectors, and the Petition of Right, against the infringers of liberties. And yet, as if the law had been the author of them, there have been within these few years more monopolies and infringement of liberties than have been in any age since the Conquest. And if all those vile harlots, as
70 Queen Elizabeth called them, that have been the authors of those evils, and the troublers of our Israel, do go unpunished, it will never be better with us. For now during parliament, like frozen snakes their poison dries up; but let the parliament dissolve, and then their poison melts and scatters abroad and doth more hurt
75 than ever . . . Let them be made examples of punishment, who have been the authors of all those miseries, according to the counsel of Solomon: Take away the wicked from before the king and his throne shall be established in righteousness.

J. Rushworth, *Historical Collections* (10 vols, 1680–1722), vol
III, part i, pp 25–7

Questions

a Explain, in your own words, the nature of the complaints made against the king's government.
b What is the tone of the speeches? Are they both equally optimistic about the outcome of events?
c 'The king can do no wrong.' Which lines suggest this?
d Explain the meaning of palliate (line 5); foment (line 5).
e What were: the Statute of Monopolies (line 65); the Petition of Right (line 66)?
f Is there any evidence that liberties were infringed in the 1630s?

B   Charges against Strafford, Laud and Finch

(*a*)
These articles have expressed the character of a great and dangerous treason, such a one as is advanced to the highest degree of malice and mischief. It is enlarged beyond the limits of any description or

definition, it is so heinous in itself as that it is capable of no
5   aggravation; a treason against God, betraying his truth and worship;
against the king, obscuring the glory and weakening the foundations
of his throne; against the commonwealth, by destroying the
principles of safety and prosperity. Other treasons are against the
rule of the law: this is against the being of the law. It is the law
10   that unites the king and his people, and the author of this treason
hath endeavoured to dissolve that union, even to break the mutual,
irreversible, indissoluble band [bond?] of protection and allegiance
whereby they are, and I hope ever will be, bound together. . . .
The law of this kingdom makes the king to be the fountain of
15   justice, of peace, of protection. . . . But the author of this treason
would make him the fountain of injustice, of confusion, of public
misery and calamity. . . .
          J. P. Kenyon (ed.), *Stuart Constitution* (Cambridge, 1966),
          p 206, Pym's speech against Strafford, 25 Nov 1640

(**b**)
We are now fallen upon the great man, the archbishop of Canterbury. Look upon him as he is in highness, and he is the sty of all
20   pestilential filth that hath infested the state and government of this
commonwealth. Look upon him in his dependencies and he is the
only man, the only man that hath raised and advanced all those,
that together with himself, have been the authors and causers of
all our ruins, miseries and calamities we now groan under. Who is
25   it but he only has brought the Earl of Strafford to all his great
places and employments? A fit spirit and instrument to act and
execute all his wicked and bloody designs in these kingdoms. Who
is it but he only that brought in Secretary Windebank into this
place of service, of trust, the very broker and pander to the whore
30   of Babylon? Who is it, Mr. Speaker, but he only, that hath advanced
all our popish bishops? . . . These are the men that should have
fed Christ's flock, but they are the wolves that have devoured
them; the sheep should have fed upon the mountains, but the
mountains have eaten up the sheep. It was the happiness of our
35   church, when the zeal of God's house eat up the bishops, glorious
and brave martyrs that went to the stake in defence of the Protestant
religion; but the zeal of the bishops hath been only to persecute
and eat up the church. Who is it, Mr. Speaker, but this great
Archbishop of Canterbury, that hath sat at the helm, to steer, and
40   manage all the projects that have been set on foot in this kingdom
this ten years last past? And rather than he would stand out, he
hath most unworthily trucked and chaffered in the meanest of
them, as, for instance, that of tobacco. . . . And there is scarce
any grievance, or complaint come before us in this place, wherein
45   we do not find him intermentioned, and as it were twisted into it,
like a busy, angry wasp, his sting is in the tail of everything. . . .

Rushworth, *Historical Collections*, III, part i, p 122, Harbottle
Grimston's speech in favour of Laud's sequestration, 19 Dec
1640

(c)
Here are many and mighty crimes . . . pursuing him fervently in
every several condition, being a silent speaker, an unjust judge,
and an unconscionable keeper. That his life appears a perpetual
50 warfare . . . against our fundamental laws, which by his own
confession, several conquests had left untouched; against the excellent constitution of this kingdom, which hath made it appear unto
strangers rather an idea than a real Commonwealth. . . . And this
with such unfortunate success, that as he always intended to make
55 our ruins a ground of his advancement, so his advancement is the
means of our further ruin. After that, contrary to the end of his
place, and the end of that meeting in which he held his place, he
had as it were gagged the Commonwealth, taking away (to his
power) all power of speech from that body, of which he ought to
60 have been the mouth, and which alone can perfectly represent the
condition of the people, whom that body only represents. . . . He
pursued this offence towards the Parliament, by inveighing against
the members, by scandalizing their proceedings, by trampling upon
their Acts and Declarations, by usurping and devolving the right,
65 by diminishing and abrogating the power, both of that and other
parliaments, and making them (as much as in him lay) both useless
and odious to his Majesty; and pursued his hatred to this fountain
of justice, by corrupting the streams of it, and laws, and perverting
the conduit-pipes, the judges. He practised the annihilating of
70 ancient and notorious perambulations of particular forests. . . . He
endeavoured to have all tenures, *durante bene placito*; to bring all
laws from his Majesty's courts into his Majesty's breast. He gave
our goods to the king, our lands to the deer, our liberties to his
sheriffs, so that there was no way by which we had not been
75 oppressed and destroyed, if the power of this person had been
equal with his will, or that the will of his Majesty had been equal
to his power. . . .
Ibid, pp 139–40, Lord Falkland's speech against Lord Keeper
Finch, 14 Jan 1641

Questions

a Summarise Pym's charges against Strafford.
b In your eyes was Strafford really guilty of treason? (Give
reasons)

c Why, according to Grimston, was Laud 'the sty of all pestilential filth that hath infested the state and government of this Commonwealth' (lines 19–20)?

d What, according to Falkland, were Finch's 'many and mighty crimes' (line 51)?

e Why was Falkland's attack on Finch more remarkable than Grimston's on Laud?

f What do you understand by 'he [Laud] hath most unworthily trucked and chaffered in the meanest of them [projects]' (lines 42–3); 'fundamental laws' (line 50); 'He endeavoured to have all tenures *durante bene placito*' (line 71)?

g What happened to Strafford, Laud and Finch?

C Regulating Statutes: Prerogative Courts and Royal Financial Expedients

(**a**)

And for as much as all matters examinable or determinable in the court commonly called the Star Chamber may have their proper remedy and redress, and their due punishment and correction, by the common law of the land, and in the ordinary course of justice
5 elsewhere; and for as much as the reasons and motives inducing the erection and continuance of that court do now cease: and the proceedings, censures and decrees of that court have by experience been found to be an intolerable burden to the subjects, and the means to introduce an arbitrary power and government; and for as
10 much as the Council Table hath of late times assumed unto itself a power to intermeddle in civil causes . . . by which great and manifold mischiefs and inconveniences have arisen and happened, and much incertainty by means of such proceedings hath been conceived concerning mens' rights and estates.
15 For settling whereof, and preventing the like in time to come, be it ordained and enacted by the authority of this present parliament, that the said court commonly called the Star Chamber, and all jurisdiction, power and authority belonging unto or exercised in the same court, or by any of the judges, officers or ministers
20 thereof, be from the first day of August in the year of our Lord God one thousand six hundred forty and one, clearly and absolutely dissolved, taken away and determined. . . .
And be it likewise enacted, that the like jurisdiction now used and exercised in the court before the President and Council in the
25 Marches of Wales; and also in the court before the President and Council established in the Northern parts; and also in the court commonly called the Court of the Duchy of Lancaster, held before the chancellor and council of that court; and also in the Court of Exchequer of the County Palatine of Chester, held before the

30   Chamberlain and Council of that court; the like jurisdiction being
exercised there, shall from the said first day of August one thousand
six hundred forty and one, be also repealed and absolutely revoked
and made void. . . .

> 17 Car. I, c. 10: An Act for regulating the Privy Council
> and for taking away the court commonly called the Star
> Chamber

(*b*)
And whereas by colour of some words in the aforesaid branch of
35   the said Act of Supremacy, whereby commissioners are authorized
to execute their commission according to the tenor and effect of
the king's letters patents . . . the said commissioners have, to the
great and insufferable wrong and oppression of the king's subjects,
used to fine and imprison them, and to exercise other authority
40   not belonging to ecclesiastical jurisdiction restored by that Act. . . .
be it enacted . . . that the aforesaid branch, clause, article or
sentence, contained in the said Act . . . shall from henceforth be
repealed. . . .

And be it also enacted by the authority aforesaid, that no
45   archbishop, bishop, nor vicar-general . . . nor any other person or
persons whatsoever, exercising spiritual or ecclesiastical power . . .
shall from and after the first day of August, which shall be in the
year of our Lord God one thousand six hundred forty and one,
award, impose or inflict any pain, penalty, fine, amerciament,
50   imprisonment or other corporal punishment upon any of the king's
subjects, for any contempt, misdemeanour, crime, offence, matter
or thing whatsoever, belonging to spiritual or ecclesiastical cogni-
zance or jurisdiction; or shall *ex officio*, or at the instance or
promotion of any other person whatsoever, urge, enforce, tender,
55   give or minister unto any churchwarden, side-man or other person
whatsoever, any corporal oath. . . .

And be it further enacted, that from and after the said first day
of August, no new court shall be erected, ordained or appointed
within this realm of England or dominion of Wales, which shall
60   or may have the like power, jurisdiction or authority, as the said
High Commission-Court now hath or pretendeth to have. . . .

> 17 Car. I, c. 11: An Act for repeal of a branch of a
> statute primo Elizabeth concerning commissioners for causes
> ecclesiastical

(*c*)
Whereas upon examination in this present Parliament of divers
of the farmers, customers, and collectors of the customs upon
merchandise, and likewise upon their own confession, it appeared
65   that they have taken divers great sums of money of his Majesty's
subjects, and likewise of merchants aliens for goods imported and

exported by the names of a subsidy of tonnage and poundage. . . .
Be it therefore declared and enacted . . . that it is and hath been
the ancient right of the subjects of this realm, that no subsidy,
70 custom, impost or other charge whatsoever ought or may be laid
or imposed upon any merchandise exported or imported by
subjects, denizens or aliens without common consent in Parliament. . . .

> 17 Car I, c. 8: A subsidy granted to the King of tonnage,
> poundage and other sums of money payable upon merchan-
> dise, exported and imported

(*d*)

Whereas divers writs of late time issued under the Great Seal of
75 England, commonly called ship-writs, for the charging of the ports,
towns, cities, boroughs and counties of this realm respectively, to
provide and furnish certain ships for his Majesty's service; and
whereas . . . a writ . . . was awarded out of the Court of Exchequer
to the then Sheriff of Buckinghamshire against John Hampden,
80 Esquire . . . all which writs and proceedings as aforesaid were
utterly against the law of the land. Be it therefore declared and
enacted . . . that the said charge imposed upon the subject for the
providing and furnishing of ships commonly called ship-money,
and the said extrajudicial opinion of the said justices . . . given
85 against the said John Hampden, were and are contrary to and
against the laws and statutes of this realm, the right of property,
the liberty of the subjects, former resolutions in Parliament, and
the Petition of Right. . . .

> 17 Car. I, c. 14: An Act for declaring unlawful and void the
> late proceedings touching ship-money. . . .

(*e*)

. . . whereas of late divers presentments have been made and some
90 judgments given whereby the . . . bounds of some of the said
forests have been variously extended . . . to the great grievance
and vexation of many persons having lands adjoining . . . and
whereas of late time some endeavours or pretences have been to
set on foot forests in some parts of this realm and the dominion of
95 Wales, where in truth none have been or ought to be, or at least
have not been used of long time. For remedy thereof . . . it be
declared and enacted . . . that from henceforth the . . . bounds of
all and every the forests respectively, shall be to all intents and
purposes taken, adjudged and deemed to extend no further . . .
100 than the . . . bounds of the said forests respectively in the twentieth
year of the reign of our late Sovereign Lord King James, and not
beyond in any wise . . . and that all and every the presentments
since the said twentieth year made, and all and every other

presentment and all and every fine and fines, and amercement and
105 amercements, upon by reason or colour of any such presentment
or presentments, shall from henceforth be adjudged, deemed and
taken to be utterly void and of no force or effect. . . .
17 Car. I, c. 16: An Act for the certainty of forests. . . .

(f)
Whereas upon pretext of an ancient custom or usage of this realm
of England, that men of full age being not knights, and being
110 seized of lands or rents of the yearly value of forty pounds or more
. . . might be compelled by the king's writ to receive, or take upon
them the order of knighthood, or else to make fine for the discharge
or respite of the same . . . many of which were altogether unfit,
in regard either of estate or quality, to receive the said order or
115 dignity. And very many were put to grievous fines and other
vexations for the same, although in truth it were not sufficiently
known how, or in what sort, or where they, or any of them,
should or might have addressed themselves for receiving the said
order or dignity, and for saving themselves thereby from the said
120 fines, process and vexations. And whereas it is most apparent that
all and every such proceeding, in regard of the matter therein
pretended, is altogether useless and unreasonable: may it therefore
. . . be . . . declared and enacted . . . that from henceforth no
person or persons of what condition, quality, estate or degree
125 soever, shall at any time be distrained or otherwise compelled by
any writ or process of the Court of Chancery or Court of
Exchequer, or otherwise by any means whatsoever, to receive or
take upon him or them respectively the order or dignity of
knighthood, nor shall suffer or undergo any fine, trouble or
130 molestation whatsoever by reason or colour of his or their having
not received or not taken upon him or them the said order or
dignity. . . .
17 Car. I, c.20: An Act for the prevention of vexatious
proceedings touching the order of Knighthood
Statutes of the Realm, V. 104 ff.

Questions

a   What suggestions are made in the statutes that the king's servants
had acted arbitrarily?
b   To what extent were these allegations true?
c   What do you understand by: the *ex officio* oath; tonnage and
poundage; ship-writs; the forest laws; Knighthood fines.
d   What happened in Hampden's case?

e Were any of these statutes reversed at the Restoration?

D Regulating Statutes: Parliaments

(*a*)
Whereas by the laws and statutes of this realm the parliament ought
to be holden at least once every year for the redress of grievances,
but the appointment of the time and place for the holding thereof
hath always belonged, as it ought, to his Majesty and his royal
5 progenitors. And whereas it is by experience found that the not
holding of Parliaments accordingly hath produced sundry and great
mischiefs and inconveniences to the King's Majesty, the Church
and Commonwealth. For the prevention of the like mischiefs and
inconveniences in time to come, be it enacted . . . that in case there
10 be not a parliament summoned by writ under the Great Seal of
England, and assembled and held before the 10th of September,
which shall be in the third year next after the last day of the last
meeting and sitting in this present Parliament . . . the Parliament
shall assemble, and be held in the usual place at Westminster . . .
15 on the second Monday, which shall be in the month of November,
then next ensuing. And in case this present Parliament now
assembled and held, or any other Parliament . . . hereafter,
assembled . . . shall be prorogued, or adjourned, or continued by
prorogation or adjournment, until the 10th day of September,
20 which shall be in the third year next after the last day of the last
meeting and sitting in Parliament . . . that then in every such case,
every such parliament . . . shall from the said 10th day of September
be thenceforth clearly and absolutely dissolved . . . [and writs
issued for elections for a new parliament to meet on the second
25 Monday in November, at Westminster].
   And it is further enacted, that no parliament henceforth to be
assembled shall be dissolved or prorogued within fifty days at least
after the time appointed for the meeting thereof, unless it be by
assent of his Majesty, his heirs or successors, and of both Houses
30 in Parliament assembled. . . .
        17 Car. I, c. 1: An Act for the preventing of inconveniences
        happening by the long intermission of parliaments
        Statutes of the Realm V, 54 ff.

(*b*)
Whereas great sums of money must of necessity be speedily
advanced and provided for the relief of his Majesty's army and
people in the northern parts of this realm, and for preventing the
imminent danger it is in, and for supply of other his Majesty's
35 present and urgent occasions, which cannot be so timely effected

as is requisite without credit for raising the said monies; which credit cannot be obtained until such obstacles be first removed as are occasioned by fears, jealousies and apprehensions of divers his Majesty's loyal subjects, that this present parliament may be
40 adjourned, prorogued, or dissolved, before justice shall be duly executed upon delinquents, public grievances redressed, a firm peace between the two nations of England and Scotland concluded, and before sufficient provision be made for the re-payment of the said monies so to be raised; all which the Commons in this present
45 parliament assembled, having duly considered, do therefore most humbly beseech your Majesty that it may be declared and enacted.

And be it declared and enacted . . . that this present parliament now assembled shall not be dissolved unless it be by Act of Parliament to be passed for that purpose; nor shall be, at any time
50 or time, during the continuance thereof, prorogued or adjourned, unless it be by Act of Parliament to be likewise passed for that purpose. . . .

> 17 Car I, c. 7: An Act to prevent inconveniences which may happen by the untimely adjourning, proroguing or dissolving this present parliament
> Ibid pp 103 ff.

Questions

a In what ways was the king's prerogative infringed by these statutes?
b 'Parliament ought to be holden at least once every year' (lines 1–2). In how many years had Parliament been held under the early Stuarts (up to and including 1640)? What does this suggest about its importance in government hitherto?
c Distinguish between 'adjournment', 'proroguing', 'dissolving' (lines 19, 23, 48, 50).
d How far were the problems outlined in the preamble to the Second Act simply excuses to enable the enactment to be imposed on the king?
e To what extent were these Acts modified in later years?

2 The Search for a Settlement

The crown stratagem of winning men over by place had been the traditional way for the crown to placate opponents and one which had been used successfully by Charles I himself. Both Strafford and Attorney-General Noy, for example, had been prominent in opposition to crown policies in the early parliaments of Charles's reign, prior to their being given office in 1628 and 1631. The history of this scheme of Francis Russell, fourth Earl of Bedford, goes back to the early days of the Long Parliament, when, in the absence of a strong Court party (fewer than fifty officials and courtiers had been elected to the Commons) Bedford came forward with a proposal to manage Parliament for the king. Negotiations proceeded slowly but on 19 February 1641 the king named Bedford and four associates – Hertford, Essex, Saye, Saville and Mandeville – to the Privy Council. This marked the closest Bedford's undertaking ever came to success. The plan, as reported by Hyde (document A), for 'the Great Patriots' to be brought into office in return for paying off the king's debts and augmenting his revenues never materialised. Bedford died of smallpox on Sunday 9 May 1641, the same day on which Charles resolved to sign Strafford's attainder. Lord Saye, who became Master of the Wards on 18 May, continued negotiations with the Court but the stratagem failed once again. By then the king had begun to turn towards a military solution, if indeed he had ever been serious about the Bedford scheme. The king's refusal to disband the Irish Army, moreover, perhaps provided the breaking point for John Pym – the man upon whom the undertaking hinged. Thereafter Pym turned to a policy of confrontation and to a demand for the parliamentary nomination of the king's ministers.

Pym's Ten Propositions (document B) need to be set against the tense political atmosphere at Westminster during May–June 1641. Indeed they were formulated by the 'close committee', a small, select Commons committee, established by Pym to investigate the army 'Plot' to overcome Parliament. The committee had met in secret and had reported its findings to the Commons on 8 June, little more than two weeks before these propositions were adopted. In these circumstances the king's proposed journey to Scotland seemed highly dangerous, as was pointed out in the second proposition. The propositions, then, should be seen as emergency proposals to deal with a specific crisis – an attempt to break the political deadlock rather than an attempt to overthrow the constitution. Paradoxically, however, the adoption of the propositions made compromise more difficult: firstly because both their tone and their insistence on parliamentary approval were bound further to alienate the king (although the propositions were never presented to the king as a whole); and secondly because Pym and his colleagues were unlikely to retreat from a programme on which they had staked their political reputations – indeed the Nineteen Propositions of 1 June 1642 were not so very different in essentials from the Ten Propositions of the previous year. The Ten Propositions thus became both the sticking-point and the crux of the parliamentary programme.

A 'Bridge' Appointments: Bedford's Scheme, spring 1641

The Great Patriots thought they might be able to do their country better service if they got the places and preferments in the Court, and so prevented the evil counsels which had used to spring from thence. And they had a fast friend then there, the Marquis of
5 Hambleton, who could most dexterously put such an affair into agitation with the least noise, and prepare both king and queen to hearken to it very willingly: and in a short time all particulars were well adjusted for every man's accommodation.

The Earl of Bedford was to be Treasurer: in order to which the
10 Bishop of London had already desired the king to receive the staff into his hand, and give him leave to retire to the sole care of his bishopric. And so the Treasury was for the present put into commission. Mr. Pym was to be Chancellor of the Exchequer, which office the Lord Cottington was likewise ready to surrender
15 upon assurance of indemnity for the future. These two were engaged to procure the king's revenue to be liberally provided for and honourably increased and settled.

And that this might be the better done the Earl of Bedford prevailed with the king . . . to make Oliver St. John . . . his
20 Solicitor-General, which his Majesty readily consented to, hoping [that], being a gentleman of an honourable extraction (if he had been legitimate) he would have been very useful in the present exigence to support his service in the House of Commons, where his authority was then great; at least, that he would be ashamed
25 ever to appear in any thing that might prove prejudicial to the Crown. And he became immediately possessed of that office of great trust, and was so well qualified for it by his fast and rooted malignity against the government that he lost no credit with his party, out of any apprehension or jealousy that he would change
30 his side: and he made good their confidence, not in the least degree abating his malignant spirit or dissembling it, but with the same obstinacy opposed every thing which might advance the king's service when he was his Solicitor as ever he had done before.

The Lord Saye was to be Master of the Wards, which place the
35 Lord Cottington was likewise to surrender for his quiet and security. And Denzil Hollis was to be Secretary of State, in the place of Secretary Wynnibank.

Thus far the intrigue for preferment was entirely complied with, and it is great pity that it was not fully executed, that the king
40 might have had some able men to have advised him or assisted; which probably these very men would have done, after they had been so thoroughly engaged: whereas the king had none left about him in any immediate trust in business . . . who either did not betray or sink under the weight or reproach of it.
45 But the Earl of Bedford was resolved that he would not enter

into the Treasury till the revenue was in some degree settled, and at least the bill for tonnage and poundage passed, with all decent circumstances and for life; which both he and Mr. Pym did very heartily labour to effect, and had in their thoughts many good
50 expedients by which they intended to raise the revenue of the Crownn. And none of them we're very solicitousto take their promotions before some other accommodations were provided for some of the rest of their chief companions. . . .

Hambden was a man they could not leave unprovided for; and
55 therefore there were several designs, and very far driven, for the satisfaction and promotion of him and Essex and Mandevill, and others, though not so fully concluded as those before mentioned. For the king's great end was, by these compliances, to save the life of the Earl of Strafford and to preserve the Church from ruin: for
60 nobody thought the archbishop in danger of his life. And there were few of the persons mentioned before who thought their preferments would do them much good if the earl were suffered to live; but in that of the Church, the major part even of those persons would have been willing to have satisfied the king, the
65 rather because they had no reason to think the two Houses, or indeed either of them, could have been induced to have pursued the contrary. And so the continued and renewed violence in the prosecution of the Earl of Strafford made the king well contented (as the other reasons prevailed with the other persons) that the
70 execution of those promotions should be for a time suspended.

Edward Hyde, Earl of Clarendon, *The History of the Rebellion and Civil Wars in England* (Oxford, 1888), vol I, pp 280–2

Questions

a Explain why Hyde was not unsympathetic towards the scheme.
b Which parliamentarian, according to Hyde, actually gained preferment in 1641? Which other one also gained office?
c Why was it necessary for 'Hambleton' to act as 'a fast friend' for Bedford at Court?
d What happened to the Bishop of London; Cottington; 'Wynnibank'?
e What reasons, other than those mentioned by Hyde, can you suggest for the scheme's failure?

B The Ten Propositions, 24 June 1641

Next, the Lord Bishop of Lincoln reported the conference this morning with the House of Commons. . . .

'He [Pym] told your lordships, he was commanded by the House

of Commons to present unto your lordships their continued care
5   and endeavour for the good of the kingdom; that, as your affections
are united with them in one great end, to serve God, the King,
and the Commonwealth, so your counsels might be likewise jointly
co-operative thereunto. . . . And as a way to this common and
general end, he was to make unto your lordships several proposi-
10 tions. Because they had lately found out very malignant and
pestiferous designs set on foot, or plotted, to trouble the peace of
the kingdom, the which though they were prevented, yet were
still pursued; which is the reason why the House of Commons do
present your Lordships with these several propositions, in ten
15 several Heads. . . .
First Head, concerning the disbanding of the Armies: That is in
the first front, because it is first to be done, and to make way for
all the rest. . . .
Second Head: That his Majesty will be pleased to allow a convenient
20 time before his journey into Scotland, that so the army may be
first disbanded; and that some of the important affairs now
depending in parliament, some in both Houses, and other some in
the House of Commons, may be dispatched before his Majesty's
journey. . . .
25 Third Head, about his Majesty's Counsels: That his Majesty may
be humbly petitioned to remove such evil counsellors against whom
there shall be any just exceptions, and for the committing of his
own business, and the affairs of the kingdom, to such counsellors
and officers as the parliament may have cause to confide in. . . .
30 Here he told your lordships a tale of a gardener, who, being
demanded why the weeds grew so fast, and the flowers so thin, in
his ground-plot, answered, that the weeds were true children, but
the flowers were but so many slips and bastards. So, saith he, it is
written, that the Kings should be our nursing fathers, and Queens
35 our nursing mothers; but we have found here of late, by reason of
bad counsellors, no nurses, but hirelings, of the public state. . . .
Howbeit this request is by the House of Commons recommended
but in general for this present, without pointing out or designing
of particulars, in hope the King will find them out of himself;
40 otherwise it will cause the House of Commons to reduce this
petition to names of particulars. . . .
The Fourth Head concerns the Queen's Majesty. Several Branches:
1. That his Majesty will be graciously pleased, by advice of his
parliament, to persuade the Queen to take some of the nobility,
45 and others of truth, into her service, in such places as are now of
her disposing. . . .
2. That no Jesuit be entertained into her Majesty's service, nor any
priest native of any of his Majesty's Dominions. . . .
3. That the College of Capuchins at Denmark House may be
50 dissolved, and the persons sent away out of the kingdom. . . .

Fifth Head, concerning the Prince, and the rest of the Royal Issue: That some person of public trust, and well affected in religion, may, by advice of Parliament, be placed about the Prince, and may take care of his education, especially in matters of religion; and the
55 like care be taken of the rest of his Majesty's children.
Sixth Head, of papists coming to the Court. . . . That his Majesty would be sparing in licensing of Papists to come to the Court. . . . That English ladies, papists, be removed from the Court. His Majesty [be] moved for His assent, that the persons of the most
60 active papists be so restrained, as shall be necessary for the safety of the kingdom, even lords as well as others.
Seventh Head, concerning the Nuncios. That it may be declared, by an Act of Parliament, that, if any man shall presume to come to this kingdom, with instructions from the Pope or Court of
65 Rome, that he shall be in case of high treason, and out of protection of the king and the laws.
Eighth Head, concerning the security and peace of the Kingdom. Four Branches:
1. That men of honour and trust be placed Lords Lieutenants in
70 every county; and that direction be given to the Lieutenants to be careful in the choice of their Deputies.
2. That the trained bands be furnished with arms, powder, and bullets, and that they be exercised and made ready for service; also that an oath be prepared, to pass both the Houses of Parliament
75 . . . to be taken by the Lord Lieutenants, Deputy Lieutenants, and other officers of trained bands, and to secure their fidelity in these dangerous times.
3. That the Cinque Ports, and other ports of the kingdom, may be put into good hands; and a list of those who govern them now,
80 may be presented to the Parliament; and that those persons may be altered upon reason; and that especial care be taken for reparation and provision of the forts.
4. That my Lord Admiral, that noble lord of whose honour the House of Commons stands secure, be desired to inform the Parliament
85 in what care the Navy is, that, if there be any defect, it may be provided for out of the money, which is to come upon the bill of Tonnage and Poundage; and that, if any suspended person have any command in any of his Majesty's ships, that he may be removed.
The Ninth Head: That his Majesty would be pleased to give directions
90 to his learned counsel to draw a general pardon, in such a large and beneficial manner as may be for the security of his subjects.
The Tenth Head: A select committee of the Lords to join with a proportionable number of the House of Commons, from time to time, to confer about these particular courses as shall be most
95 effectual for the reducing of these propositions to effect for the public good.
Lords Journal (hereafter *LJ*), IV, 285–7

Questions

a   How convincing is Pym's explanation of the reasons for the propositions (lines 1–15)?
b   Which passages suggest that Pym was still loyal to the king in June 1641?
c   Which *one proposition* do you consider to have been the most radical? (State reasons)
d   Explain: 'Kings should be our nursing feathers . . . [to] hirelings of the public state' (lines 34–6).
e   Who was 'my Lord Admiral' (line 83)? And why in Pym's eyes, was he 'that noble lord, of whose honour the House of Commons stands secure' (lines 83–4)?

3   The Resurgence of Loyalism

As John Morrill has observed: 'There could be no civil war before 1642 because there was no royalist party. The origins of the English civil war are really concerned less with the rise of opposition than the resurgence of loyalism.' The selection of documents in this section focuses on this theme. In the first session of the Long Parliament, as we have seen, the dismantling of prerogative government had won the support of a large section of the Commons. In the famous Commons vote on 21 April only fifty-nine men had the courage to oppose Strafford's attainder. It would be wrong to assume, however, that there was a strong degree of unanimity in the Commons on all issues in the first session of the Long Parliament. Document A shows that the proposal for the abolition of espiscopacy 'root and branch', for example, was vehemently opposed. This issue provided one rallying point for those 'constitutional Royalists' who were later to join the King – as S. R. Gardiner long ago observed there was an episcopalian party before there was a Royalist one, although not all episcopalians, of course, were Royalists *ipso facto*. The king's right to appoint his own counsellors was another divisive issue. This question had been raised – although not pressed – by Pym and his colleagues in the first session. By the time of Goodwin's initiative of 28 October, the 'Royalists' were both confident enough to out-argue, and strong enough to defeat, any motion for guaranteeing parliamentary approval of the king's servants. It was only the accident of the Irish Rebellion – the news of which filtered through to the House on 1 November, over a week after the event – that enabled Pym to extricate himself from a very difficult position on 8 November (document B). By the time of the Grand Remonstrance debates (document C) the Royalist tide was flowing swiftly. On 22 November, in the most dramatic of all the Long Parliamentary debates, the Royalist cause – based on the Prayer Book and episcopacy as the bulwarks of order and the revolutionary intent of the 'Opposition' – was stoutly defended. The sincerity and plausibility of leading 'constitutional Royalists' clearly influenced many who had absented themselves from the vote on Strafford or had then voted with the majority out of fear – although in this extract D'Ewes himself perhaps found it convenient not to be present when the vote was taken. Although the Grand Remonstrance was passed by a handful of votes, the Royalist faction – perhaps for the first and last time in the Long Parliament – had asserted itself as effectively as the parliamentary leadership. Not all those who had opposed the Remonstrance were necessarily committed Royalists, but if the battle lines had not yet been drawn, after the vote in the early hours of 23 November, it became increasingly unlikely that a parliamentary consensus would emerge.

A   Lord George Digby's Speech, 9 February 1641, against the Root and Branch Petition

Sir, if I thought there were no further design in the desires of some, that this London Petition should be committed, than merely to make use of it as an index of grievances, I should wink at the faults of it and not much oppose it. There is no man within these walls
5   more sensible of the heavy grievance of Church government than myself; nor whose affections are keener to the clipping of these wings of the prelates, whereby they have mounted to such insolencies; nor whose zeal is more ardent to the searing them so as they may never spring again. But having reason to believe that
10   some aim at a total extirpation of bishops which is against my heart; and that the committing of this petition may give countenance to that design, I cannot refrain myself from labouring to divert it or at least to set such notes upon it as may make it ineffectual to that end. . . .
15   . . . first, let me recall to your mind the manner of its delivery; and I am confident there is no man of judgment that will think it fit for a parliament under a monarchy, to give countenance to irregular and tumultuous assemblies of people, be it for never so good an end . . .
20   Contemptible things, Sir, swarm in the 8, 13, 14, 15, 16, 17 articles of this petition. Did ever anybody think that the gayeties of Ovid or Tom Coryet's muse should by 15,000 have been presented to a Parliament as a motive for the extirpation of bishops?

The scandal of the rochet, the lawn-sleeves, the four-corner cap,
25 the cope, the surplice, the tippet, the hood, the canonical coat etc.
may pass with arguments of the same weight, only thus much let
me observe upon it, Mr. Speaker. Wise counsels, Mr. Speaker,
must square their resolutions by another measure, by what's most
just, most honourable, most convenient. Believe me, Sir, great
30 alterations of government are rarely accompanied with any of these.
Mr. Speaker, we all agree upon this, that a reformation of Church
government is most necessary; – and our happy unity of opinions
herein should be one argument unto us to stay there. But, Sir, to
strike at the root, to attempt a total alteration, before ever I can
35 give my vote unto that, three things must be made manifest unto
me. First, that the mischiefs which we have felt under episcopal
government flow from the nature of the function, not from the
abuses of it only; that is, that no rules, no boundaries, can be set
to bishops, able to restrain them from such exorbitances. Secondly,
40 such a frame of government must be laid before us as no time, no
corruption, can make liable to proportionable inconveniences with
that which we abolish. And thirdly, it must be made to appear that
this Utopia is practicable that one would swear the penners of the
article had the pluming of some bishops already, they are so
45 acquainted with every feather of them. In a word, I know not
whether it be more preposterous to infer the extirpation of bishops
from such weak arguments, or to attribute as they do to church
government all the civil grievances, not a patent, not a monopoly,
not the price of a commodity raised, but these men make bishops
50 the cause of it. . . . There is no logic, no reasoning in their
demands. It were want of logic in me to expect it from a multitude,
but I consider the multitude in this is led by implicit faith to that
which hath been digested and contrived but by a few; and in them
truly, I cannot but wonder at the want of reconciliation here. . . .
55   For the bold part of this petition, Sir, what can there be of greater
presumption than for petitioners, not only to prescribe to a
parliament what and how it shall do; but for a multitude to teach a
parliament what is, and what is not the government, according to
God's word? Besides, what is the petition against? Is it not against
60 the government of the Church of England established by Acts of
Parliament? Is it not against the Liturgy, against several forms of
divine service ratified by the same authority? 'Tis true, Mr. Speaker,
the parliament may mend, may alter, may repeal laws, may make
new, and I hope in due season we shall do so in point of Church
65 government; but in the mean time let me tell you, Sir, I cannot
but esteem it an irreverence, and high presumption in any, to
petition point blank against a law or government in force. . . .
For my part, though no statesman, I will speak my mind freely
in this. I do not think a King can put down bishops totally with
70 safety to monarchy. Not that there is any such alliance as men talk

of 'twixt the mitre and the Crown, but from this reason, that upon
the putting down of bishops, the government of assemblies is like
to succeed it. That, to be effectual, must draw to itself the supremacy
of ecclesiastical jurisdictions that, consequently, [has] the power of
75 excommunicating kings as well as any other brother in Christ. And
if a king chance to be delivered over to Satan, judge whether men
are likely to care much what becomes of him next.

These things considered, Mr. Speaker, let us lay aside all thoughts
of such dangerous, such fundamental, such unaccomplished alter-
80 ations, and all thoughts countenancing those thoughts in others.
Let us all resolve upon that course where (with union) we may
probably promise ourselves success, happiness, and security that is
in a thorough reformation. To that, no man's vote shall be given
with more zeal, with more heartiness than mine. Let us not destroy
85 bishops, but make bishops such as they were in the primitive
times. . . .

Rushworth, *Historical Collections, III, part i, pp 170–4*

Questions

a Outline *the main points* of Digby's cases against the Root and
Branch petition.
b How justified was his attitude towards Laudian bishops?
c Explain the significance of the third paragraph.
d What does Digby mean by 'but make bishops such as they were
in primitive times (lines 85–6)?

**B   The Appointment of Ministers: Commons Debates, 28
October, 5–8 November 1641**

28 OCTOBER Mr. Robert Goodwin moved touching ill councillors
that if we did not take a course to remove such as now remained
and to prevent others from coming in hereafter, all we had done
this parliament would come to nothing and we should never be
5 free from danger. Mr. Strode seconded Mr. Robert Goodwin's
motion with great violence saying all we had done this Parliament
was nothing unless we had a negative voice in the placing of the
great officers of the King and of his councillors, by whom his
Majesty was led captive. I think most he said was premeditated
10 but it was so extreme a strain as Mr. Hyde did upon the sudden
confute most of it, showing that the choice of the great officers of
the Crown were to be appointed by the King being an hereditary
flower of the Crown . . . Others spake pro and con. I moved in
effect following: That I perceived our debate now grew to this

15 narrow point or compass that either the appointing of the great
     officers of the kingdom did wholly appertain to his Majesty by
     virtue of his prerogative as an hereditary right of his Crown, or
     the parliament had a negative voice in the constitution of them.
     For mine own part I did conceive this was an ancient and undoubted
20   right of the Crown; which rights I shall ever maintain whilst I sit
     in this House, being thereto bound not only by my general duty
     as a subject but particularly also by the Oaths of Allegiance and
     Supremacy which I have taken and by the late protestation of this
     House. . . . After I had spoken divers seconded me that we should
25   leave the disposition of the great officers to the King, only to move
     by way of petition. But others would have us prevent the choice
     of ill ones by getting a negative voice in the election of them, till
     at last it was resolved upon the question to have the heads of this
     debate to be referred to a committee to draw into a petition to be
30   presented to his Majesty. . . .

     5 NOVEMBER Mr. Pym stood up and moved that no man should be
     more ready and forward than himself to engage his estate, person,
     life and all for the suppression of this rebellion in Ireland or for the
     performance of any other service for his Majesty's honour and
35   safety. But he feared that as long as he gave ear to those evil
     councillors about him all that we did would prove in vain, and
     therefore he desired that we might add some declaration in the end
     of these instructions: that howsoever we had engaged ourselves for
     the assistance of Ireland, yet unless the King would remove his evil
40   councillors and take such councillors as might be approved by
     parliament, we should account ourselves absolved from this engage-
     ment. Divers would have had it speedily assented unto but Mr.
     Hyde stood up and first opposed it and said amongst other things
     that by such an addition we should as it were prevail the King.
45   Mr. Waller spake also against it and said that as the Earl of Strafford
     had advised the King that because we did not relieve him he was
     absolved from all rules of government. So by this addition on the
     contrary we should pretend that if the King did not remove his ill
     councillors we were absolved from our duties in assisting him in
50   the recovery of Ireland. . . .

     6 NOVEMBER A long Article [was presented] to remonstrate to his
     Majesty the danger of the state from ill councillors, and to desire
     the removal of them or else that we would not be obliged to bind
     ourselves to relieve Ireland. This last Article occasioned a great deal
55   of debate and divers spake to it. Mr. Perd said that we might well
     add this clause, for it was no more than if he had a friend or a
     brother an ill husband, and he should tell him he would not lend
     him any money or be bound for him unless he would leave his ill
     courses. Sir John Culpepper said that he thought Ireland to be a
60   part of England that we ought to defend it . . . and after some two

or three had spoken I moved in effect following. That I took the first part of this Article which declared and set forth our sufferings by ill councillors to be so clear and evident as every one will assent unto it. . . . For that latter clause in the sixth Article touching our
65 declaration that we would not give his Majesty aid without a redress of our grievances it is no more then the ancient and undoubted right of parliament . . . but whether the manner of the expression now read unto us be fit in itself or seasonable at this time is the only question. For if we shall now tell his Majesty that
70 unless he will remove evil councillors at the instant we will not assist him in the suppression of the present rebellion in Ireland, though his Majesty should grant what we ask yet it may certainly occasion the loss of that Kingdom. . . . I therefore desire that we may for our countrymens' sake and for our religion sake go through
75 with the assistance of Ireland. And for the condition which we may propose to his Majesty in the sixth Article we may follow the old parliamentary way and either to propose it of the Bill of Tunnage and Poundage, which is shortly again to pass, or else with such other aids and subsidies as his own necessities require from us. . . .

80 8 NOVEMBER Mr. Pym brought in the Instructions to be sent into Scotland to our committee there, of which we had agreed the first five Articles on Saturday last, and had long debated the sixth Article then. Wherein we desired the removal of evil councillors and that no new might be chosen or great officers of state placed without the
85 approbation of parliament, or else we would not be bound to assist his Majesty for the recovery of Ireland. But now Mr. Pym had left out that last condition and had added this new one, viz: that if his Majesty would not be graciously pleased to grant it, though we would continue in that obedience and loyalty to him which was due
90 by the laws of God and this kingdom, yet we should take such a course for the securing of Ireland as might likewise secure ourselves. Divers spake to this and most against the sixth Article and some for it. Mr. Bridgeman began and spake against it, whom divers others followed, some speaking for it and some against it till at last it came
95 to a question. And though the Ayes were apparently more than the Noes yet neither side yielding, the Speaker appointed Sir Thomas Barrington and Sir Anthony Irby tellers out of the Ayes who went forth, and Mr. John Belasyse and Sir John Culpepper out of the Noes. The Ayes were 151 and the Noes were 110, and so it was ordered
100 that the said sixth Article should be sent into Scotland as part of our instructions to be sent to our Committee there. (I was a No, conceiving this article to be of very dangerous consequence.)

W. H. Coates (ed.), *The Journal of Sir Simonds D'Ewes* . . . (Yale, 1942), pp 45–7, 94–5, 99–102, 104–5

Questions

a Which of the above parliamentarians were (i) in favour of
   retaining the king's prerogative of ministerial appointment, (ii)
   in favour of dismantling it? Outline the *main points* of their
   arguments.
b Which side do you think had the best of the debate?
c How did the Irish Rebellion help Pym's clause?
d How do the above passages illustrate Pym's tactical skills as a
   parliamentarian?
e Explain (i) 'the Oaths of Allegiance and Supremacy' (lines 22–
   3), (ii) 'the late Protestation of this House' (lines 23–4), (iii) the
   reference to Strafford (lines 45–7).
f Why did D'Ewes think the sixth Article, as passed, was 'of very
   dangerous consequence' (line 102)?

C The Grand Remonstrance Debate, 22–23 November 1641

(a)

It being past twelve of the clock . . . we then began to fall into the
debate of the remonstrance or declaration. Mr. Hyde stood first
up and desired that the Sergeant might go with his mace and call
up all the members of the House who were walking in Westminster
5 Hall, which after it had been much debated was at last done
accordingly. The Sergeant being returned and the mace laid upon
the table where also lay the said declaration or remonstrance ready
engrossed, which had been read through on Saturday foregoing,
the House fell into the debate of it. Mr. Hyde began and spake
10 very vehemently against it, who was seconded by the Lord Falkland,
Sir John Culpepper and divers others. The substance of that which
was objected was in effect following. That it was sans precedent,
nor by the power given us by the words of the writ for election
could we make a remonstrance to the people, and that alone without
15 the concurrence of the Lords. That it was of very dangerous
consequence at this time, considering the affairs of Ireland and the
many disturbances in this kingdom, to set out any remonstrance
or at least such remonstrance as this that contains many harsh
expressions and declarations what we intend to do hereafter etc.
20 viz: to petition his Majesty to take the advice of his Parliament in
the choice of his Privy Council etc. Likewise they declare that they
have already committed a Bill to take away bishops etc. Mr. Pym
and others answered most the said objections, and yet he inclined
that this declaration might be directed to his Majesty, when it had
25 been objected by some that it ought to be directed to him and not
to the people. A little after 4 of the clock in the afternoon I withdrew
out of the House. . . . After I was departed the debate continued

till about 12 of the clock at night, before which time those who
desired the declaration might pass were compelled, contrary to
30   their resolution, of which Sir Christopher Yelverton had informed
me, to suffer many particulars to be altered – and amongst the rest
that which I could not have assented unto – or else without doubt
the said declaration had been cast out of the House. For when it
came to be put to the question it passed but by the plurality of 11
35   voices for there were 148 Noes against it and but 159 Ayes for it.
The Ayes went out of the House and the Noes sat still. After the
question had been put it was again moved that the declaration
might be directed to his Majesty but that was not condescended
unto. Mr. Peard moved that this declaration might be printed but
40   Mr. Hyde and Sir John Culpepper and divers others offered to
enter their protestations against printing of it. But that was gainsaid
for no protestation can be entered without the consent of the
House. So this matter was laid aside until a further time of debate.
Everybody thought that the business had been agreed upon and
45   that the House should have risen, it being about one of the clock
of the morning ensuing. Mr. Geoffrey Palmer, a lawyer of the
Middle Temple, stood up and desired that a protestation might be
entered in the name of himself and all the rest. Upon which, divers
cried All, All, and some waved their hats over their heads, and
50   others took their swords in their scabbards out of their belts and
held them by the pommels in their hands setting the lower part on
the ground, so as if God had not prevented it there was very great
danger that mischief might have been done. All those who cried
All All and did the other particulars were of the number of those
55   that were against the remonstrance. Some who were against the
printing of the remonstrance yet disavowed Mr. Palmer's desiring
to have a protestation entered in their names, and Mr. Hampden
demanded of him how he could know other mens' minds. To who
Mr. Palmer answered, having leave of the House to speak, that he
60   having once before heard them cry All All he had thereupon desired
to have the said protestation entered in all their names. But at last
it was agreed of all hands to leave the said matter touching the
printing of the declaration undetermined, and so it was only ordered
that it should not be printed without the special order of the House.
65   And then the House arose just when the clock struck two the
ensuing morning.
        Coates, *Journal of Sir Simonds D'Ewes*, pp 184–7

(**b**)
The next morning, the debate being entered upon about nine of
the clock in the morning, it continued all that day; and candles
being called for when it grew dark (neither side being very desirous
70   to adjourn it till the next day; though it was evident very many
withdrew themselves out of pure faintness, and disability to attend

the conclusion) the debate continued till after it was twelve of the clock, with much passion. And the House being then divided upon the passing or not passing it, it was carried for the affirmative by
75   nine voices and no more. And as soon as it was declared, Mr. Hampden moved 'that there might be an order entered for the present printing it', which produced a sharper debate than the former. It appeared then that they did not intend to sent it up to the House of Peers for their concurrence, but that it was upon the
80   matter an appeal to the people, and to infuse jealousies into their minds. It had never been the custom to publish any debates of determinations of the House which [were] not regularly first transmitted to the House of Peers, nor was it thought, in truth, that the House had authority to give warrant for the printing of
85   any thing. All which was offered by Mr. Hyde with some warmth, as soon as the motion was made for the printing it. And he said he did believe the printing it in that manner was not lawful, and he feared it would produce mischievous effects, and therefore desired the leave of the House that, if the question should be put and
90   carried in the affirmative, he might have liberty to enter his protestation. Which he no sooner said than Geoffrey Palmer (a man of great reputation, and much esteemed in the House) stood up and made the same motion for himself, that he might likewise protest, when immediately together many afterwards, without
95   distinction and in some disorder, cried out, 'They did protest', so that there was after scarce any quiet and regular debate.

W. Dunn Macray (ed.), *The History of the Rebellion and Civil Wars in England* by Edward, Earl of Clarendon (Oxford, 1888), I, 419–20.

Questions

a   What was the Grand Remonstrance?
b   Compare and contrast D'Ewes' and Clarendon's accounts of the debate.
c   Which account is likely to have been the most accurate and why?
d   What evidence is there from these passages that this was an *exceptional* debate?
e   Which lines suggest that the Remonstrance, as passed, was not as revolutionary as it might have been?
f   Explain, in your own words, why there was such a disturbance after the Grand Remonstrance vote had been taken.

II *War Preliminaries, 1642*

1 An Abortive Coup, 4 January 1642

The king was not passive in the drift towards civil war. It was Charles I who originally introduced an army into the British Isles by his attempts to subdue Scotland in the Bishops' Wars; similarly, it was Charles who in the Army Plot of April and May 1641 first threatened to use armed force to resolve the deadlock at Westminister and it was he who brought armed guards to arrest the five members. But in all these instances – however rash and imprudent they were – the king was provoked by the hostile actions of his opponents. Specifically, in the case of the five members, Charles was moved to action by the rumour current at the end of the previous year that the Commons intended to impeach the queen, although it was probably the counsel of Lord Digby – characterised by Hyde as 'being too easily inclined to sudden enterprises' – that was decisive. The decision was taken late on 3 January after the cautious response of the Lords to the treason charges that had been brought against the five men earlier that day. It was Parliament's refusal to hand over the accused that prompted the king to apprehend them personally. Such a move could only have been justified by success but the king's delay of some eighteen hours ensured a humiliating and costly defeat. As Captain Robert Slyngsby observed, within a few days the king's action had been declared a high breach of privileges and the five members 'so vindicated in print that, with greater honour and applause than ever, they now sit in the House again, the City and seamen magnificently guarding them by land and water to the Parliament House at Westminster'. Charles's decision to leave London a week later, moreover, was a direct consequence of the failed coup, and it was this that separated the combatants into armed camps and made civil war all the more likely.

A Some Contemporary Accounts of the Attempted Arrest of the Five Members

(*a*)

As soon as the House met again, 'twas moved, considering there was an intention to take these five men away by force, to avoid all tumult, let them be commanded to absent themselves. Upon this, the House gave them leave to absent themselves, but entered no
5 order for it, and then the five gentlemen went out of the House. A little after the king came, with all his guard, and all his pensioners, and two or three hundred soldiers and gentlemen. The king commanded the soldiers to stay in the hall, and sent us word he was at the door. The Speaker was commanded to sit still, with the
10 mace lying before him, and then the king came to the door, and took the Palsgrave in with him, and commanded all that came with him, upon their lives not to come in. So the doors were kept open, and the Earl of Roxborough stood within the door, leaning upon it. Then the king came upwards, towards the chair, with his hat
15 off, and the Speaker stepped out to meet him. Then the king stepped up to his place, and stood upon the step, but sat not down in the chair. And after he had looked a great while, he told us he would not break our privileges but treason had no privilege; he came for those five gentlemen for he expected obedience yesterday
20 and not an answer. Then he called Mr. Pym and Mr. Holles, by name, but no answer was made. Then he asked the Speaker if they were here or where they were. Upon that the Speaker fell on his knees, and desired his excuse for he was a servant to the House, and had neither eyes, nor tongue, to see or say anything but what
25 they commanded him. Then the king told him, he thought his own eyes were as good as his, and then said, his birds were flown, but he did expect the House should send them to him, and if they did not he would seek them himself, for their treason was foul, and such a one as they would all thank him to discover. Then he
30 assured us they should have a fair trial, and so went out, putting off his hat till he came to the door. . . .

J. Bruce (ed.), *Notes of Proceedings in the Long Parliament by Sir Ralph Verney* (Camden Society, XXXI, 1845), pp 138–9

(*b*)

The king came in person into the Commons House attended with his servants and pensioners, and about 400 or 500 desperate soldiers, captains and commanders, of papists, ill-affected persons, being
35 men of no rank or quality, divers of them being traitors in France, Frenchmen fled hither, panders and rogues, in a hostile manner with arms forced to the parliament door not suffering it to be shut, expecting when the word should be given that the king coming thither was to demand those accused of treason; but those that

40   came with him, that is to say the soldiers, papists, and others of
        the queen's servants being French papists and English as is proved,
        came with a resolution that in case the Commons should deny to
        render these that were accused, to fall upon the House of Commons
        and to cut all their throats. And because the 5 men accused were
45   not in the House when the king was there, a proclamation was
        printed and proclaimed at Whitehall for the apprehension of Mr.
        Holles and the other 4. . . .

W. H. Coates, Vernon F. Snow and Mrs W. W. Young
(eds), *The Private Journals of the Long Parliament* (Yale, 1982),
pp 11–12 (Roger Hill's account)

(c)

Whereas the chambers, studies, and trunks of Mr. Holles, Sir
Arthur Haselrig, Mr. Pym, Mr. Hampden, and Mr. Strode,
50   members of the House of Commons, upon Monday the third of
        this instant January, by colour of his Majesty's warrant, have been
        sealed up . . . which is not only against the privileges of Parliament,
        but the common liberty of every subject. Which said members,
        afterward the same day, were, under the like colour, by Serjeant
55   Francis, one of his Majesty's Serjeants at Arms, contrary to all
        former precedents, demanded of the Speaker sitting in the House
        of Commons, to be delivered unto him, that he might arrest them
        of high treason. And whereas afterwards, the next day, his Majesty
        in his royal person came to the said House, attended with a great
60   multitude of men, armed in warlike manner with halberds, swords,
        and pistols, who came up to the very floor of the House, and
        placed themselves there and in other places and passages near to
        the said House, to the great terror and disturbance of the members
        then sitting, and according to their duty, in a peaceable and orderly
65   manner, treating of the great affairs of England and Ireland. And
        his Majesty, having placed himself in the Speaker's chair, demanded
        of them the persons of the said members to be delivered unto him,
        which is a high breach of the rights and privileges of Parliament
        and inconsistent with the liberties and freedoms thereof. And
70   whereas afterwards his Majesty did issue forth several warrants to
        divers officers, under his own hand, for the apprehension of the
        persons of the said members; which, by law, he cannot do, there
        being not, all this time any legal charge or accusation, or due
        process of law, issued against them, nor any pretence of charge
75   made known to that House. All which are against the fundamental
        liberties of the subject, and the right of Parliament. . . .

Commons Journal (hereafter *CJ*), II, 373, Mr Glynn's report,
6 Jan 1642

Questions

a   Using the contemporary sources above, write a short paragraph
    in your own words on what happened in the Commons on the
    afternoon of 4 January 1642.
b   How do these accounts differ? Explain the differences.
c   Which privileges of the House were abused by the king on 3
    and 4 January 1642?
d   Write a defence of the king's actions.

2   The Paper War

The beginning of the long propaganda war between king and
Parliament may be traced back at least to late December of the
previous year when the king gave a shrewd and conciliatory answer
to the petition accompanying the Grand Remonstrance (documents
A). This was the first of a series of Royalist propaganda pieces,
designed to appeal to the moderate centre, which was to culminate
in the king's answer to the Nineteen Propositions of 23 June. By
this time, the king's reunion with his eldest son in late February,
his failure to retake Hull from Sir John Hotham, which incident
itself produced a long and vehement paper skirmish – the first part
of which is produced here (documents B) – and the separate call to
arms by both Parliament and king (section 3) had intensified the
debate, so the June propositions argument was conducted in a very
different political atmosphere from that of December. The Nineteen
Propositions debate is well known and is not reproduced here. The
content of the Nineteen Propositions, moreover, was not new for
they contained elements of Pym's old Ten Propositions of the
previous June and had been first drafted as an unpublished 'declaration of fears and jealousies' more than three months earlier.
Nevertheless, their extreme nature should not be overlooked – in
Professor Fletcher's words they should be seen as 'an ultimatum
. . . rather than a serious agenda for negotiation' – and it is not
surprising that the king rejected this demand for parliamentary
sovereignty, just as he had rejected a milder parliamentary petition,
about affairs at York, the previous day. The king's answer to the
Nineteen Propositions is a masterly defence of constitutional
royalism against an innovatory parliament, but it demonstrated the
gulf which separated the king from his opponents. At this stage,
and perhaps for several months, it was clear that neither side would
compromise and that the political will to achieve a constitutional
settlement was lacking, despite the successful efforts of the peace
party in Parliament to amend the original propositions. This became
apparent in mid July when Holland presented to Charles the final
parliamentary petition to 'compose differences' (document C,a).

The king verbally dismissed it as 'like a pill well gilded' but he condescended to reply formally in words which were far removed from the smooth reassurances of earlier protestations. The time for soft language had passed and the king himself refused to dispense with the acerbic preamble (document C,b) in his answer to the Holland petition. When the body of the king's reply contained such words as: 'Let all the world judge who began this war and upon whose account the miseries which may follow must be cast', war was openly recognised as inevitable.

A The Petition Accompanying the Grand Remonstrance, presented 1 December, and the King's Answer, 23 December 1641

(*a*)

Most Gracious Sovereign, your Majesty's most humble and faithful subjects, the Commons in this present Parliament assembled, do with much thankfulness and joy acknowledge the great mercy and favour of God, in giving your Majesty a safe and peaceful return
5 out of Scotland into your kingdom of England. . . . The duty which we owe to your Majesty and our country cannot but make us very sensible and apprehensive that the multiplicity, sharpness and malignity of those evils under which we have now many years suffered, are fomented and cherished by a corrupt and ill-affected
10 party, who amongst others their mischievous devices for the alteration of religion and government, have sought by many false scandals and imputations, cunningly insinuated and dispersed amongst the people, to blemish and disgrace our proceedings in this Parliament and to get themselves a party and faction amongst
15 your subjects. . . . And because we have reason to believe that those malignant parties . . . have so far prevailed as to corrupt divers of your bishops and others in prime places of the Church, and also to bring divers of these instruments to be of your Privy Council, and other employments of trust and nearness about your
20 Majesty, the Prince, and the rest of your royal children. And by this means have had such an operation in your counsel and the most important affairs and proceedings of your government. . . . For preventing the final accomplishment whereof, your poor subjects are enforced to engage their persons and estates to the
25 maintaining of a very expensive and dangerous war. . . . And because all our most faithful endeavours and engagements will be ineffectual for the peace, safety and preservation of your Majesty and your people, if some present, real and effectual course be not taken for suppressing this wicked and malignant party, we, your
30 most humble and obedient subjects, do with all faithfulness and humility beseech your Majesty:

1. That you will be graciously pleased to concur with the humble
desires of your people in a parliamentary way, for the preserving
the peace and safety of the kingdom from the malicious designs of
35   the Popish party. For depriving the bishops of their votes in
Parliament, and abridging their immoderate power usurped over
the clergy and other your good subjects. . . . For the taking away
such oppressions in religion, church government and discipline, as
have been brought in and fomented by them. For uniting all such
40   your loyal subjects as join in the same fundamental truths against
the Papists, by removing some oppressive and unnecessary ceremonies . . . for the due execution of those good laws which have been
made for securing the liberty of your subjects.
2. That your Majesty will likewise be pleased to remove from
45   your council all such as persist to favour and promote any of
those pressures and corruptions wherewith your people have been
grieved; and that for the future your Majesty will vouchsafe to
employ such persons in your great and public affairs, and to take
such to be near you in places of trust, as your Parliament may have
50   cause to confide in. . . .
3. That you will be pleased to forbear to alienate any of the forfeited
and escheated lands in Ireland which shall accrue to your Crown
by reason of this rebellion. . . .
Which humble desires of ours being graciously fulfilled by your
55   Majesty, we will, by the blessing and favour of God, most
cheerfully undergo the hazard and expenses of this war, and . . .
lay a sure and lasting foundation of the greatness and prosperity of
your Majesty, and your royal posterity in future times.
        S. R. Gardiner (ed.), *Constitutional Documents of the Puritan*
        Revolution 1625–1660 (Oxford 1889), pp 202–5

(**b**)
To the petition, we say that although there are divers things in the
60   preamble of it which we are so far from admitting that we profess
we cannot at all understand them . . . yet, notwithstanding, we
are pleased to give this answer to you.
    To the first, concerning religion, consisting of several branches,
we say that for preserving the peace and safety of this kingdom
65   from the design of the Popish party, we have, and will still, concur
with all the just desires of our people in a parliamentary way; that
for the depriving of the bishops of their votes in Parliament, we
would have you consider that their right is grounded upon the
fundamental law of the kingdom and constitution of Parliament.
70   . . . As for the abridging of the inordinate power of the clergy, we
conceive that the taking away of the High Commission Court hath
well moderated that; but if there continue any usurpations or
excesses in their jurisdictions, we therein neither have nor will

protect them . . . that for any illegal innovations which may have
75 crept in, we shall willingly concur in the removal of them; that, if
our Parliament shall advise us to call a national synod, which may
duly examine such ceremonies as give just cause of offence to any,
we shall take it into consideration, and apply ourself to give due
satisfaction therein. But we are very sorry to hear, in such general
80 terms, corruption in religion objected, since we are persuaded in
our consciences that no Church can be found upon the earth that
professeth the true religion with more purity of doctrine than the
Church of England . . . which, by the grace of God, we will with
constancy maintain (while we live) in their purity and glory, not
85 only against all invasions of Popery, but also from the irreverence
of those many schismatics and separatists. . . .

To the second prayer of the petition, concerning the removal
and choice of councillors, we know not any of our Council to
whom the character set forth in the petition can belong; that by
90 those whom we had exposed to trial, we have already given you
sufficient testimony that there is no man so near unto us in place
or affection, whom we will not leave to the justice of the law, if
you shall bring a particular charge and sufficient proofs against
him; and of this we do again assure you, but in the meantime we
95 wish to forbear such general aspersions as may reflect upon all our
Council, since you name none in particular. That for the choice of
our councillors and ministers of state, it were to debar us that
natural liberty all freemen have; and as it is the undoubted right of
the Crown of England to call such persons to our secret counsels,
100 to public employment and our particular service as we shall think
fit, so we are, and ever shall be, very careful to make election of
such persons in those places of trust as shall have given good
testimonies of their abilities and integrity, and against whom there
can be no just cause of exception whereon reasonably to ground a
105 diffidence; and to choices of this nature, we assure you that the
mediation of the nearest unto us hath always concurred.

To the third prayer of your petition concerning Ireland, we
understand your desire of not alienating the forfeited lands thereof,
to proceed from much care and love, and likewise that it may be a
110 resolution very fit for us to take; but whether it be seasonable to
declare resolutions of that nature before the events of a war be
seen, that we much doubt of. Howsoever, we cannot but thank
you for this care, and your cheerful engagement for the suppression
of that rebellion; upon the speedy affecting whereof, the glory of
115 God in the Protestant profession, the safety of the British there,
our honour, and that of the nation, so much depends. . . .

Ibid, pp 233–6

Questions

a   What is the tone of (i) Parliament's petition (ii) the King's
    Answer?
b   How far do Parliament's requests differ from Pym's Ten
    Propositions of June 1641? (see pp 19–21)
c   Which things would the king have found difficult to accept
    (first lines of his answer) in the preamble to Parliament's
    petition?
d   Comment on:
    (i) 'a safe and peaceable return out of Scotland' (lines 4–5);
    (ii) 'For preventing the final accomplishment whereof, your
         poor subjects are enforced to engage their persons and
         estates in the maintaining of a very expensive and dangerous
         war' (lines 23–5);
    (iii) 'For depriving the bishops of their votes in Parliament, and
          abridging their immoderate power usurped over the clergy
          and other your good subjects' (lines 35–7);
    (iv) 'As for abridging the inordinate power of the clergy, we
         conceive that the taking away of the High Commission
         Court hath well moderated that' (lines 70–2);
    (v) 'no Church can be found upon the earth that professeth the
        true religion with more purity of doctrine than the Church
        of England' (lines 81–3);
    (vi) 'we know not any of our Council' to 'justice of the law'
         (lines 88–92).

B   The Debate Over Hull, April 1642

(*a*)

His Majesty having received the petition enclosed from most of
the chief of the gentry near about York, desiring the stay of his
Majesty's arms and munitions in his magazine at Hull, for the
safety not only of his Majesty's person and children, but likewise
5   of all these northern parts (the manifold rumours of great dangers
inducing them to make their said supplication) thought it most fit
to go himself in person to his town of Hull to view his arms and
munition there; that thereupon he might give directions what part
thereof might be necessary to remain there for the security and
10 satisfaction of his Northern subjects, and what part thereof might
be spared for Ireland, the arming of his Majesty's subjects that are
to go thither, or to replenish his chief magazine of the Tower of
London. Where being come upon the 23rd. of this instant and
much contrary to his expectation, he found all the gates shut upon
15 him, and the bridges drawn up by the express command of Sir
John Hotham (who for the present commands a garrison there)

and from the walls flatly denied his Majesty entrance into his said town, the reason of the said denial being as strange to his Majesty as the thing itself; it being that he could not admit his Majesty
20 without breach of trust to his Parliament. Which did the more incense his Majesty's anger against him, for that he most seditiously and traitorously would have put his disobedience upon his Majesty's parliament, which his Majesty being willing to clear, demanded of him, if he had the evidence, to aver that the parliament had directed
25 him to deny his Majesty entrance, and that if he had any such order that he should show it in writing for otherwise his Majesty could not believe it. Which he could no ways produce but maliciously made that false interpretation according to his own inferences, confessing that he had no such positive order, which his Majesty
30 was ever confident of. But his Majesty, not willing to take so much pain in vain, offered to come into that his town only with twenty horse, finding that the main of his pretence lay that his Majesty's train was able to command the garrison. Notwithstanding, his Majesty was so desirous to go thither in a private way that he gave
35 warning thereof but overnight. Which he refusing, but by way of condition (which his Majesty thought much behove him) held it most necessary to declare him traitor (unless upon better thoughts he should yield obedience) which he doubly deserved, as well for refusing entrance to his natural sovereign as by laying the reason
40 thereof groundlessly and maliciously upon his Parliament.

One circumstance his Majesty cannot forget, that his son, the Duke of York, and his nephew, the Prince Elector, having gone thither the day before, Sir John Hotham delayed the letting of them out to his Majesty till after consultation.

45 Hereupon his Majesty hath thought it expedient to demand justice of this parliament against the said Sir John Hotham, to be exemplarily inflicted upon him according to the laws; and the rather, because his Majesty would give them a fit occasion to free themselves from this imputation by him so injuriously cast upon
50 them, to the end his Majesty may have the easier way for the chastising of so high a disobedience.

Rushworth, *Historical Collections*, III, part i, pp 567–8, the king's message to Parliament, 24 April 1642

(*b*)
The Lords and Commons in Parliament finding just cause to fear not only the desperate designs of papists and others of the malignant party at home but also the malice of enemies incited by them from
55 abroad, thought it necessary for the safety of this kingdom to secure the town of Kingston-upon-Hull, being one of the most considerable places for strength and affording the best convenience for landing of foreign forces, and where a part of the magazine of the kingdom for that time was placed. And for that end appointed

60   Sir John Hotham, one of the members of the House of Commons, being a gentleman of the same county of a considerable fortune and approved integrity, to take upon him the government of the town, and to draw thither some of the trained bands for the guard thereof. . . .

65   They further conceiving that the magazine there, being of so great importance to this kingdom, would be more secure in the Tower of London, did petition his Majesty to give his consent [that] the same might be removed. Which, notwithstanding, his Majesty did refuse. And thereupon some few ill-affected persons

70   about the city of York, took upon them the presumption, in opposition to our desires and in contempt of both Houses, to petition his Majesty to contain the magazine at Hull, alleging it to be for the safety of his Majesty (as if there could be a greater care in them of his Majesty's royal person than in Parliament). And his

75   Majesty the next day, after the delivery of that petition, being the 23rd of this instant April, took occasion thereupon to go to the town of Hull, attended with about 400 horse (the Duke of York and the Prince Elector being gone thither the day before) and required Sir John Hotham to deliver up the town into his hands.

80   Who, perceiving his Majesty to be accompanied with such force as might have mastered the garrison of the town; and having received intelligence of an intention to deprive him of his life, in case the King should be admitted, informed his Majesty of the trust reposed in him by both Houses of Parliament, and that he could not,

85   without breach of that trust, let him in; beseeching his Majesty to give him leave to send to the Parliament to acquaint them with his Majesty's command, and to receive their directions therein which he would do with all expedition. Which answer his Majesty was not pleased to accept of, but presently caused him and his officers

90   to be proclaimed traitors before the walls of the town. And thereupon dispatched a message to the Houses, therein charging Sir John Hotham with high treason, and aggravating his offence because he pretended the Parliament's command, in the meanwhile hindering him of all means of intelligence with the Parliament, for

95   his Majesty caused all passages to be stopped between him and them. And in pursuance of the same, one of his servants, who was sent by him with letters to the Parliament to inform them of the truth of those proceedings, was apprehended, his letters taken from him and his person detained. Whereby (contrary to the common

100   liberty of every subject) he was not only deprived of means to clear himself of that heavy accusation, but of all ways of intercourse, either to receive directions from them that trusted him or to inform them what had happened.

      The Lords and Commons, finding the said proceedings to be a

105   high violation of the privileges of Parliament (of which his Majesty had in several messages impressed himself to be so tender) a great

infringement of the liberty of the subject and the law of the land, which his Majesty had so often lately professed would be his rule to govern by, and tending to the endangering of his Majesty's
110 person and the kingdom's peace, thought fit, as well for the vindication of their own rights and privileges and the indemnity of that worthy person employed by them, as for the clearing of their own proceedings, to published these ensuing votes, which were made upon a former relation that came from the King.
115   Die Jovis, April 28 1642. Resolved upon the question: That Sir John Hotham, Knight, according to this relation, hath done nothing but in obedience to the command of both Houses of Parliament.
. . . That this declaring of Sir John Hotham traitor, being a Member of the House of Commons, is a high breach of the privilege of
120 Parliament. . . . That this declaring Sir John Hotham traitor, without due process of law, is against the liberty of the subject and against the law of the land.
      Ibid, pp 570–1, Parliament's declaration concerning Hull, 28 April 1642

Questions

a What was the importance of Hull (i) for the king (ii) for Parliament?

b Explain in your own words what happened at Hull, 22–23 April 1642.

c How did the incident worsen relations between king and Parliament?

d Who gets the better of this argument? (Justify your answer.)

e What was so special about parliamentary votes being published?

C Parliament's Petition of 12 July (presented 16th) and the Preamble to the King's Answer, 17 July 1642

(*a*)
May it please your Majesty, although we, your Majesty's most humble and faithful subjects, the Lords and Commons in Parliament assembled, have been very unhappy in many former petitions and supplications to your Majesty, wherein we have represented our
5 most dutiful affections, in advising and desiring those things which we held most necessary for the preservation of God's true religion, your Majesty's safety and honour, and the peace of the kingdom; and with much sorrow do perceive that your Majesty, incensed by many false calumnies and slanders, doth continue to raise forces
10 against us and your other peaceable and loyal subjects, and to make

great preparations for war, both in the kingdom and from beyond the seas, and by arms and violence to overrule the judgment and advice of your Great Council, and by force to determine the questions there depending, concerning the government and liberty of the kingdom; yet such is our earnest desire of discharging our duty to your Majesty and the kingdom, to preserve the peace thereof, and to prevent the miseries of civil war amongst your subjects, that, notwithstanding we hold ourselves bound to use all the means and power which by the laws and constitutions of this kingdom we are trusted with, for defence and protection thereof, and of the subjects, from force and violence, we do in this our humble and loyal petition prostrate ourselves at your Majesty's feet, beseeching your royal Majesty that you will be pleased to forbear and remove all preparations and actions of war, particularly the forces from about Hull, from Newcastle, Tynmouth, Lincoln, and Lincolnshire, and all other places. And that your Majesty will recall the commissions of array, which are illegal, dismiss troops and extra-ordinary guards by you raised. That your Majesty will come nearer to your Parliament, and hearken to their faithful advice and humble petitions, which shall only tend to the defence and advancement of religion, your own royal honour and safety, the preservation of our laws and liberties. And we have been, and ever shall be, careful to prevent and punish all tumults, and seditious actions, speeches, and writings, which may give your Majesty just cause of distaste or apprehension of danger. From which public aims and resolutions no sinister or private respect shall ever make us to decline. That your Majesty will leave delinquents to the due course of justice; and that nothing done or spoken in Parliament, or by any person in pursuance of the command and direction of both Houses, be questioned anywhere but in Parliament.

And we, for our parts, shall be ready to lay down all those preparations which we have been forced to make for our defence. And for the town of Hull, and the ordinance concerning the militia, as we have in both these particulars only sought the preservation of the peace of the kingdom and the defence of the Parliament from force and violence, so we shall most willingly leave the town of Hull in the state it was before Sir John Hotham drew any forces into it; delivering your Majesty's magazine into the Tower of London, and supplying whatsoever hath been disposed by us for the service of the kingdom. We shall be ready to settle the militia by a bill, in such a way as shall be honourable and safe for your Majesty, most agreeable to the duty of Parliament, and effectual for the good of the kingdom; that the strength thereof be not employed against itself, and that which ought to be for our security applied to our destruction; and that the Parliament, and those who profess and desire still to preserve the Protestant religion both in this realm and in Ireland, may not be left naked and indefensible

to the mischievous designs and cruel attempts of those who are the
professed and confederated enemies thereof in your Majesty's
60 dominions and other neighbour nations. To which, if your
Majesty's courses and counsels shall from henceforth concur, we
doubt not but we shall quickly make it appear to the world, by
the most eminent effects of love and duty, that your Majesty's
personal safety, your royal honour and greatness, are much dearer
65 to us than our own lives and fortunes, which we do most heartily
dedicate, and shall most willingly employ, for the support and
maintenance thereof.
Clarendon, *History of the Rebellion*, II, pp 230–1.

(**b**)
Though his Majesty had no great reason to believe that the
directions sent to the Earl of Warwick to go to the river of Humber
70 with as many ships as he should think fit, for all possible assistance
to Sir John Hotham (whilst his Majesty expected the giving up of
the town unto him) and to carry away such arms from thence as
his discretion thought fit to spare out of his Majesty's own
magazine; the choosing a general by both Houses of Parliament,
75 for the defence of those who have obeyed their orders and
commands (be they never so extravagant and illegal); their declaration that in that case they would live and die with the Earl of
Essex, their general (all which were voted the same day with this
petition); and the committing the Lord Mayor of London to prison
80 for executing his Majesty's writs and lawful commands, were but
ill prologues to a petition which might compose the miserable
distractions of the kingdom. Yet his Majesty's passionate desire of
the peace of the kingdom, together with the preface of the
presenters, 'That they had brought a petition full of duty and
85 submission to his Majesty, and which desired nothing of him but
his consent to peace' (which his Majesty conceived to be the
language of both Houses too) begot a greedy hope and expectation
in him that this petition would have been such an introduction to
peace that it would at least have satisfied his message of the eleventh
90 of this month, by delivering up Hull unto his Majesty. But, to his
unspeakable grief, his Majesty hath too much cause to believe that
the end of some persons by this petition is not in truth to give any
real satisfaction to his Majesty, but, by the specious pretences of
making offers to him, to mislead and seduce his people, and lay
95 some imputation upon him of denying what is fit to be granted.
Otherwise, it would not have thrown those unjust reproaches and
scandals upon his Majesty for making necessary and just defence
for his own safety; and so peremptorily justified such action[s]
against him as by no rule of law or justice can admit the least
100 colour of defence; and, after so many free and unlimited acts of
grace passed by his Majesty without any condition, have proposed

such things which in justice cannot be denied unto him, upon such
conditions as in honour he cannot grant. However, that all the
world may see how willing his Majesty would be to embrace any
105 overture that might beget a right understanding between him and
his two Houses of Parliament (with whom he is sure he shall have
no contention when the private practices and subtle insinuations of
some few malignant persons shall be discovered, which his Majesty
will take care shall be speedily done) he hath with great care
110 weighed the particulars of this petition. . . .
     Ibid, p 232

Questions

a Which petition is the most convincing and why?
b What evidence is presented here that civil war is near at hand?
c Comment on the following parliamentary requests:
    (i) 'that your Majesty will recall the commissions of array,
       which are illegal' (lines 26–7);
    (ii) 'that your Majesty will leave delinquents to the due course
       of justice' (lines 37–8);
    (iii) 'And for the town of Hull and the ordinance concerning
       the militia . . . we have . . . only sought the preservation
       of the peace of the kingdom and the defence of the
       Parliament' (lines 43–5);
d Complete (in a short paragraph, using your own words) the
    king's reply.

3 The Call to Arms

Parliament had been concerned with the question of the control of
the militia ever since the revelation of the Army Plot of April/May
1641 – as we have seen (pp 19–21) the eighth of Pym's Ten
Propositions had included a proposal for securing the loyalty of
the militia officers – but early attempts to secure a militia bill failed.
It was Oliver Cromwell who had first suggested that the best way
forward would be by ordinance. A militia ordinance to put the
trained bands into a posture of defence and to give the command
of them to the Earl of Essex, whom the king had temporarily made
Captain General of forces south of the Trent during his absence in
Scotland, had been drafted by the Commons and sent up to the
Lords in mid November. The decision of the committee of the
whole House on 18 January to appoint new Lord Lieutenants who
would exercise 'a standing power for the commanding of military
forces in every county' may thus be seen as a logical outcome of
the deliberations of the previous November. Yet it took several

weeks of hard work, notably by William Pierrepoint who chaired the committee responsible for naming the Lord Lieutenants, and gentle persuasion that the Militia Ordinance was an essentially defensive precaution, before it passed both Houses (document A,a). Technically this did not happen until 5 March but the crucial decision was taken three days earlier when, in the light of the king's refusal to agree to parliamentary requests for the disposal of the militia (see document B,a), the Commons resolved to put the kingdom 'into a posture of defence by authority of both Houses' without the king's concurrence.

With the exception of the City of London, the implementation of the Militia Ordinance was a slow business. Pym and the parliamentary leaders purposely played a waiting game: it was not until 2 April that the Lords were requested to execute the Ordinance, a message that had to be repeated more than five weeks later. The delay may also be explained by the time taken over the king's own Militia Bill. So it was not until late May that the first Lord Lieutenants and their deputies went into the counties to enforce the Ordinance. Meanwhile many of the old Lieutenancy commissions were surrendered and numerous deputies appointed. Between late May and mid July the Ordinance was executed in fourteen counties and between mid August and late October in a further nine. As these letters from four counties indicate (document A,b), the Lieutenants and their deputies generally reported that the militia was near full strength and well armed (although there was a noticeable shortage in Lincolnshire because of the Scots war) and that a goodly number of men had volunteered 'for the defence of the king and parliament'. Yet no indication of the impending military struggle was given in these reports. The military preparations reported here were seen as essentially defensive measures to save the king and the kingdom from the 'bloody counsels of papists', the target of parliamentary propaganda ever since the opening days of the Long Parliament. Much more innovating than the Militia Ordinance, but no less defensive in tone, was the propositions scheme of early June (document A,c). This invited subscriptions of money and plate, as well as offers to maintain cavalry and arms, and became the basis of the parliamentary war effort, although the immediate response of the counties was never more than lukewarm.

The king's response to the militia question was, in some ways, masterly. In a series of broadsides he denounced the early parliamentary initiatives but did not exclude the possibility of compromise. The February answer to Parliament, for example, declared his willingness to grant 'such commissions as he hath done this parliament to some Lord Lieutenants by your advice' (London and the corporations only excepted) but urged 'if that power be not thought enough' that the militia be regulated by statute. It was this message that must have persuaded the parliamentary leaders to proceed by ordinance, a device which, as the king later observed, was of dubious legality and not binding without his consent. Charles responded with his own Militia Bill and it was only when this was amended out of all recognition that he exercised his veto. Yet it was one thing for the king to countermand the parliamentary ordinance, it was quite another to devise adequate machinery to call men to arms after Parliament had precluded the use of the Lord Lieutenants and their deputies in the counties. In the circumstances, the device opted for – the commission of array – was by no means a bad choice for it offered Charles a much more flexible system of recruitment than was available to the Lord Lieutenants empowered by the Militia Ordinance. (See document B,a.) But the use of such commissions posed two distinct problems for the king: first, the statute on which these commissions were based (5 Henry IVc.25) was of dubious legality; and second, the instruments had not been employed since 1557 (although Charles had toyed with the idea of using them in the West Country to raise troops for the Scottish War in 1640) so that when they were again issued in late May/June 1642 Englishmen were totally unfamiliar with their use. Moreover, as we can see from the Hereford report (document B,b,2) they were issued in Latin so few people would have understood them when they were publicly read out at town market places. It is hardly surprising, therefore, that some commissioners of array should meet with a hostile reception, particularly in a county like Warwickshire (document B,b,1) where the gentry community was split in allegiance. By contrast, in Herefordshire and Cornwall (document B,b,2,3) the gentry were more solidly Royalist and the commissioners were loyally received, although as Judge Foster observed at the end of his arduous circuit, a desire for peace was paramount among most West Countrymen, even as late as August 1642.

A   The Parliamentary Call to Arms

(a)   The Militia Ordinance, 5 March 1642

An Ordinance of the Lords and Commons in Parliament, for the Safety and Defence of the Kingdom of England, and Dominion of Wales

Whereas there hath been of late a most dangerous and desperate design upon the House of Commons, which we have just cause to
5   believe to be an effect of the bloody counsels of papists and other ill-affected persons who have already raised a rebellion in the kingdom of Ireland, and, by reason of many discoveries, we cannot but fear they will proceed not only to stir up the like rebellion and

insurrections in this kingdom of England, but also back them with
10   forces from abroad. For the safety, therefore, of his Majesty's
person, the Parliament, and kingdom, in this time of imminent
danger, it is ordained by the Lords and Commons now in Parliament
assembled, that Henry Earl of Holland shall be Lieutenant of the
County of Berks . . . [the other Lord Lieutenants are then listed]
15   and severally and respectively have power to assemble and call
together all and singular his Majesty's subjects, within the said
several and respective counties and places, as well within liberties
as without, that are meet and fit for the wars; and them to train,
exercise, and put in readiness; and them, after their abilities and
20   faculties, well and sufficiently, from time to time, to cause to be
arrayed and weaponed, and to take the muster of them in places
most fit for the purpose. And the aforesaid . . . shall severally and
respectively have power, within the several and respective counties
and places aforesaid, to nominate and appoint such persons of
25   quality as to them shall seem meet, to be their Deputy Lieutenants,
to be approved of by both Houses of Parliament. And that any
one or more of the said Deputies, so assigned and approved of, in
the absence, or by the command of the said Henry Earl of Holland
[etc.] . . . shall have power to make colonels and captains, and
30   other officers, and to remove them out of their places, and make
others from time to time, as they shall think fit for that purpose.
And the said Henry Earl of Holland [etc.] . . . their Deputy or
Deputies, in their absence, or by their command, shall have power
to lead, conduct, and employ the persons aforesaid, arrayed and
35   weaponed, for the suppression of all rebellions, insurrections, and
invasions that may happen within the several and respective counties
and places . . . as within any other part of this realm of England
or dominion of Wales . . . according as they from time to time
shall receive directions from the Lords and Commons assembled
40   in Parliament.

And be it further ordained, that Sir John Gaire, Sir Jacob Garrett,
knights and aldermen [etc.] . . . citizens of London, or any six or
more of them, shall have such power and authority, within the
city of London and the liberties thereof, as any of the Lieutenants
45   before named are authorised to have, by this Ordinance, within
their said several and respective counties (the nomination and
appointment of Deputy Lieutenants only excepted).

And it is further ordained, that such persons as shall not obey in
any of the premises shall answer their neglect and contempt of the
50   Lords and Commons in a parliamentary way, and not otherwise,
nor elsewhere; and that every the powers granted as aforesaid shall
continue until it shall be otherwise ordered or declared by both
Houses of Parliament, and no longer.

   LJ, IV, pp 625–7, 5 March 1642

Questions

a   What is an ordinance and how does it differ in authority from a
    statute?
b   How revolutionary were the proposals of the Militia Ordinance?
c   Comment on the first lines of the Ordinance (from 'whereas'
    to 'abroad').
d   Why was separate provision made for the City of London?
    What had happened to the City government in 1641–2?

(b) Its Implementation

(1)

. . . This morning, ten of my Deputy Lieutenants met me here at
55 Northampton, whereof of the trained bands of this county (consisting but of three hundred men) were summoned to appear. The
captains affirm that their companies were never fuller upon any
other summons. Here appeared likewise about five hundred and
fifty volunteers, not inferior either in arms or readiness to the
60 trained bands, besides many other able bodies of meaner condition
(which were not numbered, but did far exceed the armed men, as
was generally agreed on amongst us). Who, being not able to
compare arms, yet offered their service with the greatest alacrity,
some having swords, some clubs, and all good hearts for the
65 defence of the king and Parliament. . . .

> *LJ*, v. p 139, Lord William Spencer to the Earl of Leicester,
> 14 June 1642

(2)

I have now perfected your Lordship's commands in putting the
Ordinance in execution concerning the militia of this county, and
have taken a muster of all the trained bands, with much contentment
in the assurance I have received of their fidelity and affection to
70 serve the Parliament, which they have fully expressed in this
particular of the militia, in their ready appearance, so that, of
eighteen companies, very few or none failed to appear. Their want
of arms, which were taken away in the last northern expedition, is
their only discouragement, but those I intend shortly to supply by
75 your Lordship's order to the Committee at Hull. For the horse, I
cannot give your Lordship so good an account of their appearance
as I desired, the warning being short and many of them at soil;
but I cannot doubt of their forwardness in any service to the
Commonweath, having received a full testimony of their affections
80 by this enclosed declaration. . . .

> Ibid, p 155, Lord Willoughby to the Speaker, Lincoln, 19
> June 1642

This being the first day of our mustering the regiments within this county, having the opportunity of this bearer's address to you, we thought it worth your Lordship's knowledge that calling Sir Thomas Jervoise and Mr. Wellopp's regiments before us, consis-
85 ting, by their old muster books, of eighteen hundred, we had so ready an obedience to your commands, by the Ordinance of Parliament, that the full number made their appearance, completely armed, before us, with a hundred volunteers out of the town of Basingstoke and divers others from other adjacent parts. . . .

> Ibid, p 156, Deputy Lieutenants of Hampshire to Earl of Pembroke, Rooksdowne, 21 June 1642

(4)
90 . . . The County of Warwick being divided into four hundreds, the Lord Lieutenant, for the ease thereof, did appoint for each hundred a several day, and convenient place of meeting for their view and training . . . so as the total sum of the volunteers amounts unto two thousand eight hundred and fifty. And whereas the
95 trained bands of the county of Warwick, and city and county of Coventry are in the whole six hundred; there appeared of them . . . five hundred and fifty. And besides the aforesaid appearance, the Earl of Northampton being in the county, upon a report that he would oppose the said service at Coleshill, there was a ready
100 and affectionate appearance of about eight hundred horse that accompanied the Lord Lieutenant thither, for the securing of his person and advancing the cause. And in these meetings and concourse of people, we found a most free and clear expression of their affections to the King and Parliament. . . .

> Ibid, p 195, Deputy Lieutenants of Warwick to the Speaker, Coventry, 5 July 1642

Questions

a Explain how the Militia Ordinance was implemented at a local level.
b Why was the opposition in these counties to the activities of the Lord Lieutenants and their Deputies not more extensive? How far was the reaction of these counties typical of the whole country?
c How do you explain the fact that the authors of these letters were not conscious that they were about to fight a civil war against the king?
d How did these musters in the summer of 1642 differ from those

in previous years? What do they show about the king's quest for a 'perfect militia' in the 1630s?

(c) The Propositions Scheme, 9 June 1642

105 . . . the Lords and Commons . . . excite all well-affected persons to contribute their best assistance, according to their solemn vow and protestation, to the preparations necessary for the opposing and suppressing of the traitorous attempts of these wicked and malignant councillors, who seek to engage the King in so dangerous
110 and destructive an enterprise, and the whole kingdom in a civil war, and destroy the privileges and being of parliaments. This recourse to the good affections of those that tender their religion and just liberties, and the enjoyment of the blessed fruits of this present Parliament, which were almost ready to be reaped and are
115 now as ready to be ruined by those wicked hands, being the only remedy left them under God, and without which they are no longer able to preserve themselves, or those by whom they are entrusted:

1. They, the said Lords and Commons, do declare, that whosoever shall bring in any proportion of ready money, or plate, or shall
120 underwrite to furnish and maintain any number of horse, horsemen, and arms, for the preservation of the public peace, and for the defence of the King and both Houses of Parliament from force and violence, and to uphold the power and privileges of Parliament, according to this Protestation; it shall be held a good and acceptable
125 service to the Commonwealth, and a testimony of his good affection to the Protestant religion, the laws, liberties, and peace of this kingdom, and to the Parliament and privileges thereof. And because a considerable aid cannot be raised by few hands, and the condition of all men's estates and occasions is not always proportionable to
130 their affection, the Lords and Commons do declare that no man's affection shall be measured according to the proportion of his offer, so that he express his good-will to this service in any proportion whatsoever.

2. And it is further declared, by the Lords and Commons in
135 Parliament, that whosoever shall bring in any money or plate, or shall furnish and maintain any horse, horsemen, and arms, for the purposes aforesaid, shall have their money repaid, with the interest according to eight pounds *per cent*. And the full value of their plate, with consideration for the fashion, not exceeding one shilling per
140 ounce, and shall have full recompense for all their charge in finding, furnishing, and maintaining of horse, horsemen, and arms; and for this both Houses of Parliament do engage the public faith.

3. And it is ordained, that Sir John Wallaston, Knight and Alderman . . . [and three other Aldermen] shall be treasurers, to receive all

145 such money and plate as shall be brought in for the purposes
aforesaid. . . .
4. It is ordered that . . . shall be commissaries, to value the horse
and arms that shall be furnished for this service; and that a
signification, under the hands of them, or any two of them, of
150 such value of the horse and arms, and of the time when they were
first brought in, shall be a warrant to demand satisfaction, according
to the said values; and they shall keep an account of the time from
the first enrolment of any such horse and horsemen, that such as
find and maintain them may be repaid, according to the rate of
155 two shillings and six pence *per diem*. . . .
5. It is ordered, that whosoever shall bring in money or plate, or
shall provide and maintain horse, horsemen, and arms, for this
service, shall do according to their duty therein; and the Lords and
Commons do engage the power and authority of Parliament to
160 save them harmless from all prejudice and inconvenience that may
befall them by occasion thereof.
6. It is ordered that members of either House who are present shall
be desired to declare in their Houses respectively what money or
plate they will bring in; or what horse, horsemen, and arms, they
165 will find and maintain.
7. It is desired, that all such as have their residence in or about
London, or within eighty miles, will bring in their money, plate,
or horse, within a fortnight after notice; and they that dwell further
off, within three weeks. . . .
170 And lastly, it is declared, that whatsoever is brought in shall not
at all be employed upon any other occasion than to the purposes
aforesaid; which are, to maintain the Protestant religion, the King's
authority and his person in his royal dignity; the free course of
justice, the laws of the land, the peace of the kingdom, and the
175 privileges of Parliament, against any force which shall oppose them;
and this by the direction of both Houses of Parliament.
    Ibid, pp 121–2, 9 June 1642

Questions

a How convincing do you find the argument of the preamble and
   last declaration?
b In what ways was this a more revolutionary document than the
   Militia Ordinance?
c How good a deal were the inducements to lend to Parliament?
   Why was the local response to this measure so reticent in the
   first instance?
d How important was this scheme in the winning of the civil
   war?

B The King's Response

(a) The Commission of Array

Whereas it hath been declared by the votes of both Houses of
Parliament the 15th of March last, that the kingdom hath of late
and still is in so evident and imminent danger, both from enemies
abroad and a popish discontented party at home, that there is an
5 urgent and inevitable necessity of putting our subjects into a posture
of defence for the safeguard both of our person and people; and
that sithence divers inhabitants of divers counties have addressed
their petitions to that purpose. And whereas a small number of
both Houses (after it had been rejected by the Lords in a full House,
10 and without our royal assent, or the opinion of the judges
concerning the legality of it) have attempted by way of Ordinance,
to put in execution the militia of the kingdom, and to dispossess
many of our ancient nobility of the command and trust reposed in
them by us, and have nominated divers others who have no interest,
15 nor live near to some of the counties to which they are nominated
for the lieutenancy, whereby they cannot be properly serviceable
to the counties wherewith they are entrusted; nor our people receive
that content and security which we desire they should. To submit
to the execution of which power by the way of Ordinance, without
20 it were reduced into a law by Act of Parliament established by our
royal assent, were to reduce and expose our subjects to a mere
arbitrary government, which by God's grace we shall never permit.
We therefore, considering that by the laws of the realm it
belongeth to us to order and govern the militia of the kingdom,
25 have thereupon by our proclamation of the 27th of May last,
prohibited all manner of persons whatsoever upon their allegiance
to muster, levy, or summon upon any warrant, order or ordinance
from one or both Houses of Parliament, whereunto we have not,
or shall not give our express consent to any of the trained bands or
30 other officers without express warrant under our hands. . . . And
considering that in ancient time the militia of the kingdom was
ever disposed of by the commissioner of array, and that by a
particular statute upon record in the Tower, made in the fifth year
of Henry the fourth, by full consent . . . we have thought fit to
35 refer it to that ancient legal way of disposing the power of the
militia by commissions of array for defence of us, our kingdom
and our county; authorizing you, or any three or more of you, to
array and train our people, and to apportion and assess such persons
as have estates and are not able to bear arms, to find arms for other
40 men in a reasonable and moderate proportion; and to conduct them
so arrayed as well to the coasts, as to other places, for the opposition
and destruction of our enemies in case of danger, as to your
discretions, or any three or more of you shall seem meet, whereof

you Henry Earl of Huntington, and in your absence, William Earl
45   of Devonshire, or Henry Hastings Esq. to be one. And being both
confident in a great measure both of the loyal affections of our
people, and very tender to bring any unnecessary burden or charge
on them by augmenting the number of the trained bands, we do
for the present only require that you do forthwith cause to be
50   mustered and trained all the ancient trained bands and freehold
bands of the county, carefully seeing that they be supplied with
able and sufficient persons, and completely armed; unless you find
that there be just cause, and that it shall be with the good liking of
the inhabitants for their own better security to make any increase
55   in their number; and over such bands to appoint and set such
colonels, captains and officers as you shall think most fit for the
discharge of that service being such persons as have considerable
interest in the county and not strangers. And in case of any
opposition, you are to raise the power of the county to suppress
60   it, and to commit all such persons as are found rebellious herein
into the custody of our sheriff, whose care and assistance we
especially require. And that he shall from time to time issue forth
such warrants for the assembling of our people at such times and
places as by you shall be agreed on, according to the trust reposed
65   in him by our said commission. And we have authorized you our
commissioners, or any three of you, after such array made, from
time to time to train and take musters of our said bands; and to
provide beacons and other necessaries for the better exercising of our
people, and discovery of sudden invasions and commotions. . . .
Rushworth, *Historical Collections*, III, part i, pp 657–8, the
king's letter sent with the Commission of Array to Leices-
tershire, dated (at York) 12 June 1642

Questions

a   Explain the meaning of 'array'.
b   How good is this document as a piece of propaganda?
c   How valid are the king's arguments in favour of the Commission
of Array?
d   How wide are the powers given to the commissioners of array?
How do they differ from those bestowed on the Lord Lieutenants
under the Militia Ordinance? (see document A,a above).

(b) Its Implementation

(1)
70   This Saturday, about eleven of the clock in the morning, there

came intelligence to the mayor and aldermen of the city of Coventry that the Earl of Northampton was come to the said city. The mayor desired three of the aldermen to visit the Earl of Northampton, as recorder of that city; and the Earl certified these three gentlemen
75 that he came from York, from the King, and brought with him a proclamation from his Majesty, which he affirmed was sealed about three of the clock in the afternoon upon Thursday last; which proclamation was directed to all his loving subjects within the kingdom of England and dominion of Wales, to authorize all his
80 Majesty's said subjects to obey the Commission of Array (which Commission, his lordship informed, was warranted per divers statute laws yet unrepealed). At that instant, he requested the said aldermen to acquaint the mayor that he would meet the mayor and aldermen at the Council House of that city, and there he would
85 declare his Majesty's mind to them. At the time appointed, the Earl came and certified the mayor and aldermen that he had received a commission of array from his Majesty, and would put it speedily in execution in the county of Warwick, and city and county of Coventry. His lordship, being desired that his commission might
90 be viewed, answered [that] it was not finished at his coming from York, but he should receive it from thence speedily. . . . After the said Earl was gone from this city, the sheriffs of the said city and county came, and certified me that they would serve the King and Parliament, and observe the Ordinances of both Houses concerning
95 the militia, with their lives and fortunes, according to their late protestation. . . . [But] The Earl of Northampton made known that the mayor, with some others, was joined with him in the commission. And I am persuaded they will show readiness in obeying that commission (the mayor refusing to accept of your
100 lordship's deputation for the militia), if they be not prevented by the wisdom of the Parliament. . . .

LJ, V, pp 164–5, John Barker to Lord Brooke, dated (at Coventry) 25 June 1642

(2)
The trained bands being come into Hereford, the drums beat up to call together the soldiers, then the commissioners read the Commission of Array, under the town hall in the presence of a
105 few of the soldiers and many others, which Commission was read in Latin . . . few understanding it. After which, the drums beat up, and having drawn each company to wait upon their colours, the commissioners going down to Wigmarsh, the bands marching after them; which being come thither, each captain sets the band
110 in order. Which being done, the commissioners together with the sheriff, who is one in commission, viewed Captain Scudamore's band, which appeared very fully. Then Captain Scudamore and his officers called over his band by the list, and viewed their arms.

After which, he told them he would have them all in readiness if
115 there were any occasion to use them, as he hoped there would not,
and that they should go no further than he went. So in like manner,
the rest of the captains, viz., Captain Wigmore and Captain
Slaughter called over their bands, all which made a very good
appearance. Then the commissioners, joining together, called up
120 that band which was Sir Robert Harley's and called it over by the
list, first called the captain, Sir Robert Harley, then the officers of
the band amongst which only one drum and the ancient appeared.
In calling over the soldiers, many were found absent and so
defaulted to the number, as was conceived, of forty or fifty. This
125 being done, the commissioners authorised Mr. Coningsby to be
captain of the said band, in the room of Sir Robert Harley, and so
gave notice of it to the ancient and some others, who said if they
must lose their old captain, they willingly embraced Mr. Coningsby
rather than any man. . . . After this all the trained bands were
130 drawn into one entire body, a table being placed in the midst of
them, the commissioners standing about it, the crier from them
command[ed] silence. Then Mr. Edmonds, Clerk of the Peace,
stood upon the table and read a letter from his Majesty, declaring
that he had had a declaration of the good affection of this county,
135 so he doubted not of a further manifestation or expression of their
loyalty in doing him service. There was also declared his Majesty's
pleasure in authorising Mr. Robert Croft for the command of what
horse shall be sent in to his Majesty out of this county in a free
and voluntary way, as I conceive. Moreover, it was declared that
140 what money or plate shall be sent in to his Majesty, by his loving
subjects of this county, it must go to York and be delivered to the
Controller of his Majesty's Household who is authorised for the
purpose. After this, was read the resolution of Herefordshire,
against which no man that I heard of objected, which being done,
145 they all cried 'God save the King,' and then departed the field. The
band of volunteers marching first into town, when they came to
enter the gate of the city, put all their hats under their stick ends
and held them up with a great acclamation for the King. . . .

Historical Manuscripts Commission, Portland III, pp 90–1,
report on Herefordshire, 14 July 1642

(*3*)
In obedience to your commands, we ended our long journey before
150 the assizes of Cornwall began, where we found my Lord Mohun
and the greatest number of commissioners of the array, who openly
began their work on the fast day, the Wednesday before, at
Lostwithiel; but also at several private meetings at my Lord
Mohun's and Sir Nicholas Slanning's castle, as we are informed.
155 . . . The names as we learned of the commissioners of array, the
new justices and the names of these put out, we have placed in the

foot of this letter. The first proceed we made was to Judge Foster, and delivered him the commands, and required his performance. He told us, he would do his duty. From thence we went to the
160 church, where one Mr. Nicholas Hatch, whose devotions were out, praying for Charles Lord Mohun, his patron, and our worthy sheriff, who are two commissioners of array, in his sermon did declare that the militia was in the King, with some rotten stories that are too troublesome to write or hear. From thence we went
165 to the Bench, to hear the judge's discharge, which made a little noise, of these commands; and we had as little respect as we did expect. But when my Lord came to declare his Majesty's directions, he had vigour, voice and rhetoric to act that home. Thence we went abroad, to understand how our country was possessed. . . .
170 Most of the new justices are of the Commission of Array and they go opposite to our way. We have waited three days here, labouring a right understanding of the power of Parliament. . . . As we are now writing, this hour, at ten of the clock, at the ending of the assizes. . . . they read his Majesty's proclamation and resolution
175 against Hull, the proclamations against the militia, the Commission of Array, the warrants to the sheriffs for their proceeds; and they have appointed the execution of it. . . .

Ibid, p 275, the committee in Cornwall to the Speaker, dated (at Launceston) 5 Aug 1642

(4)
. . . whereas I had been in several places pressed to deliver my own opinion touching the illegality of the Commissions of Array, and
180 was pressed upon the votes in both Houses of Parliament, and other for the judges to declare and publish the same votes, for that both votes and order were so generally well known, and in all men's mouths, I conceived it no way against his Majesty's service nor my own duty to declare such vote and order were made and
185 passed. But, for my own part, I expressly declared myself that I forbore to deliver any opinion of my own; nor have I as yet declared myself to any what my opinion is, touching the legality or illegality thereof. Although I find the contrary in print, yet [it is] false and accompanied with many other untruths, wherein I
190 shall refer myself to all that were present. The truth is, the counties are much possessed with the illegality of the commissions of array, and the unlimited power, as is alleged, in the commissioners, and by reason thereof infinitely averse thereunto. Yet, on the other side, I cannot find but they are possessed with contentment in his
195 Majesty's declaration for maintenance of religion and laws of the kingdom, and the liberty of Parliament, and his great care of the good of his subjects. . . . And, for anything I could perceive, the general desire of the countries is [that] both the Commissions of Array and Militia be laid down, and some way to be established

200 by Act of Parliament for the quiet settling of the militia of the kingdom. And truly the several contradictory commands make so great distraction (as they say) amongst them, that they fear if it should so continue it will be exceeding mischievous to many particular persons whose hearts stand well affected both to his
205 Majesty's service and love of the public good; so will it bring great confusion to the general if not speedily prevented by some settled course.

> *CSPD 1641–43*, pp 375–6, Sir Robert Foster, justice of assize for the western circuit, to Secretary Nicholas, 21 Aug 1642

Questions

a   What were the political views of (i) the Earl of Northampton (ii) Sir Robert Harley (iii) Judge Foster? Support your answer by reference to the above passages.

b   Compare and contrast the reception given to the commissioners of array in Warwickshire, Herefordshire and Cornwall. Explain the different reactions of these counties.

c   How do you reconcile Foster's account of activities in the West Country with the parliamentary committee report on Cornwall?

III Military Conflict and the Parliamentary Army

I Early Hostilities and the Scottish Alliance

By 1642, defensive preparations for civil war were gaining momentum although many Parliamentarians and Royalists continued to believe that conflict could be avoided. The crude division of England into opposing camps was symbolised by the king's departure from London to Hampton Court on 10 January. By February, as Royalists from the capital gradually slipped away to join him, Charles began to move northwards – attempting to rally loyal supporters and financial aid away from the Parliamentary strongholds in the south. The drift to war was accelerating, and civil war officially broke out when the king raised his standard at Nottingham in August.

The immediate task for Parliamentarians was to ensure themselves against military defeat by organising an effective militia. Responsibility for the Parliamentary forces was entrusted to the Earl of Essex, who embodied 'everything that stood for respectability and conservatism'. However, while preventing an armed debacle was an objective all Parliamentarians could accept, no unanimity existed at Westminster over the ultimate goals of the civil war. As the early battles proved inconclusive, and neither side gained a substantial advantage, the internal dissonance over the nature of conflict increased. This was eventually to prove the cause of a profound dispute between Oliver Cromwell and his commanding officer, the Earl of Manchester. The disagreements among the Parliamentary officers were mirrored by arguments at Westminster between those who favoured peace, and those who wished to see the king defeated in battle.

While the attitudes of an ambivalent 'peace party' caused Parliament to prevaricate over this crucial issue, military developments caused concern at Westminster. At the Battle of Edgehill (23 October 1642), Essex's army had been unable to stop the Royalist march from Shrewsbury to London, despite much loss of life on both sides. The subsequent battle of Brentford was indecisive, and parliament's cause was under close military threat until the king, realising the impossibility of controlling London at this stage, withdrew to establish Royalist headquarters at his 'alternative capital' – Oxford. By early 1643, the king had established command over most of the north and west of England, although several Parliamentary garrisons were effectively resisting siege within the Royalist area. The king's military options were restricted by the existence of these garrisons in Plymouth, Hull and Gloucester – for Royalist commanders felt unable to move against London while the threat of disruption remained in the rear.

On the Parliamentary side, the early months of 1643 represented the nadir of the military campaign. Most of England was in Royalist hands, and the Parliamentary forces had failed to make a significant impact in the conflict. Only one course remained open to Parliament, short of actually negotiating a peace settlement with King Charles: the construction of a military alliance with the Scots. The Scots had already shown an inclination to the Parliamentary cause in the events of 1641, and had been instrumental in organising opposition to the Prayer Book of 1637 and in the calling of the Long Parliament. However, it was widely recognised that the Scots would only consider lending military aid if Parliament undertook to reform the Anglican church – and so the price of Scottish support was to be the strict imposition of Presbyterian religious uniformity. Parliament's position was, nonetheless, calamitous, and an alliance was forged in September 1643 despite the doubts expressed by many at Westminster. The main principles were defined in *The Solemn League and Covenant* (document A,a). The detailed reform of existing clerical practice was referred to a new body – the Westminster Assembly of Divines – which consisted of 125 ministers (mainly Presbyterian), 30 laymen, and several Scots observers (document A,b).

A   Ecclesiastical Reform

(*a*)
A solemn league and covenant for reformation and defence of religion, the honour and happiness of the king, and the peace and safety of the three kingdoms of England, Scotland and Ireland.

We noblemen, barons, knights, gentlemen, citizens, burgesses,
5   ministers of the gospel, and commons of all sorts in the kingdoms of England, Scotland and Ireland, by the providence of God living under one king, and being of one reformed religion; having before our eyes the glory of God and the advancement of the kingdom of Our Lord and Saviour Jesus Christ, the honour and happiness of
10   the King's Majesty and his posterity, and the true public liberty, safety and peace of the kingdom, wherein everyone's private condition is included; and calling to mind the treacherous and

bloody plots, conspiracies, attempts and practices of the enemies
of God against the true religion and professors thereof in all places,
15 especially in these three kingdoms, ever since the reformation of
religion; and how much their rage, power and presumption are of
late at this time increased and exercised, whereof the deplorable
estate of the Church and kingdom of Ireland, the distressed estate
of the Church and kingdom of England, and the dangerous estate
20 of the Church and kingdom of Scotland are present and public
testimonies . . . each one of us for himself, with our hands lifted
up to the most high God, do swear:

I That we shall sincerely, really and constantly, through the
grace of God, endeavour in our several places and callings, the
25 preservation of the reformed religion in the Church of Scotland,
in doctrine, worship, discipline and government, against our
common enemies; the reformation of religion in the kingdoms of
England and Ireland in doctrine, worship, discipline and
government, according to the word of God and the example of the
30 best reformed churches; and we shall endeavour to bring the
churches of God in the three kingdoms to the nearest conjunction
and uniformity in religion, confessing of faith, form of church
government, directory for worship, and catechising, that we and
our posterity after us may, as brethren, live in faith and love, and
35 that the Lord may delight to dwell in the midst of us.

II That we shall in like manner, without respect of persons,
endeavour the extirpation of Popery, prelacy (that is, Church
government by archbishops, bishops, their chancellors and commissaries, deans, deans and chapters, archdeacons, and all other
40 ecclesiastical officers depending on that hierarchy), superstition,
heresy, schism, profaneness, and whatsoever shall be found to be
contrary to sound doctrine and the power of godliness, lest we
partake in other men's sins, and thereby be in danger to receive of
their plagues; and that the Lord may be one and his name one in
45 the three kingdoms.

III We shall with the same sincerity, reality and constancy in our
several vocations endeavour with our estates and lives mutually to
preserve the rights and privileges of the parliaments, and the
liberties of the kingdoms, and to preserve and defend the King's
50 Majesty's person and authority, in the preservation and defence of
the true religion and liberties of the kingdoms, that the world may
bear witness with our consciences of our loyalty, and that we have
no thoughts or intentions to diminish his Majesty's just power and
greatness.

55 IV We shall also with all faithfulness endeavour the discovery of
all such as have been or shall be incendiaries, malignants, or evil

instruments, by hindering the reformation of religion, dividing the King from his people, or one of the kingdoms from another.

> Reprinted in J. P. Kenyon, *The Stuart Constitution* (1978), pp 263–4

(b)

Whereas it hath been declared and resolved by the Lords and
60 Commons assembled in Parliament that the present Church government by archbishops, bishops, their chancellors, commissaries, deans, deans and chapters, archdeacons, and other ecclesiastical officers depending upon the hierarchy is evil, and justly offensive and burdensome to the kingdom, a great impediment to reformation
65 and growth of religion, and very prejudicial to the State and government of this kingdom, and that therefore they are resolved that the same shall be taken away, and that such a government shall be settled in the Church as may be most agreeable to God's Holy Word, and most apt to procure and preserve the peace of the
70 Church at home, and nearer agreement with the Church of Scotland, and other reformed churches abroad; and for the better effecting hereof, and for the vindicating and clearing of the doctrine of the Church of England from all false calumnies and aspersions, it is thought fit and necessary to call an assembly of learned, godly
75 and judicious divines, to consult and advise of such matters and things, touching the premises, as shall be proposed unto them by both or either of the Houses of Parliament, and to give their advice and counsel therein to both or either of the said Houses when and as often as they shall be thereunto required.

> An Ordinance for the calling of an Assembly of learned and Godly Divines . . . (12 June 1643)

Questions

a Explain the reasons for the establishment of the Westminster Assembly (document b).
b What features of Anglican Church government were opposed both by the Scottish Presbyterians and most of the Parliamentarians?
c How could Parliament claim that it had 'no thoughts or intentions to diminish his Majesty's just power and greatness' (lines 53–4)?
d Explain the significance of the phrase 'according to the word of God' (line 29).

2 The Consequences of Marston Moor (2 July 1644)

The battle of Marston Moor was a turning point in the civil war, although it did not seriously deplete the king's military resources. The immediate cause of the battle was Prince Rupert's attempt to break the Parliamentary siege of York where the king's northern commander – the Earl of Newcastle – was trapped with his army. Marching from Lancashire, Rupert managed to evade the Parliamentary forces and relieve the city on 18 July 1644. Rupert's military genius now deserted him – instead of resting his troops and devising a joint strategy with Newcastle, he immediately assumed the command and turned to attack the Parliamentary army under Lord Leven, Lord Fairford and the Earl of Manchester. On the following evening, the two armies drew up opposite each other on Marston Moor – due west of the city of York. It was improbable that battle should commence so late in the day, and both commanders seem to have been content to exchange cannon–shot and wait until the morrow. But unexpectedly, Cromwell's cavalry of the Eastern Association charged – some reports claim that Cromwell perceived a momentary tactical advantage; others that he was infuriated by the death of his nephew, a victim of the Royalist artillery. Cromwell mentions the latter event in his account of the battle in correspondence with his bereaved brother-in-law (document A,a).

The main events of the subsequent struggle are reasonably clear. The battle continued from around 8 p.m. to midnight: Cromwell's horse, with the advantage of surprise, defeated Rupert's celebrated cavalry on the Royalist right flank; but the Parliamentary right collapsed under attack from the king's northern cavalry. Cromwell, crucially, reassembled his 'Ironsides' and launched a second assault against the jubilant northern horse – who were rapidly dispersed in disarray. The Scots infantry, despite heavy losses, stood firm in the middle of the field; and the rout of the Royalist cavalry made the position of the king's infantry hopeless. About 4000 Royalists were killed in the conflict, and Prince Rupert fled to York with Newcastle.

The significance of the Parliamentary victory lay in the restoration of civilian morale (particularly given the defeat of the 'invincible' Rupert), rather than in any decisive shift in the military balance. Newcastle's defeat left Parliament with effective control over the North of England, although isolated pockets of Royalist resistance held out for over a year. But Parliament, and her allies, were not united by a military victory which also served to emphasise some of the disputes and jealousies which divided the victors. The Scots commissioners were keen to stress the important role played by their own forces in the victory. Many in England, however, viewed Cromwell as the hero of the hour (document A,b).

A Accounts of the Battle

(*a*)

'To my loving Brother, Colonel Valentine Walton: These'
'Leaguer before York', 5th July 1644
Dear Sir,

It's our duty to sympathise in all mercies; that we may praise
5   the Lord together in chastisements or trials, that so we may sorrow
together.

Truly England and the Church of God hath had a great favour
from the Lord, in this great victory given unto us, such as the like
never was since this war began. It had all the evidences of an
10   absolute victory obtained by the Lord's blessing upon the godly
party principally. We never charged but we routed the enemy. The
left wing, which I commanded, being our own horse, saving a few
Scots in our rear, beat all the Prince's horse. God made them as
stubble to our swords, we charged their regiments of foot with
15   our horse, routed all we charged. The particulars I cannot relate
now, but I believe, of twenty-thousand, the Prince hath not four-
thousand left. Give glory, all the glory, to God.

Sir, God hath taken away your eldest son by a cannon-shot. It
brake his leg. We were necessitated to have it cut off, whereof he
20   died. . . . At his fall, his horse being killed with the bullet, and as
I am informed three horses more, I am told he bid them open to
the right and left, that he might see the rogues run. Truly he was
exceedingly beloved in the Army, of all that knew him. But few
knew him, for he was a precious young man, fit for God. You
25   have cause to bless the Lord. He is a glorious saint in Heaven,
wherein you ought exceedingly to rejoice. Let this drink up your
sorrow; seeing these are not feigned words to comfort you, but
the thing is so real and undoubted a truth. You may do all things
by the strength of Christ. Seek that, and you shall easily bear your
30   trial. Let this public mercy to the Church of God make you to
forget your private sorrow. The Lord be your strength: so prays
Your truly faithful and loving brother,
Oliver Cromwell

Cromwell to Colonel Valentine Walton (5 July 1644) *The
Letters and Speeches of Oliver Cromwell*, introduced by Thomas
Carlyle (1904), pp 176–7

(*b*)

Sir Thomas Fairfax, having again taken the field with his father,
35   after a miraculous victory they had gained over the Irish army
which the king had brought over, joined the Scots; and the Earl of
Manchester, having raised a force in the associated counties, with
which he made an expedition to Lincoln, having Colonel Cromwell

for his lieutenant–general, marched into Yorkshire, and uniting
40   with the other two armies, they all besieged the Earl of Newcastle
in York. To raise this siege, Prince Rupert came with a great army
out of the south; the besiegers rose to fight with the prince, and
Newcastle drew all his force out of York to join with him, when
both armies, on a great plain called Marston Moor, had a bloody
45   encounter, and the Scots and Lord Fairfax had been wholly routed,
and the battle lost, but that Cromwell, with five thousand men
which he commanded, routed Prince Rupert, restored the other
routed parliamentarians, and gained the most complete victory that
had been obtained in the whole war. The victors possessed all the
50   prince's ordnance, carriages and baggage; whereupon the prince
fled, with as many as he could save, back into the south; the Earl
of Newcastle, with some of his choice friends, went into Germany,
and left Sir Thomas Glenham governor of York, which he soon
surrendered, and then the three generals parted; Leven went back
55   into the north, and took the town of Newcastle, Fairfax remained
in Yorkshire, and Manchester returned into the south, taking in
many small garrisons by the way as he passed through the counties.
        Lucy Hutchinson, *Memoirs of Colonel Hutchinson (1664–1671)*
        (1968 edn), pp 182–3

Questions

a   Are there any reasons (in document a) to suspect some inaccur-
      acies in Cromwell's account of Marston Moor?
b   Why should Cromwell particularly wish to deprecate the efforts
      of the Scots?
c   Who were the Scots Commissioners, and why were they
      important?

3   Cromwell and Manchester

The victory at Marston Moor restored Parliament's hopes of a
military victory, but these were not to be immediately realised.
On the contrary, Parliament was soon to suffer an important
reverse in the campaign. While three Parliamentary armies had
been engaged at York, the Earl of Essex's force concentrated on
the south-west of England. Intending to effect a propaganda coup
by capturing the queen, Essex was lured further westwards – into
Devon and Cornwall. Henrietta Maria evaded her pursuers, and
escaped to exile in France. Meanwhile, the Royalist trap closed
around Essex's isolated army – now cut off in hostile territory by

the king's forces marching from Oxford. Essex retreated along the peninsula, and was finally cornered at Lostwithiel, supported only by the Parliamentary fleet under the Earl of Warwick. Realising the impossibility of relief, Essex decided to rescue what he could from this hopeless position. Accordingly, on 31 August 1644, he instructed his cavalry to break out of the siege under cover of darkness, while he made his own escape by rowing out to one of the Parliamentary ships. By so doing, Essex effectively abandoned his infantry and artillery to the king's pleasure – a fact gleefully exploited by Royalist propagandists. The king proved magnanimous in victory; after plundering their munitions and equipment, he allowed the disconsolate Parliamentarians to disperse. This embarrassing episode was a major blow to Parliament's hopes of victory.

Significantly, the members at Westminster did not censure Essex for his folly and tactical naivety (documents A,a,b). However, other Parliamentarians (particularly in the army) felt strongly about this issue, believing that the military campaign was not being conducted effectively. This question was brought sharply into focus by the publication of a long-standing dispute between Cromwell and the Earl of Manchester, his commanding officer. Cromwell had been alarmed by Manchester's decision not to attack Newcastle or to disrupt Rupert's forces regrouping in Chester. This impending crisis finally emerged following the second indecisive Battle of Newbury (27 October 1644): the king, the Prince of Wales, and the main body of the Royalist army were allowed to slip away unopposed from Donnington Castle, largely because the Earl of Manchester refused to authorise pursuit until the following day. This caused great resentment, and the disagreement between Cromwell and Manchester – first aired when the Parliamentary commanders met in Council of War – was soon causing passionate debate in the Commons. It is not surprising that the Royalist perception of the Earl of Manchester should be sympathetic (document A,c).

Cromwell's charges against Manchester (documents B,a,b) bore directly upon the Parliamentary division between 'peace' and 'war' factions. Manchester's riposte included not only a defence of his military conduct, but also an attack on Cromwell's political and religious affiliation (documents C,a,b). This was again significant, for Manchester's remarks expressed the increasing concern felt by Parliamentary leaders (such as Holles and Whitelocke) about the social and religious composition of the army. Many were aghast at the elevation of non-propertied soldiers to officer status – for example, the notorious John Lilburne was already Lieutenant-Colonel and second in command of Lord Brooke's cavalry regiment. Manchester's remarks were a symptom of the uneasy and suspicious scrutiny of the army by conservative Parliamentarians, who feared independent or sectarian religion and the threat of social revolution even more than they feared a Royalist resurgence.

A   Assessments of the Conduct of the War

(*a*)

. . . The Earl of Essex, having given an account of the misfortune of the Army, and offered to come up to justify himself, if required, the two Speakers wrote thus to him: The Committee of both Kingdoms having acquainted the Houses with your letters from
5   Plymouth, they have commanded us to let you know, that as they apprehend the misfortune of that accident, and submit to God's pleasure in it, so their good affections to your Lordship, and their opinion of your fidelity in the public service, is not at all lessened. They resolve not to be wanting in their best endeavours for
10 repairing this loss: To which purpose they have written to the Earl of Manchester to march with all speed towards Dorchester with all the forces he can, and Sir W. Waller is likewise ordered to march speedily thither with all his Horse and Foot. The Houses have appointed 6000 Foot-Arms, 500 pair of pistols, and 6000 suits of
15 clothes, etc. to meet you at Portsmouth for encouraging your forces: And they are confident your Lordship's presence in those parts will much conduce to the public advantage.

     J. Rushworth, *Historical Collections* (1703–8) Vol 5, p 355

(*b*)

That violent party, which had at first cozened the rest into the war, and afterwards obstructed all the approaches towards peace, found
20 now that they had finished as much of their work, as the tools which they had wrought with could be applied to; and what remained to be done, must be despatched by new workmen. They had been long unsatisfied with the Earl of Essex, and he was as much with them; both being more solicitous to suppress the other,
25 than to destroy the King. They bore the loss and dishonour he had sustained in Cornwall very well; and would have been glad, that both he and his army had been quite cut off, instead of being dissolved; for most of his officers and soldiers were corrupted in their affections towards them, and desired nothing but peace: so
30 that they resolved never more to trust or employ any of them.

     Edward Hyde (Earl of Clarendon) in *Selections from the History of the Rebellion*, introduced by H. Trevor-Roper (1978), p 202

(*c*)

By his natural civility, good manners, and good nature, which flowed towards all men, he was universally acceptable and beloved;

and no man more in the confidence of the discontented and factious
party than he, and [none] to whom the whole mass of their designs,
35 as well what remained in chaos as what was formed, was more
entirely communicated, and more consulted with . . . [How-
ever]. . . .

The Earl of Manchester, of the whole cabal, was, in a thousand
respects, most unfit for the company he kept. He was of a gentle
40 and a generous nature; civilly bred; had reverence and affection for
the person of the King, upon whom he had attended in Spain;
loved his country with too unskilful a tenderness; and was of so
excellent a temper and disposition, that the barbarous times, and
the rough parts he was forced to act in them, did not wipe out, or
45 much deface, those marks: insomuch as he was never guilty of any
rudeness towards those he was obliged to oppress, but performed
always as good offices towards his old friends, and all other persons,
as the iniquity of the time, and the nature of the employment he
was in, would permit him to do; which kind of humanity could
50 be imputed to very few.

And he was at last dismissed, and removed from any trust, for
no other reason, but because he was not wicked enough.

Edward Hyde, Earl of Clarendon, op cit, pp 202, 204

Questions

a What evidence exists for Clarendon's Royalist sympathies in
documents b and c?
b Explain what is meant by the final sentence of document b
(lines 25–30).
c Why did Parliament adopt such a deferential approach to Essex
(documents a and b)?
d Use documents a and b to illustrate the major divisions within
Parliament in late 1644.

B Cromwell's Attack on the Military Leaders

(*a*)
In the House of Commons, on Monday 25th November, 1644,
Lieutenant-General Cromwell did, as ordered on the Saturday
before, exhibit a charge against the Earl of Manchester, to this
effect:
5   That the said Earl hath always been indisposed and backward to
engagements, and the ending of the War by the sword; and always
for such a peace to which a victory would be a disadvantage; and
hath declared this by principles express to that purpose, and by a
continued series of carriage and actions answerable.

10　　And since the taking of York, as if the Parliament had now
advantage full enough, he hath declined whatsoever tended to
further advantage upon the enemy; hath neglected and studiously
shifted off opportunities to that purpose, as if he thought the King
too low, and the Parliament too high, especially at Donnington
15　　Castle.
　　　　That he hath drawn the Army unto, and detained them in, such
a posture as to give the enemy fresh advantages; and this, before
his conjunction with the other Armies, by his own absolute will,
against or without his Council of War, against many commands
20　　of the Committee of both Kingdoms, and with contempt and
vilifying of those commands; and, since the conjunction, sometimes
against the Councils of War, and sometimes by persuading and
deluding the Council to neglect one opportunity with pretence of
another, and this again of a third, and at last by persuading them
25　　that it was not fit to fight at all.
　　　　The Letters and Speeches of Oliver Cromwell, op cit, Vol I
　　　　(Fragments from a speech to the Commons, 25 Nov 1644),
　　　　pp 184–5

(b)
Cromwell accused the Earl of Manchester 'of having betrayed the
Parliament out of cowardice; for that he might, at the King's last
being at Newbury, when he drew off his cannon, very easily have
defeated his whole army, if he would have permitted it to have
30　　been engaged: that he went to him, and showed him evidently
how it might be done; and desired him that he would give him
leave, with his own brigade of horse, to charge the king's army in
their retreat; and the Earl, with the rest of his army, might
look on, and do as he should think fit: but that the Earl had,
35　　notwithstanding all importunity used by him and other officers,
positively and obstinately refused to permit him; giving no other
reason, but that, he said, if they did engage, and overthrow the
King's army, the King would always have another army to keep
up the war; but if that army which he commanded should be
40　　overthrown, before the other under the Earl of Essex should be
reinforced, there would be an end of their pretences; and they
should be all rebels and traitors, and executed and forfeited by the
law.'
　　　　This pronunciation what the law would do against them was
45　　very heavily taken by the Parliament, as if the Earl believed the
law to be against them, after so many declarations made by them,
'that the law was on their side, and that the King's arms were taken
up against the law'. The Earl confessed 'he had used words to that
effect, that they should be treated as traitors, if their army was
50　　defeated, when he did not approve the advice that was given by
the lieutenant general; which would have exposed the army to

greater hazard, than he thought seasonable in that conjuncture, in the middle of the winter, to expose it to.

Edward Hyde, Earl of Clarendon, op cit, pp 202–3

Questions

a Use document (a) to examine Cromwell's objections to Manchester's military leadership.
b Why did Manchester refuse to continue the Battle of Newbury (document b)?
c Analyse Manchester's view of the legality of the Parliamentary cause (document b).

C Manchester's Reply

(a)

As might have been expected, Manchester took fire. On the 26th he asked leave of the Peers to defend himself in the House of which he was a member. On the 28th, having obtained the required permission, he assailed Cromwell in return.

5   The narrative thus laid before the Commons consisted of two sections. In the first, which related entirely to the military side of the dispute, Manchester passed lightly over his own part in the recent failure, painted Cromwell as a factious and somewhat inert officer, and laid stress upon his own habit of confirming himself

10 to the resolutions of the Council of War, and upon Cromwell's acknowledgement that this had been the case. As a personal reply this section of the narrative was to a certain extent effective, but it offered no serious defence of those errors which had ruined the last campaign. In the second section Manchester attacked his accuser

15 on the political side. After urging that Cromwell's own position in the army was sufficient evidence that no attempt had been made in it to depress Independents, he held him up to scorn as the despiser of the nobility and the contemptuous assailant of the Assembly of Divines. Cromwell, it seemed, had actually spoken of these

20 reverend gentlemen as persecutors. What was still worse, he had expressed a desire to have an exclusively Independent army, with the help of which he might be enabled to make war on the Scots if they attempted to impose a dishonourable peace on honest men.

    On both sides the larger political dispute threatened to swallow

25 up the question of military action. The Scots were especially irritated by Cromwell's attack upon themselves, now for the first time revealed to them. 'This fire', wrote Baillie, 'was long under the embers; now it's broken out, we trust, in a good time. It's like,

for the interest of our nation, we must crave reason of that darling
30   of the sectaries, and, in obtaining his removal from the army,
which himself by his over-rashness has procured, to break the
power of that potent faction. This is our present difficile exercise:–
we had need of your prayers.'
        S. R. Gardiner, *The History of the Civil War* (1894), pp. 83–
        4

(*b*)
After speaking of the discontents of his army; of his endeavours to
35   quiet them and of the value and esteem he has always had for many
of those in his army who have differed from him in judgment,
Manchester proceeds, 'Lieut.-General Cromwell shall be my com-
purgator in this matter. He knows that I always placed him in
chiefest esteem and credit with me. But it is true that of late I have
40   not given so free and full a power unto him as formerly I did,
because I heard that he used his power so as in honour I could not
avow him in it, and indeed I grew jealous that his designs were
not as he made his professions to me; for his expressions were
sometimes against the nobility; that he hoped to live to see never a
45   nobleman in England, and he loved such better than others because
they did not love lords. He hath further expressed himself with
contempt of the Assembly of Divines, to whom I pay a reverence
as to the most learned and godly convention that hath been this
many ages, yet these he termed persecutors; and that they persecuted
50   honester men than themselves. His animosity against the Scotch
nation . . . was such as he told me that in the way they now carried
themselves, pressing for their discipline [i.e. urging the taking of
the covenant], he could as soon draw his sword against them as
against any in the King's army; and he grew so pressing for his
55   designs as he told me that he would not deny but that he desired
to have none in my army but such as were of the Independent
judgment, giving me this reason:– That in case there should be
propositions for peace or any conclusion of a peace such as might
not stand with those ends that honest men should aim at, this army
60   might prevent such a mischief.
        Manchester to the House of Lords: reprinted in *Camden
        Miscellany* (No. 8) and *Letters and Speeches of Oliver Cromwell*,
        op cit, p 184

Questions

a   How did the Earl of Manchester reply to Cromwell's attack?
b   Explain the significance of Manchester's comments about Inde-
    pendency in the army.

c Why were the Scots 'especially irritated' by Cromwell, and how did they attempt to remove the irritant?

4 'New Modelling' the Army

One of the consequences of the public scandal and disaffection produced by the dispute between Cromwell and Manchester was the crucial decision to reform military organisation. The growing strength of the 'war party' at Westminster was also instrumental in this change – to those who believed that a favourable settlement could only be procured by the defeat of the king, the vital prerequisite was an army adequately prepared and determined to conquer its opponents in the field. Evidently the ambivalent leadership of Essex and Manchester proved incapable of securing decisive victory; it followed that the Parliamentary forces required not only restructuring at regimental level, but also firm and dedicated generals to exploit whatever military advantages might be offered to Parliament. Cromwell raised the issue of the army leadership and prosecution of the campaign in the House of Commons on 9 December 1644, claiming that rapid reform was necessary before localities became unable to bear the costs of civil war (document A,a). The immediate effect was the proposal by Zouch Tate of a Self-Denying Ordinance which had two primary objectives: the least important being the easing of 'tender consciences' by allowing individuals to serve in the Parliamentary army without adopting the Covenant (much to the dismay of the Scots but the enthusiastic approval of Cromwell). Secondly, the Ordinance provided that members of either Parliamentary chamber should relinquish simultaneous military commands – the intention was to remove the moderate nobility from positions dominating the military hierarchy (document A,b). Contemporary views of the Self-Denying Ordinance are recorded by Lucy Hutchinson and Richard Baxter (documents A,c,d). The Bill passed the House of Commons on 19 December, but the Lords proved obstinate before finally approving the measure on 3 April 1645. By the spring of 1645, however, the new modelling of Parliamentary forces was already well under way. The army was divided into twelve regiments of foot (14,400 men); eleven regiments of horse (6600 men), and one dragoon regiment (1000 men) under the overall command of Sir Thomas Fairfax from January 1645. Cromwell, exceptionally, retained his commission, becoming Lieutenant-General in command of horse. The Self-Denying Ordinance ensured Cromwell's victory over Parliamentary opponents, but the political complexion of the New Model Army remained unclear, and a source of no little concern to the moderate faction at Westminster.

A   The Debate on 'New Modelling'

(*a*)

It is now a time to speak, or forever hold the tongue. The important occasion now is no less than to save a nation out of a bleeding, nay almost dying condition to which the long continuation of this war has already brought it; as without a more speedy, vigorous
5   and effective prosecution of the war – casting off all lingering proceedings like those of soldiers of fortune beyond the seas to spin out a war – we shall make the kingdom weary of us, and hate the name of a parliament.

For what do the enemy say? What do many say that were friends
10   at the beginning of the parliament? Even this, that the members of both Houses have got great places and commands, and the sword into their hands and by interest in the parliament and by power in the army will perpetually continue themselves in grandeur, and will not permit the war speedily to end, lest their own power
15   should determine with it. This that I speak here to our own faces, is but what others do utter abroad behind our backs. I am far from reflecting on any. I know the worth of those commanders, members of both Houses, who are yet in power – but if I may speak my conscience without reflection upon any, I do conceive if the army
20   be not put into another method, and the war more vigorously prosecuted, the people can bear the war no longer and will enforce you to a dishonourable peace.

But this I would recommend to your prudence – not to insist upon any complaint or oversight of any commander-in-chief upon
25   any occasion whatsoever; for as I must acknowledge myself guilty of oversights, so I know they can rarely be avoided in military matters. Therefore waiving a strict inquiry into the cause of these things let us apply ourselves to the remedy which is most necessary. And I hope we have such true English hearts and zealous affections
30   towards the general weal of our mother country, as no members of either House will scruple to deny themselves and their own private interests for the public good.

Letters and Speeches of Oliver Cromwell, op cit, pp 186–7

(*b*)
An Ordinance of the Lords and Commons assembled in Parliament for
the discharging of the Members of both Houses from all offices both
35   *military and civil.*

Be it ordained by the Lords and Commons assembled in Parliament, that all and every of the members of either House of Parliament shall be, and by authority of this Ordinance are discharged at the end of forty days after the passing of this Ordinance of and from
40   all and every office or command military or civil, granted or

conferred by both or either of the said Houses of this present
Parliament or by any authority derived from both or either of them
since the 20th day of November, 1640.
    And be it further ordained that all other governors and comman-
45 ders of an island, town, castle or fort, and all other colonels and
officers inferior to colonels in the several armies, not being members
of either of the Houses of Parliament shall, according to their
respective commands, commissions, continue in their several places
and commands wherein they were employed and entrusted the
50 20th day of March 1644, as if this Ordinance had not been made.
And that the vice-admiral, rear-admiral, and all other captains and
inferior officers in the fleet shall, according to their several and
respective commissions continue in their several places and commands wherein they were employed and entrusted the said 20th
55 day of March, as if this Ordinance had not been made.
    Provided always, and it is further ordained and declared, that
during this war the benefit of all offices being neither military nor
judicial hereafter to be granted, or in any way to be appointed to
any person or persons by both or either House of Parliament, or
60 by authority derived from thence, shall go and inure to such public
uses as both Houses of Parliament shall appoint. And the grantees
and persons executing all such offices shall be accountable to the
Parliament for all the profits and perquisites thereof and shall have
no profit out of any such office other than a competent salary for
65 the execution of the same in such manner as both Houses of
Parliament shall order and ordain.
    Provided that this Ordinance shall not extend to take away the
power and authority of any Lieutenancy or Deputy-Lieutenancy in
the several counties, cities or places, or of any *custos rotulorum,* or
70 of any commission for Justices of Peace, or sewers, or any
commission of *Oyer* and *Terminer,* or gaol-delivery.
    Provided always, and it is hereby declared, that those members
of either House who had offices by grant from His Majesty before
this Parliament and were by His Majesty displaced sitting this
75 Parliament and have since by authority of both Houses been
restored, shall not by this Ordinance be discharged from their said
offices or profits thereof, but shall enjoy the same – anything in
this Ordinance to the contrary thereof notwithstanding.
        Gardiner, *Constitutional Documents,* pp 287–8

(*c*)
It was too apparent how much the whole parliament cause had
80 been often hazarded, how many opportunities of finishing the war
had been overslipped by the Earl of Essex's army; and it was
believed that he himself with his commanders rather endeavoured
to become arbiters of war and peace than conquerors for the
parliament, for it was known that he had given out such expressions.

85   Wherefore those in the parliament who were grieved at the prejudice
of the public interest, and loath to bring those men to public shame
who had once well merited it of them, devised to new model the
army, and an ordinance was made called the self-denying ordinance
whereby all members of parliament of both houses were discharged
90   of their commands in the army. Cromwell had a particular
exception, when Essex, Manchester and Denbigh surrendered their
commissions and Sir Thomas Fairfax was made general of the new-
modelled army; Cromwell lieutenant-general, and Skippon major-
general. The army was reduced to twenty-one thousand, who
95   prosecuted the war not with design of gain and making it their
trade, but to obtain a righteous peace and settlement for the
distracted kingdom, and accordingly it succeeded in their hands.

Lucy Hutchinson, *Memoirs,* op cit, pp 183–4

(*d*)

And these things made the new modelling of the army to be
resolved on. But the question was how to effect it without stirring
100   up the forces against them which they intended to disband. And
all this was notably despatched at once by one vote, which was
called the Self-Denying Vote, viz., that because commands in the
army had much pay and parliament men should keep to the service
of the House, therefore no parliament men should be members of
105   the army. This pleased the soldiers, who looked to have more pay
to themselves, and at once it put out the two generals the Earl of
Essex and the Earl of Manchester, and also Sir William Waller (a
godly, valiant major-general of another army), and also many
colonels in the army and in other parts of the land, and the governor
110   of Coventry, and of many other garrisons, and to avoid all suspicion
Cromwell was put out himself.

When this was done the next question was who should be lord-
general, and what new officers should be put in or old ones continued.
And here the policy of Vane and Cromwell did its best. For general
115   they chose Sir Thomas Fairfax . . . this man was chosen because they
supposed to find him a man of no quickness of parts, of no elocution,
of no suspicious plotting wit, and therefore one that Cromwell could
make use of at his pleasure. And he was acceptable to sober men
because he was religious, faithful, valiant and of grave sober resolved
120   disposition, very fit for execution and neither too great not too
cunning to be commanded by the parliament.

And when he was chosen for the general, Cromwell's men must
not be without him, so valiant a man must not be laid by. The
Self-Denying Vote must be thus far only dispensed with. Cromwell
125   only, and no other member of either House, must be excepted,
and so he is made lieutenant-general of the army. . . .

N. H. Keeble (ed), *Autobiography of Richard Baxter* (1985),
p 46

Questions

a Why was the Self-Denying Ordinance proposed, and what were its primary intentions?

b Assess Richard Baxter's reasons for opposing the Self-Denying Ordinance.

c How did the 'new modelling' of Parliamentary forces contribute to the military campaign against the Royalists?

5 The Growth of Military Radicalism

Dating from the *Solemn League and Covenant* (1643) religious tensions were evident within the Parliamentary militia, and such divisions gradually became more pronounced towards the conclusion of the first civil war. The imposition of Presbyterian church government was resented by many officers (including Cromwell who professed no enthusiasm for the Scottish model), not to mention the heterogeneous elements of the common soldiery. The regiments of the Eastern Association and cavalry regiments generally were notorious for their Independent sympathies, while many foot soldiers were recruits from apprentice classes in London and provincial towns – often despising tithes and professing no voluntary allegiance to any national church. It is practically impossible to estimate the strength of irreligion in the Parliamentary camp, but it is evident that by 1645 the old antipathies towards Laud and the episcopalian hierarchy had been replaced by opposition to Presbyterian domination and the Assembly of Divines. This sentiment was more pronounced in some regiments than others, but for moderate opponents of royal absolutism (already concerned about Parliament's growing dependence on the army) gradual realisation of the religious complexion of the militia came as an unwelcome surprise. Reports by contemporary observers of religious opinions in the army are extremely unreliable, but certainly served to increase the gulf between Parliament and its military agents. Hugh Peter, a radical army chaplain, wrote in glowing terms to Parliament: 'Your army is under a blessed conduct, their counsels Godly and faithful . . . whereas soldiers usually spend and make forfeiture even of the civility they bring into other armies; here men grow religious, and more spiritual-thriving than in any place of the kingdom.' A more sober and orthodox minister, Richard Baxter, responded quite differently to his brief experience of chaplaincy in the Parliamentary army (document A).

A Religious Heterodoxy

When the court newsbook told the world of the swarms of
Anabaptists in our armies, we thought it had been a mere lie,
because it was not so with us nor in any of the garrison or county
forces about us. But when I came to the army, among Cromwell's
5   soldiers, I found a new face of things which I never dreamed of. I
heard the plotting heads very hot upon that which intimated their
intention to subvert both church and state. Independency and
Anabaptistry were most prevalent; Antinomianism and Arminian-
ism were equally distributed. . . . Abundance of the common
10 troopers, and many of the officers, I found to be honest, sober,
and orthodox men, and others tractable, ready to hear the truth
and of upright intentions. But a few proud, self-conceited, hot-
headed sectaries had got into the highest places and were Cromwell's
chief favourites, and by their very heat and activity bore down the
15 rest (being indeed not one to twenty throughout the Army; their
strength being in the General's and Whalley's and Rich's regiments
of horse, and in the new-placed officers in many of the rest).
    I perceived that they took the king for a tyrant and an enemy,
and really intended absolutely to master him or ruin him; and that
20 they thought if they might fight against him they might kill him
or conquer him; and if they might conquer, they were never more
to trust him than he was in their power. . . . They said, what were
the Lords of England but William the Conqueror's colonels, or the
barons but his majors, or the knights but his captains? They plainly
25 showed me that they thought God's providence would cast the
trust of religion and the kingdom upon them as conquerors. They
made nothing of all the most wise and godly in the armies and
garrisons that were not of their way. Per fas aut nefas, by law or
without it, they were resolved to take down not only bishops and
30 liturgy and ceremonies, but all that did withstand their way. They
were far from thinking of a moderate episcopacy, or of any healing
way between the Episcopal and the Presbyterians. They most
honoured the Separatists, Anabaptists, and Antinomians. . . .
    When I had informed myself, to my sorrow, of the state of the
35 army, Captain Evanson (one of my orthodox informers) desired
me yet to come to their regiment, telling me that it was the most
religious, most valiant, most successful of all the army but in as
much danger as any whatsoever. I was loath to leave my studies
and friends and quietness at Coventry to go into an army so contrary
40 to my judgement, but I thought the public good commanded me
and so I gave him some encouragement; whereupon he told his
Colonel (Whalley), who also was orthodox in religion, but engaged
by kindred and interest to Cromwell. He invited me to be chaplain
to his regiment, and I told him I would take but a day's time
45 to deliberate and would send him an answer or else come to

him. . . . As soon as I came to the army Oliver Cromwell coldly bid me welcome, and never spake one word to me more while I was there; nor once all that time vouchsafed me an opportunity to come to the headquarters where the councils and meetings of the
50 officers were, so that most of my design was thereby frustrated. And his secretary gave out that there was a reformer come to the army to undeceive them, and to save church and state, with some other such jeers. . . .

Here I set myself from day to day to find out the corruptions of
55 the soldiers, and to discourse and dispute them out of their mistakes, both religious and political. My life among them was a daily contending against seducers and gently arguing with the more tractable, and another kind of militia I had than theirs. . . . Because I perceived that it was a few men that bore the bell that did all the
60 hurt among them, I acquainted myself with those men and would be oft disputing with them in the hearing of the rest.

Richard Baxter, *Relinquiae Baxterianae* cited in A.S.P. Woodhouse, *Puritanism and Liberty* p 388 and *The Autobiography of Richard Baxter* pp 50–2

B Political Radicalism

Parliamentary concern about the composition and objectives of certain regiments in the army was not long confined to purely religious matters. Following the end of the first civil war in 1646, radical elements in the new Model Army began to press for consideration of various grievances associated primarily with the years of military conflict. In 1647 a series of pamphlets and petitions originating in the army were directed towards Westminster in an attempt to draw legislative attention to the perceived shortcomings of military and social organisation. Moreover, the petitioners became more radical as their initial entreaties were dismissed and ceremoniously destroyed by the House of Commons – so military pamphlets came to include overtly critical commentary on the nature of contemporary society, and explicit attacks on several decisions of Parliament. In relation to military grievances, pamphleteers demanded the payment of arrears due to troops of the New Model Army; by the summer of 1647, soldiers in foot regiments were eighteen weeks in arrears of pay while the situation in regiments of horse was even worse – some troopers being more than ten months in arrears. Furthermore, the soldiers requested that Parliament legally indemnify all members of the New Model against future prosecution for acts committed in time of war. Parliament prevaricated, but the regiments were increasingly aware of the collective political strength of the victorious army, arranging a mass rendezvous of regiments on Newmarket Heath (5 June 1647) to proclaim their intention not to disband until grievances had been fully resolved. The autonomous strength of the army was confirmed by the seizure of Charles I from Holmby House in Northamptonshire by Cornet Joyce and other junior troopers apparently acting under Cromwell's instruction. This act represented a direct attempt to influence negotiations between Charles and Parliament, which the army viewed with immense suspicion and hostility. To support their demand for redress of grievances, the army additionally refused to conform to Parliamentary directives ordering several regiments to Ireland to prevent Catholic rebellion. Such commands were perceived by officers and soldiers as a means of dividing the New Model and thereby diffusing its collective authority. It is also evident that service in Ireland was universally unpopular in the army. Finally, remnants of previous disputes re-emerged in some of the military pamphlets of 1647 – the soldiers wished Parliament to confirm the justice of the armed campaign against the king by formally decreeing monarchical actions illegal, approving the military campaign and providing the security of a general indemnity for all except royalists. These demands were outlined in several pamphlets, the most important being *A Declaration, or Representation; A Solemne Engagement of the Army* (both June 1647), and *The Case of the Armie Truly Stated* (October 1647) (documents B,b,c).

Of all these statements, *A Declaration, or Representation* was the most profound, not only demanding constitutional alterations such as shorter regular Parliaments purged of corrupt members or Royalist interests, but also proclaiming the legitimate right of the army to exercise political influence: 'We were not a mere mercenary army, hired to serve any arbitrary power of a state, but called forth and conjured by the several Declarations of Parliament to the defence of our own and the people's just rights and liberties'. The army also proposed a detailed plan for a settlement of outstanding disputes between the king and Parliament known as *The Heads of the Proposals*, which would also have resolved disagreements between Parliament and the army. *The Heads of the Proposals* were tendered to Parliament in August 1647, but only produced friction within the New Model as radicals were dissatisfied with the nature of this document.

In the later part of 1647, internal disputes between officers and soldiers within the Parliamentary army became more pronounced, and the New Model Army was unable to present a united front in suggestions for social, political and military reform. Paradoxically, the coherence of the army was impaired by its democratic tendencies. In an attempt to produce mutually-agreed policies, the common soldiers were permitted to elect two agents (or 'agitators') for each regiment – so that representatives of the soldiers would sit together with officers in the General Council of the Army. Edward Hyde was unimpressed by the establishment of a military debating forum (document B,d). While thoroughly supported by the army, this novel arrangement proved impractical in many respects; many ordinary soldiers had been influenced by Leveller propaganda and so the political aspirations of the agitators were generally considerably more radical than the policies favoured by Cromwell, Ireton and the other senior officers. The famous Putney Debates involving the General Council of the Army between 28 October and 1 November 1647 reveal a mature division of aspirations. The radical tendency in the Parliamentary army was now fully exposed, but only at the expense of the inevitable fragmentation of the army as a coherent political entity (document B,e) plus irreconcilable discord between the New Model and the remaining moderates at Westminster – a tension which ultimately led to Pride's Purge and the Rump Parliament.

(*a*)

We the officers and soldiers of the army subscribing hereunto; do hereby declare, agree and promise, to and with each other, and to and with the parliament and kingdom as follows:

1. That we shall cheerfully and readily disband when thereunto
5 required by the parliament, or else many of us shall be willing to engage in further services either in England or Ireland, having first such satisfaction to the army in relation to our grievances and desires heretofore presented, and such security that we of ourselves, when disbanded, and in the condition of private men, or other the
10 free born people of Engalnd, to whom the consequence of our case does easily extend, shall not remain subject to the like oppression, injury or abuse, as in the premisses has been attempted and put upon us; while an army by the same mens continuance, in the same credit and power, especially if as our judges, who have in these
15 past proceedings against the army so far prevailed to abuse the parliament and us, and to endanger the kingdom; and also such security that we ourselves, or any member of this army or others, who have appeared to act anything on behalf of the army, in relation to the premisses before recited, shall not after disbanding
20 be any way questioned, prosecuted, troubled or prejudiced for any thing so acted, or for the entering into or necessary prosecution of this necessary agreement: (we say) having first such satisfaction and security in these things as shall be agreed unto by a Council to consist of those general officers in the army (who have concurred
25 with the army in the premisses) with two commission officers and two soldiers to be chosen for each regiment who have concurred and shall concur with us in the premisses and in this agreement. And by the major part of such of them who shall meet in Council for that purpose when they shall be thereunto called by the general.

30   2. That without such satisfaction and security as aforesaid, we shall not willingly disband, nor divide, nor suffer ourselves to be disbanded or divided.

And whereas we find many strange things suggested or suspected to our great prejudice concerning dangerous principles, interests

35   and designs in this army (as to the overthrow of magistracy, the suppression or hindering of presbytery, the establishment of Independent government, or upholding of a general licentiousness in religion under pretence of liberty of conscience, and many such things); we shall very shortly tender to the parliament a vindication

40   of the army from all such scandals to clear our principles in relation thereunto. And in the mean time we do disavow and disclaim all purposes or designs in our late or present proceedings to advance or insist upon any such interest, neither would we (if we might and could) advance or set up any other particular party or interest

45   in the kingdom (though imagined never so much our own) but shall much rather (as much as may be within our sphere or power) study to promote such an establishment of common and equal right and freedom to the whole, as all might equally partake of but those that do by denying the same to others, or otherwise render

50   themselves incapable thereof.

(Anon.) *A Solemn Engagement of the Army* (5 June 1647) in A. S. P. Woodhouse, *Puritanism and Liberty* (London, 1974), pp 402–3

(*b*)

In the Declaration of June 14 it was declared that the army would adhere to their desires of full and equal satisfaction to the whole soldiery of the kingdom in arrears, indemnity, and all other things mentioned in the papers that contained the grievances,

55   disatisfactions and desires who did then or should afterwards concur with this army in these desires.

But many thousands who have concurred with this army are now to be sent for Ireland, or to be disbanded with two months pay before any security for arrears, or sufficient indemnity, or

60   any satisfaction to any desires as soldiers or commoners then propounded; so now our declaration is forgotten and the faith of the army and his Excellency broken, for it may be remembered that his Excellency often promised that the same care should be taken for those that concurred, that should be for this army,

65   therefore if this course be driven on, what better can we expect for ourselves in the end?

In the same Declaration . . . it is declared that the army took up arms, in judgement and conscience, for the people's just rights and liberties and not as mercenary soldiers, hired to serve an arbitrary

70   power of the state, and . . . it was declared that they proceeded upon the principles of right and freedom and upon the law of

nature and nations: but the strength of the endeavours of many hath been, and are now, spent to persuade the soldiers and agitators that they stand as soldiers only to serve the state and may not as free commoners claim their right and freedom as due to them, as those ends for which they have hazarded their lives and that the ground of their refusing to disband, was only the want of arrears and indemnity. . . .

The love and affection of the people to the army (which is the armies greatest strength) is decayed, cooled and near lost. It is already the common voice of the people: what good have our new saviours done for us? What grievances have they procured to be redressed? Wherein is our condition bettered, or how are we more free than before?

Not only so, but the army is rendered as a heavy burden to the people in regard more pay is exacted daily for them and the people find no good procured by them that is . . . equivalent to the charge; so that now the people begin to cry louder for disbanding the Army than they did formerly for keeping us in arms, because they see no benefit accruing. They say they are as likely to be oppressed and enslaved both by king and parliament as they were before the army engaged – professedly to see their freedoms cleared and secured. . . . You will do nothing for us (say they) we are vexed by malignant judges, for conscience sake by arbitrary committees in the country, and at the parliament ordering one thing this day and recalling it the next to our intolerable vexation. Injustice in the law is the same, and we buy our right at as dear a rate as ever; tithes are enforced from us double and treble, excise continues, we can have no accounts of all our monies disbursed for the public; more is daily required, and we do not know what is become of all we have paid already, the soldiers have little pay, and the maimed soldiers, widows and orphans are thrust upon us to be parish charges. . . .

All those large sums of money that were allowed to needless pretended officers of the court which did but increase wickedness and profanity may be reserved for a public treasure to be expended in paying those forces that must be maintained for the peoples safety, so that through a good and faithful improvement of all the lands pertaining to the court, there might be much reserved for leaving public charges, and easing the people. . . .

And its further offered that forest lands, and Deans and Chapters lands be immediately set apart for the arrears of the army, and that the revenue of these and the residue of the Bishops lands unsold . . . may be forthwith appointed to be paid unto our treasury, to be reserved for the soldiers constant pay.

(Anon.) *The Case of the Army Truly Stated* (18 October 1647). Also in William Haller and Godfrey Davies, *The Leveller Tracts 1647–1653* (Massachusetts, 1964), pp 68–81

(c)

So that about this time, that they might be upon a nearer level with the parliament, the army made choice of a number of such officers as they liked; which they called the general's council of officers; who were to resemble the house of peers; and the common
120 soldiers made choice of three or four of each regiment, mostly corporals or sergeants, and none above the degree of ensign, who were called agitators, and were to be as a house of commons to the council of officers. These two representatives met severally, and considered all of the acts and orders made by the parliaments
125 towards settling the kingdom, and towards reforming, dividing or disbanding of the army: and upon mutual messages and conferences between each other they resolved in the first place and declared, 'that they would not be divided or disbanded before their full arrears were paid, and before full provision was made for liberty
130 of conscience; which, they said, was the ground of the quarrel and for which so many of their friends' lives had been lost, and so much of their own blood had been spilt; and hitherto there was so little security provided in that point that there was a greater persecution now against religious and godly men, than ever had
135 been in the king's government, when the bishops were their judges'.

Clarendon, *History of the Rebellion* (Selections), op cit, p 285

(d)

Take heed of crafty politicians and subtle Machiavellians and be sure to trust no man's painted words, it being high time now to see actions . . . if any man (by bringing forth unexpected bitter fruits) has drawn upon himself a just suspicion, let him justly bear
140 his own blame. . . .

One of the surest marks of deceivers is to make fair, long and eloquent speeches, but a trusty or true-hearted man studies more to do good actions than utter deceitful orations. And one of the surest tokens of confederates in evil is not only, when one of his
145 fellows is vehement, fiery or hot in any of their pursuits, to be patient, cold or moderate, to pacify his partner, and like deceitful lawyers before their clients to qualify matters, but sometimes seem to discord or fall out and quarrel in counsels, reasonings and debates – and yet nevertheless in the end to agree in evil . . . if
150 such and such a man be not godly and upright, they know not whom in the world to trust, while in the meantime under the vizards of great professions, gilded with some religious actions, they both deceive the world and bring their wicked designs and self-interests to pass. . . .
155 In the council they held forth to you the bloody flag of threats and terrors, talked of nothing but faction, dividing principles, anarchy; of hanging, punishment, and impudently maintained that your regiments were abused and the aforesaid *Case* not truly

subscribed, and did appoint a committee ad terrorem. And abroad
160 they hold forth the white flag of accommodation and satisfaction,
and of minding the same thing which you mind, and to be flesh of
your flesh and bone of your bone, and to invite you to their
headquarters where they hope either to work upon you as they
have most lamentably done upon others, even to betray your trust,
165 confound both your understandings and counsels, corrupt your
judgements, and blast your actions. . . .

If you do venture to go thither beware that you are not frighted
by the word anarchy unto a love of monarchy, which is but the
gilded name for tyranny; for anarchy had never been so much as
170 once mentioned among you had it not been for that wicked end.

You need to be well armed and fortified against the devices that
will be put upon you. Ireton (you know) has already scandalised
The Case of the Army in the General Council. Where, by his own
and his confederates craft and policy, he reigns as sole master –
175 insomuch as those friends you have there (which we hope you will
see in due time not to be few) find it to little purpose to show
themselves active in opposing him. And as he undertook so has he
answered your *Case*; wherein he shows himself so full of art and
cunning, smooth delusion (being skilled in nothing more), and if
180 you did not sensibly know the things to be real and experimentally
true, which you have therein expressed and published, 'tis ten to
one but he would deceive you.

This is certain. In the House of Commons both he and his father
Cromwell do so earnestly and palpably carry on the king's design
185 that your best friends there are amazed at it, and even ready to
weep for grief to see such a sudden and dangerous alteration. And
this they do in the name of the whole army, certifying the House
that if they do not make further address to the king they cannot
promise that the army will stand by them if they should find
190 opposition. And what is this but as much in effect as in the name
of the whole army to threaten the House into a compliance with
the king, your most deadly enemy, and who (if things go on thus)
will deceive both you and them and all that act most for him.

To what purpose then should you either debate, confer or treat
195 with such false sophisters or treacherous deceivers as these who,
like the former courtiers, can always play the hypocrites without
any check of conscience? To what end should you read or spend
time to consider what they either write or speak, it being so evident
that as they did intend so they proceed to hold you in hand until
200 their work be done. But if you will show yourselves wise, stop
your ears against them: resist the devil and he will fly from you.

(Anon.) *A Call to all the Soldiers of the Army* (29 October
1647) in Woodhouse, op cit, pp 439–41

Questions

a Outline the nature of Richard Baxter's concern over the composition of the parliamentary army (document A).

b Why did the New Model Army become increasingly radical in social and political terms?

c Assess the evidence provided by these documents relating to the religious complexion of the army, and particularly of Cromwell.

d How did the objectives of officers and soldiers conflict in the General Council of the Army?

IV The Quest for Liberty

1 The Development and Decline of Radicalism

Much of the import of recent historical work on the civil war stresses the underlying conservatism of the king's Parliamentary opponents between 1640 and 1642. This is augmented by a series of local studies which emphasise the moderation of the rural gentry and the tendency towards neutralism in many counties. We are assured that opposition to the Crown in the early 1640s was naturally defensive and that future Parliamentarians desired no political or social *revolution*. However, in the course of the civil war, an unexpected but not unnatural expansion of political consciousness occurred, leading to active popular consideration of various issues which were purely latent in 1642. Moreover, the breakdown in effective censorship of press and pulpit (dating from the Parliamentary imprisonment of Laud in late 1640) enabled 'the lower sort' to participate more fully in political processes, and the focus of political debate gradually extended beyond Westminster to include churches, taverns and places of work. This chapter presents some of the prominent features of popular radicalism in the course of a civil war which inexorably took on some features of an English 'revolution.'

Those participants in the conflict who hoped for more radical change in English society tended to present their arguments in terms of freedom: liberty to express opinions verbally or in print; liberty to attend whatever form of religious service one desired; freedom of trade from monopolies, and liberty to play an active role in political affairs through the franchise. The quest for liberty was first and foremost an attack on religious uniformity and intolerance as traditionally practised by the national church – an issue which seemed crucial in the light of comparatively recent domination of the Anglican Church by English Laudians. Of course, division over ceremonies and practices within the Anglican Church was not a novelty – indeed potential for conflict existed since the Reformation. Following the Elizabethan Act of Uniformity and the Queen's Injunctions (both 1559), the term 'Puritan' gradually entered the ecclesiastical vocabulary, to denote those who objected to some Anglican ceremonies as vestiges of Catholicism, and who wished for further reform of the Church in a Protestant direction. Under Laud from 1633, however, the 'odious name of puritan' was applied with extreme liberality by the bishops to their opponents within the Church, as Henry Parker testifies (document A,a). Royalists in the 1640s were inclined to employ the term contemptuously of Parliamentarians in general, showing that at least some *perception* of religious division underpinned the military conflict.

Religious issues were to some extent complicated by the spread of continental sectarianism in England, although Anabaptists and Familists in particular were numerically insignificant. In 1640, heterodox sects were equally reviled by Royalists and Parliamentarians, but they were to gain significance as the years of struggle progressed. Initially a singular religious issue proved divisive: most Parliamentarians accepted the need to remove Laud, but it was virtually impossible to establish an acceptable post-Laudian ecclesiastical hierarchy. Most of the criticism levelled at Laud consisted of attacks on recent clerical practice (particularly the silencing of Puritan lecturers), or on the person of the archbishop, rather than concentrating upon matters of theology; in this respect, William Prynne's predestinarian work *Anti-Arminianism* (1630) is exceptional. In the aftermath of Laud's demise, the crucial issue for Parliament was the nature of the new religious settlement – some favoured the extreme solution of rejecting episcopalianism in its entirety, as advocated in the 'Root and Branch' petition. The political voice of the Lords Spiritual was effectively terminated by the Bishops' Exclusion Bill of February 1642. Parliament, realising the potential for discord over religion, deferred finalising the settlement by creating an Assembly of Divines at Westminster to consider religious issues – but the need for Scottish military assistance finally proved irresistible, and led to the establishment of a Presbyterian national church from 1643.

Racial prejudice against the Scots was common in the early seventeenth century, and the Presbyterian settlement (despite the abolition of bishops) proved immensely unpopular. The established patterns of church worship were gradually breaking down as both traditional Anglicanism *and* Puritanism began to distintegrate – although this phenomenon was localised – and London became the centre of opposition to Presbyterian intolerance, the continuation of tithes and the *Directory for Public Worship*. The Levellers drew comparisons between Laudian and Presbyterian uniformity (document A,b). Presbyterians were also opposed by the so-called 'Independent' London congregations, who distrusted the rigid centralisation of church government favoured by the Presbyterian ministry and who adopted a more tolerant approach to liberty of conscience. In his pamphlet, *Smoke in the Temple* (1646), John

Saltmarsh elaborated on a series of distinctions between Presbyterians and Independents (document A,c). John Goodwin, the prominent Independent Minister, went further and argued that religious toleration was a necessity for a godly society, in his pamphlet *Independency God's Verity* (1647).

Why was freedom of worship regarded as crucial? Saltmarsh explains: 'The liberty of the subject is that of soul as well as body, and that of the soul more clear, precious, glorious . . . be not ye then the servants of men in the things of God'. Many diverse arguments were expounded by opponents of intolerance – the Independent position was developed in the anonymous pamphlet *The Ancient Bounds* (1645) (document B,a). Presbyterians, such as Thomas Edwards and Ephraim Pagitt, began to publish incredulous compilations of heresies and rampant sectarianism, catalogues which were used by the clerical authorities to proclaim the dangers of religious toleration. In the mid-1640s, Roger Williams and William Walwyn compiled an eloquent defence of liberty of conscience – it is noticeable that attacks on Presbyterianism were no longer confined to Independent ministers but were now produced by more radical separatists and 'seekers'. It is also necessary to draw attention to the significance of debates on the role of the civil magistrate at this period; although often a confusing issue for students, in practice this refers generally to the position of civil authorities in determining religious issues and, especially, deciding punishments for heterodoxy (document B,b). John Wildman, the Leveller, feared the role of the magistrate in matters of conscience because 'the probability is greater that he will destroy what is good than prevent what is evil'.

By 1646–7, however, the unanimity of the opponents of Presbyterianism was irreparably damaged. Although Independents had initially welcomed sectarian pamphlets critical of Presbyterian uniformity (such as Richard Overton's *Arraignment of Mr Persecution*), a gulf rapidly developed between Independents and Separatists – particularly as those who rejected even congregationalism began to realise that limitations did exist to Independent toleration. The contentious issues were publicised in a series of pamphlets written by William Walwyn against personal opponents associated with Goodwin's gathered congregation. Walwyn's original piece locates the Independents firmly in the tradition of those who claim special divine insight and who subsequently seek to protect their vision by persecution of non-believers (document B,c).

The Levellers' religious perspective required freedom of worship, although many accepted contemporary prejudice and denied toleration to Catholics and Jews. The cornerstone of the Leveller argument for liberty of conscience was the idea that God had implanted in natural man the faculty of *reason*; this belief had already been conceded by prominent Anglican divines including William Perkins, Richard Hooker and Archbishop Ussher. Thus, the Levellers' concept of reason represented the logical development of a concession to natural human attributes already sanctioned by orthodox Protestant theologians. The demand for toleration was a corollary of this emphasis on human reason, for God could only reveal to each man the appropriate path of salvation if individuals were given freedom to worship God according to conscience – rather than subjected to the dictates of an autocratic national church. For this reason, the Levellers made liberty of conscience an explicit part of their major policy statements: in the *Agreement of the People*, for example, the right to determine religion is specifically excluded from government (document B,d).

The quest for liberty rapidly extended beyond the issue of conscience in the 1640s. Cromwell was believed to have said 'that the state had been more delinquent than the Church, and that the people suffered more by the civil than the ecclesiastical power; and therefore that the change of one would give them little ease, if there were not as great an alteration in the other'. Consequently, the principle of toleration inspired further related demands for *civil* rights: for freedom of speech, for liberty of printing (against the censorship of the Stationer's Company) and for the right to petition Parliament over grievances. The desire for toleration in religion naturally led to a campaign for secular liberties. Milton's tract *Areopagitica* (1644) represented an early statement of the case against censorship of publications (document B,e). A pamphlet produced by urban apprentices, *The Mournfull Cries of Many Thousand Poore Tradesmen*, requested the end of restrictions upon commerce. Parliament treated popular petitions with contempt, causing the radicals finally to advocate political remedies for their grievances. Disenchantment with the effectiveness of parliamentary government inspired a series of Leveller pamphlets, particularly *England's New Chains Discovered* by Lilburne, Overton's *Remonstrance*, and Walwyn's *The Bloody Project* (document C,a). The crux of the Leveller argument was the claim that Parliament had consciously denied the liberties of the subject. The only conceivable remedy lay in fundamental political reform – giving the common people a significant political voice by extending the franchise. Richard Overton prepared the ground for such innovation by chastising 'our now degenerate Parliament' for its failure to relieve the oppression of the people, and by suggesting that ultimate political sovereignty resided not in Parliament, but in the people (document C,b).

In practice, the nature of the extended suffrage proved a thorny issue which caused division within the Leveller movement itself. Most Levellers favoured a compromise solution which did *not* involve universal manhood suffrage, while a minority refused, on principle, to countenance any restriction of political rights. In the latter group, the position adopted by Colonel Rainsborough (an Army Leveller soon to be assassinated by Royalists) during the Army Debates in Putney Church in late October 1647, is the most extreme and democratic. The context of the debate was the Army Council's consideration of the first Leveller *Agreement of the People*, particularly the first article, dealing with more representative reapportionment of Parliamentary constituencies (document D,a). This argument for full political liberty and a democratic franchise was immediately refuted by Commissary-General Henry Ireton (Cromwell's son-in-law) on behalf of the military officers (document D,b). Eventually, fearing the effects of aristocratic manipulation of elections and viewing economic independence as the prerequisite for political autonomy, the Levellers acquiesced in a restricted franchise, while simultaneously attempting to secure more accountable and representative government through limitations upon the duration of parliaments and measures designed to eliminate corruption (document D,c). Thus, the Levellers unsuccessfully attempted to use the civil war as a method of securing religious, civil and political liberties – their failure does not obscure some of the most advanced statements of human rights written in English before the late eighteenth century – particularly one passage from the pen of Richard Overton (document D,d).

The quest for liberty in the English revolution proved ultimately unsuccessful, despite the abolition of press censorship and the temporary attainment of religious freedom. These represent dramatic concessions wrested from authority during the chaos of civil war, but it proved impossible to make further inroads in terms of individual political rights or constitutional restrictions upon the actions of government. Such progressive ideas were historically misplaced in the 1640s. By late 1648 the Presbyterian influence was largely removed from Parliament, and the House of Lords was practically moribund – but only at the expense of a new military dictatorship with the Rump becoming the instrument of army government. This development was anathema to the prophets of liberty. Upon securing power, the Grandees quickly turned against Levellers and other radicals in an attempt to stamp out internal dissent. By March 1649 all the prominent libertarians were imprisoned, including 'the four poor Sea-green Fiddlers in the Tower', still busily producing vitriolic pamphlets against Cromwell for this betrayal, such as Lilburne's *England's New Chains Discovered* and *The Baiting of The Great Bull of Bashan* by Richard Overton. Political liberty was a chimera in the 1640s, the nation was not prepared for universal suffrage and only vaguely aware of the merits of constitutional impediments to the arbitrary exercise of Parliamentary authority. The domestic events of the 1650s represent a period of retrenchment as the new regime suppressed radical opposition to secure a grudging internal consensus for the continuing struggle against Royalist restoration.

A   The Use of Religious Terminology

(a)   A Parliamentarian on religious nomenclature

Dissent in Ecclesiasticall Policie about ceremonies and other smaller matters, being not of the substance of Religion, first gave occasion to raise this reproachfull word Puritan in the Church. . . .

Those whom we ordinarily call Puritans are men of strict life,
5   and precise opinion, which cannot be hated for anything but their singularity in zeale and piety, and certainly the number of such men is too small and their condition too low, and dejected; but they which are the Devils chiefe Artificiers in abusing this word, when they please can so stretch and extend the same that scarce
10   any civill honest Protestant which is hearty and true to his Religion can avoid the aspersion of it.

[Henry Parker?] *A Discussion Concerning Puritans: A Vindication of Those Who Unjustly Suffer by the Mistake, Abuse and Misappreciation of that Name* (London, 1641), pp 8–9

(b)   The Levellers criticise religious uniformity

The great oppression of the high Commission was most evident in molesting of godly peaceable people, for non-conformity, or different opinion and practice in Religion, judging all who were
15   contrary-minded to themselves, to bee Hereticks, Sectaries, Schismaticks, seditious, factious, enemies to the State, and the like; and under great penalties forbidding all persons, not licenced by them, to preach or publish the Gospel: Even so now at this day, the very same, if not greater molestations, are set on foot, and violently
20   prosecuted by the instigation of a Clergy no more infallible than the former, to the extreame discouragement and affliction of many thousands of your faithfull adherents, who are not satisfied that controversies in Religion, can be trusted to the compulsive regulation of any: And after the Bishops were suppressed, did hope
25   never to have seen such a power assumed by any in this Nation any more. . . .

As those who found themselves aggrieved formerly at the burdens and oppressions of those times, that did not conform to the Church-government then established, refused to pay Ship-money,
30   or yeeld obedience to unjust Patents, were reviled and reproached with nicknames of Puritans, Hereticks, Schismaticks, Sectaries, or were termed factious or seditious, men of turbulent spirits,

despisers of government, and disturbers of the publike peace; even
so is it at this day in all respects, with those who shew any sensibility
35 of the fore-recited grievances, or move in any manner or measure
for remedy thereof, all the reproaches, evills, and mischiefs that
can be devised, are thought too few or too little to bee laid
upon them, as Roundheads, Sectaries, Independents, Hereticks,
Schismaticks, factious, seditious, rebellious disturbers of the publike
40 peace, destroyers of all civill relation, and subordinations; yea, and
beyond what was formerly, nonconformity is now judged a
sufficient cause to disable any person though of known fidelity,
from bearing any Office of trust in the Common-wealth, whilest
Neuters, Malignants, and disaffected are admitted and continued.

> [William Walwyn?] *The Large Petition* (March 1647) reprinted
> in Don Wolfe, *Leveller Manifestoes of the Puritan Revolution*
> (New York, 1944), pp 137–8

(c) Independents and Presbyterians

45   Presbytery so called: what it is, and what they hold

The Presbytery is set up by an alleged pattern of eldership and
presbytery of the Apostles and Elders in the first churches of the
Gospel, strengthened by such scriptures as are in the margin, and
by allusion to the Jewish government and to appeals in nature.
50 Their churches are parochial, or parishes, as they are divided at
first by the Romish prelates and the statute-laws of the state. Which
parishes and congregations are made up of such believers as were
made Christians first by baptism in infancy, and not by the Word;
and all the parishes or congregations are under them as they are a
55 classical, provincial, and national Presbytery. And over those
parishes they do exercise all church power and government which
may be called the Power of the Keys.

        Independency so called: what it is, and what they hold

The people of God are only a church when called by the Word and
60 Spirit into consent or covenant and [when] Saints by profession,
and all church-power is laid here and given out from hence into
pastorship and elders, etc.; and a just distribution of interest betwixt
elders and people. All spiritual government is here and not in any
power foreign or extrinsical to the congregation, or authoritative.
65 Their children are made Christians first by infant baptism and after
by the Word; and they are baptized by a federal or covenant-
holiness, or birth-privileges as under the Law. They may enjoy all
ordinance in this estate, and some may prophesy.

> John Saltmarsh, *Smoke in the Temple* (1646) reprinted in
> A. S. P. Woodhouse, *Puritanism and Liberty* (London, 1974),
> pp 179–80

Questions

a   What evidence is given in these extracts of pejorative use of religious nomenclature?

75 b   For what reason was critical use of the term 'Puritan' extended in the 1630s?

c   Outline the chief objections of the sects to Presbyterian church government.

d   What religious affiliation was held by Saltmarsh? (Give reasons

80   for your choice.)

B   Religious Uniformity and Toleration

(a) Independents against uniformity

There are two things contended for in this liberty of conscience: first to instate every Christian in his right of free, yet modest, judging and accepting what he holds; secondly, to vindicate a necessary advantage to the truth, and this is the main end and

5   respect of this liberty. I contend not for variety of opinions; I know there is but one truth. But this truth cannot be so easily brought forth without this liberty; and a general restraint, though intended but for errors, yet through the unskilfulness of men, may fall upon the truth. And better many errors of some kind suffered than one

10 useful truth be obstructed or destroyed. . . .
   Now then, if we keep but to this term conscience, first, all vicious and scandalous practices, contrary to the light of nature or manifest good of societies, are cut off not to trouble us in this matter, as deriving themselves not from conscience, but a malignant

15 will and unconscienced spirit. Nor yet may all principles that derive themselves from conscience have the benefit of this plea of liberty, so as to save their owners. As first, if they shall be found of a disabling nature, or wanting in their due proportion of benevolence to public peace, liberties, societies; . . . as for instance, scruple of

20 conscience cannot exempt a man from any civil duty he owes to the state or the government thereof, but it may well beseem a state to force men to contribute to their own and the public good and safety. And though God can have no glory by a forced religion, yet the state may have benefit by a forced service. Again, the

25 service of the state is outward, civil, bodily, and is perfect as to its

end without the will and conscience of that person from whom it is extorted; so is not the service of God, which is inward and spiritual, yea it must be in spirit and truth. Then much less may any such principles find favour in this discourse, as, beside the
30 former deficiency, shall be found pregnant with positive malignity (and that in a high nature and consequence too perhaps) to societies, as the doctrines of the Papists.

Anon. *The Ancient Bounds* (1645) reprinted in Woodhouse, *Puritanism and Liberty*, pp 247–8

(b) Separatists support toleration

(**1**)
It is the will and command of God that, since the coming of his Son the Lord Jesus, a permission of the most paganish, Jewish,
35 Turkish, or Antichristian consciences and worships be granted to all men in all nations and countries; and they are only to be fought against with that sword which is only, in soul matters, able to conquer, to wit, the sword of God's Spirit, the word of God. The state of the land of Israel (the kings and people thereof, in peace
40 and war) is proved figurative and ceremonial, and no pattern nor precedent for any kingdom or civil state in the world to follow. God requireth not an uniformity of religion to be enacted and enforced in any civil state; which enforced uniformity, sooner or later, is the greatest occasion of civil war, ravishing of conscience,
45 persecution of Christ Jesus in his servants, and of the hypocrisy and destruction of millions of souls. An enforced uniformity of religion throughout a nation or civil state confounds the civil and religious, denies the principles of Christianity and civility, and that Jesus Christ is come in the flesh. The permission of other consciences
50 and worships than a state professeth only can, according to God, procure a firm and lasting peace.

Roger Williams, *The Bloody Tenent of Persecution* (1644) reprinted in ibid., p 266

(**2**)
I find by myself that Christians cannot live, though they enjoy all natural freedom and content where they are not free to worship God in a way of religion, and I find also by myself that Christians
55 cannot worship God in any way but that which agreeth with their understandings and consciences.

William Walwyn, *A Word More* (May 1646) p 5

(c) The Levellers attack independency

Those, whom this discourse now deemeth worthy of reproofe did seeme to judge, when they condemned the persecuting practices, of the new raised Presbyters, whose positions and professions
60 whilst they were persecuted by the Bishops, did clearly hold forth a full and complete liberty of Conscience, in the exercise of Religion, and justly and truly did the Independents reprove them, as their many bookes, of that Subject, do sufficiently testifie: their reproofs were sharp, and their replyes driven home; whereby they put the
65 question of the utmost liberty of Conscience, out of all question, accompting nothing more base, or mis-beseeming a Christian, than to question, or vex, or reproach any man for his judgment or practice, touching matters of Religion, and inciting all men to peace, unity, love, and true friendship, though of never so many
70 severall opinions, or different wayes in Religion.

By which their ingenuity, they (as the Puritan Presbyter had done before them) gained abundance of love and respect from all men; their Congregations multiplied, and in conclusion, obtained much countenance from authority: which they no sooner tasted
75 but instantly, some of them began to pride themselves, and to despise others; and to reproach and villifie all such, as upon tryall and examination of their Churches, their Pastors and Sermons, finding all to be but fained imitations, nothing reall or substantiall, forsooke their societies, and thereupon as the Presbyters had used
80 them; so deale the Independents with these, and all that any wayes adhered unto these, raising nick-names and bitter invective reproaches against them, sparing neither art nor paines, to make them odious to others, and their lives (if it were possible) a burthen to themselves; and though reasons have been offered, and
85 conferences desired, that they might see their error, and forbeare to deale thus contrary to their positive, owned, and declared principles: yet have they persisted therein, and go on still without ceasing, manifesting a most destructive and persecuting disposition, not only towards these, but towards many others whom they now
90 (as complete Judges of other mens Consciences) judge to be erronious, or heriticall, and seeme to have placed their felicity in the ruine of those whom their own Consciences cannot deny to have been instrumentall in their preservations, and who have not thought their lives too precious, to purchase them that freedom
95 which now they enjoy. . . .

Then comes the Independents and pretend to erect, a holy, pure and undefiled worship, according to the pattern, shewed unto them by the true Spirit indeed, pleading for generall liberty of conscience, void of all compulsion or restrictions, and professing the meeknes
100 of the very Lambs of Christ, and humility towards all men; who now could have suspected what since hath been discovered? . . .

Do they not dayly spit their venom privatly and publickly, against any that either seperate from them, or joyne not with them, and that in as foul aspersions, as ever the Pope uttered against
105 Luther, the Bishops against the Puritan, or the Presbyter against the Independents, are they not high and skillfull in rayling making whom they please Atheists, Anti-scripturists, Antinomians, Anti-magistrats, Polligamists, Seekers, or what they will: and can these proceed from the true Spirit of God, or from the Spirit of Antichrist?
110 Judge impartially Yee that are yet untainted in your consciences.

> William Walwyn, *The Vanity of the Present Churches* (1649), reprinted in Haller and Davies, *The Leveller Tracts*, op. cit., pp 252–8

(d) Constitutional restrictions upon religious coercion

That we do not inpower or entrust our said representative to continue in force, or to make any Lawes, Oaths, or Covenants, whereby to compell by penalties or otherwise any person to any thing in or about matters of faith, Religion or Gods worship or to
115 restrain any person from the profession of his faith, or exercise of Religion according to his Conscience, nothing having caused more distractions, and heart burnings in all ages, than persecution and molestation for matters of Conscience in and about Religion. . . .

That it shall not be in their power to continue the Grievance of
120 Tithes, longer than to the end of the next Representative; in which time, they shall provide to give reasonable satisfaction to all Impropriators: neither shall they force by penalties or otherwise any person to pay towards the maintenance of any Ministers, who out of conscience cannot submit thereunto. That it shall not be in
125 their power to impose Ministers upon any [of] the respective Parishes, but shall give free liberty to the parishioners of every particular parish, to chuse such as themselves shall approve; and upon such terms, and for such reward, as themselves shall be willing to contribute, or shall contract for, Provided none be
130 chusers but such as are capable of electing Representatives. . . .

They shall not disable any person from bearing any office in the Common-wealth, for any opinion or practice in Religion, excepting such as maintain the Popes (or other forraign) Supremacy.

> The Third Leveller, *Agreement of the People of England* (May 1649), reprinted in G. E. Aylmer, *The Levellers in the English Revolution* (London, 1975), pp 164–6

(e) Milton's opposition to censorship of publications

And as it is particular disesteem of every knowing person alive,
135 and most injurious to the written labours and monuments of the
dead, so to me it seems an undervaluing and vilifying of the whole
Nation. I cannot set so light by all the invention, the art, the wit,
the grave and solid judgement which is in England, as that it can
be comprehended in any twenty capacities how good soever, much
140 lesse that it should not passe except their superintendence be over
it, except it be sifted and strained with their strainers, that it should
be uncurrant without their manuall stamp. Truth and understanding
are not such wares as to be monopolized and traded in by tickets
and statutes, and standards. We must not think to make a staple
145 commodity of all the knowledge in the Land, to mark and licence
it like our broad cloth, and our wooll packs. . . .
    It reflects to the disrepute of our Ministers also, of whose labours
we should hope better, and of the proficiencie which their flock
reaps by them, then that after all this light of the Gospel which is,
150 and is to be, and all this continuall preaching, they should be still
frequented with such an unprincipled, unedified, and laick rabble,
as that the whiffe of every new pamphlet should stagger them out
of their catechism, and Christian walking. This may have much
reason to discourage the Ministers when such a low conceit is had
155 of all their exhortations, and the benefiting of their hearers, as they
are not thought fit to be turned loose to three sheets of paper
without a licencer. . . .
    I could recount what I have seen and heard in other Countries, where
this kind of inquisition tyrannizes; when I have sat among their learned
160 men, for that honor I had, and been counted happy to be born in such a
place of Philosophic freedom, as they suppos'd England was, while
themselvs did nothing but bemoan the servile condition into which
learning amongst them was brought. . . . There it was that I found and
visited the famous Galileo grown old, a prisner to the Inquisition, for
165 thinking In Astronomy otherwise than the Franciscan and Dominican
licencers thought. . . .
    While things are yet not constituted in Religion, that freedom of
writing should be restrained by a discipline imitated from the Prelates,
and learnt by them from the Inquisition to shut us up all again
170 into the brest of a licencer, must needs give cause of doubt and
discouragement to all learned and religious men. Who cannot but
discern the fineness of this politic drift, and who are the contrivers;
that while Bishops were to be baited down, then all Presses might be
open; it was the peoples birthright and privilege in time of Parliament,
175 it was the breaking forth of light. But now the Bishops abrogated
and voided out of the Church, as if our Reformation sought no more,
but to make room for others into their seats under another name, the
Episcopall arts begin to bud again . . . liberty of Printing must be

enthralled again under a Prelaticall commission of twenty, the privilege
180 of the people nullified, and which is worse, the freedom of learning
must groan again, and to her old fetters: all this the Parliament yet
sitting.

> John Milton, *Areopagitica* (November 1644; Paris, 1956 edition),
> pp 174–86

Questions

a Outline the arguments against religious uniformity presented by
  Independents and Separatists.
b For what reasons were the opponents of Presbyterianism divided,
  according to document c?
c (i) Explain the Levellers' exclusion of Roman Catholics from
  toleration.
  (ii) How did the Levellers' view of tithes contrast with clerical
  authority in the 1640s?
d 'I contend not for variety of opinions; I know there is but one
  truth.' Could this Independent statement be considered appropriate
  to Milton's argument against censorship in *Areopagitica*?
e How effective was censorship of publications in (i) the 1630s (ii)
  the 1640s?

C   Leveller Grievances

(*a*)
Or was it sufficient thinke you now, that the Parliament invited you
at first upon generall termes, to fight for the maintenance of the true
Protestant Religion, the Libertyes of the People, and Privileges of
Parliament; when neither themselves knew, for ought is yet seen, nor
5 you, nor any body else, what they meant by the true Protestant
Religion, or what the Liberties of the People were, or what those
Privileges of Parliament were, for which yet neverthelesse thousands
of men have been slain, and thousands of Familyes destroyed?
    It is very like that some of you that joyned with the King upon his
10 invitation, thought, that though the King had formerly countenanced
Popery, and Superstition, had stretcht his Prerogative to the oppression
and destruction of his People, by Pattents, Projects, &c. yet for the
future he would have been more zealouse for the truth, and more
tender of his People, and not have persisted (notwithstanding his new
15 Protestations) to maintain his old Principles.
    And so likewise many of you that joyned with the Parliament,
who had formerly seen, felt, or considered the persecution of godly
conscientious people by the Bishops and their Clergy, with the

reproaches cast upon them, and their grievous and destructive
20 imprisonment, did beleeve the Parliament under the notion of
Religion, intended to free the Nation from all compulsion in matters
of Religion, and from molestation, or persecution for opinions, or
non-conformity; and that all Lawes or Statutes tending thereunto
should have been repealed: But since you find (by killing and
25 destroying their opposers) you have enabled them to performe all
things that might concern your freedome, or be conducible to the
peace of the Kingdome. But do you now find that they do mean
that, or the contrary? And will your consciences give you leave any
longer to fight or engage in the cause of Religion, when already you
30 see what fruits you and your friends reap thereby.

And no doubt many of you understood by the Liberties of the
People, that they intended to free the Commons in Parliament the
peoples Representative, from a Negative voyce, in King, or Lords,
and would have declared themselves the highest Authority, and so
35 would have proceeded to have removed the grievances of the
Common-wealth: And when you had seen Pattents, Projects, and
Shipmoney taken away, the High Commission, and Starchamber
abolished, did you ever imagine to have seen men and women
examined upon Interrogatories, and questions against themselves, and
40 imprisoned for refusing to answer? Or to have seen Commoners
frequently sentenced and imprisoned by the Lords? Did you ever
dream that the oppressions of Committees would have exceeded those
of the Councel-table; or that in the place of Pattents and Projects,
you should have seen an Excise established, ten fold surpassing all
45 those, and Shipmoney together? You thought rather that Tythes
would have been esteemed an oppression, and that Trade would have
been made perfectly free, and that Customs if continued, would
have been abated, and not raysed, for the support of domineering
factions, and enrichment of foure or five great men, as they have
50 been of late times, to the sorrow and astonishment of all honest men,
and the great prejudice of the Trade of the Nation.

Doubtlesse you hoped that both Lawes and Lawyers, and the
proceedings in all Courts should have been abreviated, and corrected,
and that you should never more have seen a Begger in England.
55 You have seen the Common-wealth enslaved for want of Parliaments, and also by their sudden dissolution, and you rejoyced that
this Parliament was not to be dissolved by the King; but did you
conceive it would have sat seven yeares to so little purpose, or that it
should ever have come to passe, to be esteemed a crime to move for
60 the ending thereof? Was the perpetuating of this Parliament, and the
oppressions they have brought upon you and yours, a part of that
Liberty of the People you fought for? Or was it for such a Privilege
of Parliament, that they only might have liberty to oppresse at their
pleasure, without any hope of remedy? If all these put together make
65 not up the cause for which you fought, what was the Cause? What

have ye obtained to the People, but these Libertyes, for they must not be called oppressions? These are the fruits of all those vast disbursements, and those thousands of lives that have been spent and destroyed in the late War.

William Walwyn, *The Bloody Project* (August 1648)

(b)

70   You were chosen to work our deliverance, and to estate us in natural and just liberty agreeable to reason and common equity; for whatever our forefathers were, or whatever they did or suffered, or were enforced to yield unto, we are the men of the present age, and ought to be absolutely free from all kinds of exorbitances, molestations or
75   arbitrary power, and you we chose to free us from all without exception or limitation. . . .

I do confidently conclude (if confidence may be derived from the just principles of nature) that the transgression of our weal by our trustees is an utter forfeiture of their trust, and cessation of their
80   power. Therefore if I prove a forefeiture of the people's trust in the prevalent party at Westminster in Parliament assembled, then an appeal from them to the people is not anti-parliamentary, anti-magisterial; not *from* that sovereign power, but *to* that sovereign power. . . . Even so may the commonalty of England reply to their
85   Parliament-members, that they are made for the people, not the people for them, and no otherwise may they deal with the people than for their safety and weal, for no more than the people are the King's, no more are the people the Parliament's [they] having no such propriety in the people as the people have in their goods, to do
90   with them as they list. As they will not grant it to be the prerogative of Kings, neither may we yield it to be the privilege of Parliaments.

Richard Overton, from *A Remonstrance of Many Thousand Citizens* (July 1646) and *An Appeale* (July 1647)

Questions

a   Elucidate and account for Walwyn's criticisms of Parliament (document a).
b   To what extent does Overton's argument rest upon principles, rather than detailed objections?
c   Account for the movement away from Parliamentary arguments based on Henry Parker's assertion of Parliamentary sovereignty to Overton's claim that the people represent the sovereign power.

D   The Putney Debates: Extension of the Franchise?

(*a*)

IRETON: 'The exception that lies in it is this. It is said they [seats in the House of Commons] are to be distributed according to the number of the inhabitants –'to the people of England' etc. And this doth make me think that the meaning is that every man that is an inhabitant is
5   to be equally considered, and to have an equal voice in the election of those representers, the persons that are for the general Representative. And if that be the meaning then I have something to say against it. . . .'

PETTY: 'We judge that all inhabitants that have not lost their birthright
10 should have an equal voice in elections.'

RAINSBOROUGH: 'I desired that those that engaged in it [might be included]. For really I think that the poorest he that is in England hath a life to live, as the greatest he. And therefore truly, sir, I think it's clear, that every man that is to live under a government ought
15 first be his own consent to put himself under that government; and I do think that the poorest man in England is not at all bound in a strict sense to that government that he hath not had a voice to put himself under; and I am confident that, when I have heard the reasons against it, something will be said to answer those reasons insomuch
20 that I should doubt whether he was an Englishman or no, that should doubt of these things.'

> Extracts from the Putney Debates. Reprinted in A. S. P.
> Woodhouse, *Puritanism and Liberty*, op cit, pp 52–3

(*b*)

I think that no person hath a right to an interest or share in the disposing of the affairs of the kingdom, and in determining or choosing those that shall determine what laws we shall be ruled by
25 here, no person hath a right to this that hath not a permanent fixed interest in this kingdom, and those persons together are properly the represented of this kingdom, who taken together, and consequently are to make up the representers of this kingdom, are the representers, who taken together do comprehend whatsoever is of real or permanent
30 interest in the kingdom, and I am sure there is otherwise (I cannot tell what), otherwise any man can say why a foreigner coming in amongst us, or as many as will coming in amongst us, or by force or otherwise settling themselves here, or at least by our permission having a being here, why they should not as well lay claim to it as
35 any other. We talk of birthright. Truly birthright there is thus much claim: men may justly have by birthright, by their very being born in England, that we should not seclude them out of England. That we should not refuse to give them air and place and ground, and the freedom of the highways and other things, to live amongst us, not
40 any man that is born here, though he in birth, or by his birth there

come nothing at all that is part of the permanent interest of this kingdom to him. That I think is due to a man by birth. But that by a man's being born here he shall have a share in that power that shall dispose of the lands here, and of all things here, I do not think it a
45 sufficient ground, but I am sure if we look upon that which is the utmost, within man's view, of what was originally the constitution of this kingdom, upon that which is most radical and fundamental, and which if you take away, there is no man hath any land, any goods, you take away any civil interest, and that is this: that those
50 that choose the representers for the making of laws by which this state and kingdom are to be governed, are the persons who taken together, do comprehend the local interest of this kingdom; that is, the persons in whom all land lies, and those in corporations in whom all trading lies. This is the most fundamental constitution of this
55 kingdom, and which if you do not allow you allow none at all. This constitution hath limited and determined it, that only those shall have voices in elections. It is true, as was said by a gentleman near me, the meanest man in England ought to have. I say this: that those that have the meanest local interest, that man that hath not forty shillings
60 a year, he hath as great voice in the election of a knight for the shire as he that hath ten thousand a year or more.

> Henry Ireton in the Putney Debates, Cf. G. E. Aylmer, *The Levellers in the English Revolution* (London 1975) pp 100–1

(*c*)
That the Supreme Authority of England and the Territories therewith incorporate, shall be and reside henceforward in a Representative of the people consisting of four hundred persons, but no more; in the
65 choice of whom (according to naturall right) all men of the age of one and twenty years and upwards (not being servants, or receiving alms, or having served the late King in Arms or voluntary Contributions), shall have their voices; and be capable of being elected to that Supreme Trust those who served the King being disabled for ten
70 years onely. . . .
    That two hundred of the four hundred Members, and not lesse, shall be taken and esteemed for a competent Representative; and the major Voyces present shall be concluding to this Nation. The place of Session, and choice of a Speaker, with other circumstances of that
75 nature, are referred to the care of this and future Representatives.
    And to the end [that] publick Officers may be certainly accountable, and no Factions made to maintain corrupt Interests, no Officer of any salary Forces in Army or Garison, nor any Treasurer or Receiver of publick monies, shall (while such) be elected a Member for any
80 Representative; and if any Lawyer shall at any time be chosen, he shall be uncapable of practice as a Lawyer, during the whole time of that Trust. And for the same reason, and that all persons may be capable of subjection as well as rule.

That no Member of the present Parliament shall be capable of being
85 elected of the next Representative, nor any Member of any future
Representative shall be capable of being chosen for the Representative
immediately succeeding: but are free to be chosen, one Representative
having intervened: Nor shall any Member of any Representative
be made either Receiver, Treasurer, or other Officer during that
90 imployment.
That for avoyding the many dangers and inconveniences apparantly
arising from the long continuance of the same persons in Authority:
We Agree, that this present Parliament shall end the first Wednesday
in August next 1649, and thenceforth be of no power or Authority:
95 and in the mean time shall order and direct the Election of a new and
equall Representative, according to the true intent of this our
Agreement: and so as the next Representative may meet and sit in
power and Authority as an effectuall Representative upon the day
following; namely the first Thursday of the same August 1649.
The (third and final) *Agreement of the Free People of England*
(1 May 1649) in G. E. Aylmer, op cit, pp 162–3

(d)
100 To every individual in nature is given an individual property by
nature not to be invaded or usurped by any. For everyone, as he is
himself, so he hath a self-propriety else could he not be himself; and
on this, no second may presume to deprive any of without manifest
violation and affront to the very principles of nature and of the rules
105 of equity and justice between man and man. 'Mine' and 'thine' cannot
be except this be. No man hath power over my rights and liberties,
and I over no man's. I may be but an individual, enjoy myself and
my self-propriety and may write [right?] myself no more than myself
or presume any further. If I do I am an encroacher and an invader
110 upon another man's right to which I have no right. For by natural
birth all men are equally and alike born to like propriety, liberty and
freedom; and as we are delivered of God by the hand of nature into
this world, everyone with a natural, innate freedom and propriety (as
it were writ in the table of every man's heart, never to be obliterated)
115 even so are we to live: everyone equally and alike to enjoy his
birthright and privilege, even all whereof God by nature hath made
him free. . . .
He that gives more sins against his own self, and he that takes
more is a thief and robber to his own kind. Every man by nature [is]
120 a King, priest and prophet in his own natural circuit and compass,
whereof no second may partake but by deputation, commission and
free consent from him whose natural right and freedom it is. . . .
The safety of the people is the sovereign law to which all must
become subject and for the which all powers human are ordained by

125 them; for [all] tyranny, oppression and cruelty whatsoever and in whomsoever is in itself unnatural, illegal, yea, absolutely anti-magisterial, for it is even destructive to all human civil society and therefore resistable.

Richard Overton, *An Arrow Against all Tyrants* (1646)

Questions

a   To what extent did Levellers and officers disagree over electoral arrangements during the Putney debates?
b   Examine Ireton's contention that the right to vote is determined by possession of a 'permanent fixed interest in the kingdom'.
c   Why did the Levellers intend to restrict parliamentary autonomy through an *Agreement of the People*?
d   Assess Overton's view of natural rights.

V Towards a New Model of Government: the Commonwealth

1 Rump Rule: The Rump Parliament, 1649–53

Pride's Purge of over 100 MPs (more than double this number withdrew voluntarily) on 6 and 7 December 1648 forestalled the Long Parliament's attempt to continue negotiations with the king and set up a 'Rump' Parliament of about 70 members. Not all these men were committed republicans. Indeed, that reluctant revolutionary, Oliver Cromwell, who was not a party to Pride's Purge, was still working for an accommodation with the king in the days before Christmas 1648, and many other MPs agreed to the purge without accepting that regicide was the inevitable sequel. Pride's Purge, however, was the essential precondition for the establishment of a Commonwealth, for the exclusion of the moderates enabled the Rump to pass the 4 January ordinance setting up the High Court of Justice to try Charles I. The sentence and execution of the king duly followed on 27 and 30 January. The House of Lords was then abolished by a Commons resolution of 6 February and on 7 February the monarchy was voted as being 'unnecessary, burdensome and dangerous to the liberty, safety and public interest of this nation', although the necessary legislation for both resolutions was not ready for a further six weeks (document A,a–b). On 14 February the council of state, the executive body of the new republic, was created. Kingdom was not finally transformed into Commonwealth, however, until the Commons resolution of 19 May 1649 which declared Parliament 'the supreme authority of this nation' (document A,c).

Radical expectations were high in the early months of the republic. The legend 'God with us' on the new coinage perhaps best symbolised the hope that a godly reformation was going to accompany the political revolution. The delay in declaring the Commonwealth, however, was an indication of disagreements within the Rump as to the way forward. These divisions had been intensified by the readiness of the radicals to broaden the base of the new regime. At least half of the nominated council of state, for example, were not whole-heartedly committed to the Revolution. Further, after 1 February, about 100 excluded MPs who had voted in favour of the 5 December motion to continue negotiations with the king were readmitted to the House. This influx of moderates was to have an enormous effect on the direction and pace of Rump legislation.

A wide measure of agreement could be anticipated for such anti-Royalist measures as the abolition of Cathedral Offices (Act of 30 April 1649), the sale of Dean and Chapter land (31 July 1649), the sale of the goods and personal estate of the royal family (4, 16 July 1649, 17 July 1651, 31 December 1652) and the making void of royal titles (4 February 1652). Similarly there was a majority in the Rump in favour of the Acts for the propagation of the gospel in New England (as well as Wales and Ireland, although a general propagation for England was not passed), and for the repeal of the Elizabethan church attendance laws (documents B). In a period of sectarian licence, a traditional Puritan morality programme for the 'reformation of manners' could also be expected to gain Rump support, especially from the Presbyterians who needed to be won over to avert a possible alliance with the Royalists. This resulted in the series of repressive (yet unenforceable) Acts passed during the summer of 1650, including the strict sabbath observance law, the famous measure imposing the death penalty for adultery and the Act against blasphemy (documents C). Limited agreement was also secured for minor reform of the law. When it came to more controversial measures, however, the fissures within the Rump were at once exposed.

So after the initial surge of legislation, the Rump lapsed into inertia, and except at times of army pressure (after Cromwell's appeals post Dunbar and Worcester and the army petition of August 1652) the Parliament concentrated on survival in a period of war, counter-revolution and economic and social dislocation. This did not matter provided the army was preoccupied, as it was until the end of the last serious Royalist insurrection at Worcester (September 1651). With the removal of this military threat and the return of officers such as Cromwell and Harrison to their seats in the Rump, the army was freer to press for the continuance of the revolution at home. Strong demands were made for the abolition of tithes, new elections and further reform of education and the law. But it was the Rump's failure to agree to the army's procedure for parliamentary reform that was to be the immediate cause of its sudden dissolution by Oliver Cromwell on 20 April 1653.

Cromwell's bitter recriminations against the Rump on that day (document D,a) were excessive and should be compared with the views of some of his other contemporaries. The Levellers were without illusions from the start as may be seen by this extract from Lilburne's 1649 tract, *Picture of the Council of State* (document D,b) Other visionaries who had looked forward in 1649 to the reign of King Jesus were totally disillusioned by 1653 and, as the Venetian ambassador reported (document D,c), were quite ready to see the back of the Rump. Such hostile contemporary portraits, however, need to be contrasted with those of the Rumpers themselves. As might be expected, these men pictured the Rump in a rather different light (documents D,d–f). Admittedly, these views are mostly retrospective but it may be that they are nearer the truth than those of other contemporaries with even greater axes to grind. Dr Worden, the foremost historian of the Rump Parliament, suggests that the Rump was not particularly corrupt, factious or inefficient when compared with other seventeenth-century parliaments. His overwhelming impression is one of 'bustle' rather than 'sloth' particularly in the early years and at times of crisis. He concedes that plans for legal, religious and electoral reform were confounded, but reminds us that reform was incidental for many Rumpers, whose prime concern was the achievement of domestic stability. That the Rump failed to provide an alternative form of government quickly enough for the army leaders should not blind us to its accomplishments. Certainly it is both unjust and unfortunate that one of the Rump's earliest detractors, the purged MP Clement Walker, should have coined the prurient sobriquet that was to gain such popular notoriety when it was restored to power in 1659–60. The roasting of the later Rump on the night of 11 February 1660, so memorably recorded by Pepys, may well have been deserved but the Parliament of 1649–53 is entitled to a better deal from history.

A The Creation of the Commonwealth

(a) The Act Abolishing the Office of King, 17 March 1649

Whereas Charles Stuart, late King of England, Ireland, and the territories and dominions thereunto belonging, hath by authority derived from Parliament been and is hereby declared to be justly condemned, adjudged to die, and put to death, for many treasons,
5   murders, and other heinous offences committed by him, by which judgement he stood, and is hereby declared to be attainted of high treason, whereby his issue and posterity, and all others pretending title under him, are become incapable of the said Crowns, or of being King or Queen of the said kingdom or dominions, or either
10   or any of them; be it therefore enacted . . . that all the people of England and Ireland, and the dominions and territories thereunto belonging, of what degree or condition soever, are discharged of all fealty, homage, and allegiance which is or shall be pretended to be due unto any of the issue and posterity of the said late King, or
15   any claiming under him; and that Charles Stuart, eldest son, and James called Duke of York, second son, and all other the issue and

posterity of him the said late King . . . are and be disabled to hold or enjoy the said Crown. . . .

And whereas it is and hath been found by experience, that the office of a King in this nation and Ireland, and to have the power thereof in any single person, is unnecessary, burdensome, and dangerous to the liberty, safety, and public interest of the people, and that for the most part, use hath been made of the regal power and prerogative to oppress and impoverish and enslave the subject; and that usually and naturally any one person in such power makes it his interest to incroach upon the just freedom and liberty of the people, and to promote the setting up of their own will and power above the laws, that so they might enslave these kingdoms to their own lust; be it therefore enacted and ordained by this present Parliament, and by authority of the same, that the office of a King in this nation shall not henceforth reside in or be exercised by any one single person. . . .

And whereas by the abolition of the kingly office provided for in this Act, a most happy way is made for this nation (if God see it good) to return to its just and ancient right, of being governed by its own representatives or national meetings in council, from time to time chosen and entrusted for that purpose by the people, it is therefore resolved and declared by the Commons assembled in Parliament, that they will put a period to the sitting of this present Parliament, and dissolve the same so soon as may possibly stand with the safety of the people that hath betrusted them, and with what is absolutely necessary for the preserving and upholding the Government now settled in the way of a Commonwealth; and that they will carefully provide for the certain choosing, meeting, and sitting of the next and future representatives, with such other circumstances of freedom in choice and equality in distribution of members to be elected thereunto, as shall most conduce to the lasting freedom and good of this Commonwealth. . . .

S. R. Gardiner, *Constitutional Documents of the Puritan Revolution 1625–1660*, pp 384–7

(b) An Act Abolishing the House of Lords, 19 March 1649

The Commons of England assembled in Parliament, finding by too long experience that the House of Lords is useless and dangerous to the people of England to be continued, have thought fit to ordain and enact, and be it ordained and enacted by this present Parliament, and by the authority of the same, that from henceforth the House of Lords in Parliament shall be and is hereby wholly abolished and taken away. . . . Nevertheless it is hereby declared, that neither such Lords as have demeaned themselves with honour,

courage, and fidelity to the Commonwealth, nor their posterities
who shall continue so, shall be excluded from the public councils
of the nation, but shall be admitted thereunto, and have their free
60 vote in Parliament, if they shall be thereunto elected, as other
persons of interest elected and qualified thereunto ought to
have. . . .

Ibid, pp 387–8

(c) An Act declaring England to be a Commonwealth, 19 May 1649

Be it declared and enacted by this present Parliament, and by the
authority of the same, that the people of England, and of all the
65 dominions and territories thereunto belonging, are and shall be,
and are hereby constituted, made, established, and confirmed, to
be a Commonwealth and Free State, and shall from henceforth be
governed as a Commonwealth and Free State by the supreme
authority of this nation, the representatives of the people in
70 Parliament and by such as they shall appoint and constitute as
officers and ministers under them for the good of the people, and
that without any King or House of Lords.

Ibid, p 388

Questions

a   Was Charles I 'justly condemned, adjudged to die and put to
    death' (lines 3–4)?
b   How much 'fealty, homage and allegiance' was shown to the
    'issue and posterity of the said late King' (lines 13–14) during
    the Rump Parliament, 1649–53?
c   How convincing do you find the arguments put forward (in
    the Act abolishing monarchy) in favour of republican rule and
    parliamentary sovereignty?
d   To what extent was the promise in the last paragraph of passage
    (a) broken?
e   How far was the House of Lords 'useless and dangerous to the
    people of England' (lines 50–1)?
f   How revolutionary was the Commonwealth Act?

B   Acts of Propagation and Toleration

(a)   An Act for the promoting and propagating the Gospel of Jesus Christ in New England, 27 July 1649

Whereas the Commons of England assembled in Parliament have received certain intelligence, by the testimonial of divers faithful and godly ministers, and others in New England, that divers the heathen natives of that country, through the blessing of God upon
5   the pious care and pains of some godly English of this nation, who preach the gospel to them in their own Indian Language, who not only of barbarous are become civil, but many of them forsaking their accustomed charms and sorceries, and other satanical delusions, do now call upon the name of the Lord, and give great testimony of
10   the power of God, drawing them from death and darkness, into the life and light of the glorious gospel of Jesus Christ; which appeareth by their diligent attending on the word so preached unto them, with tears lamenting their mis-spent lives, teaching their children what they are instructed in themselves, being careful to
15   place their said children in godly English families, and to put them to English schools, betaking themselves to one wife, putting away the rest, and by their constant prayers to Almighty God morning and evening in their families, expressed (in all appearance) with much devotion and zeal of heart. All which considered, we cannot
20   but in behalf of the nation, represent, rejoice and give glory to God, for the beginning of so glorious a propagation of the gospel of Jesus Christ amongst those poor heathen; which cannot be prosecuted with that expedition and further success as is desired, unless fit instruments be encouraged and maintained to pursue it,
25   universities, schools, and nurseries of literature settled for further instructing and civilizing them, instruments and materials fit for labour, and clothing, with other necessaries, as encouragements for the best deserving among them, be provided, and many other things necessary for so great a work; the furnishing of all which
30   will be a burthen too heavy for the English there (who although willing, yet unable) having in a great measure exhausted their estates in laying the foundations of many hopeful towns and colonies in a desolate wilderness; and therefore conceive our selves of this nation bound to be helpful in the promoting and advancing
35   of a work so much tending to the honour of Almighty God. Be it therefore enacted, that for the furthering so good a work, and for the purposes aforesaid, from henceforth there shall be a corporation in England consisting of sixteen persons (viz.) a president, treasurer, and fourteen assistances . . . and shall be called by the name of *The*
40   *President and Society for propagation of the Gospel in New England* . . . which said commissioners are hereby ordered and appointed, to dispose of the said moneys in such manner as shall best and

principally conduce to the preaching and propagating of the gospel
of Jesus Christ amongst the natives, and also for maintaining of
45 schools and nurseries of learning, for the better education of the
children of the natives.

And forasmuch as we cannot but be induced from the consideration of the premises, to recommend the furthering thereof to the
charity of all such whose hearts God shall incline thereunto, by
50 their Christian and charitable contributions, to be as the foundation
of so pious and great an undertaking; be it therefore, and it is
hereby enacted by the Parliament assembled, and by the authority
thereof, that a general collection be made for the purposes aforesaid,
in and through all the counties, cities, towns and parishes of
55 England and Wales. And for the more speedy and better affecting
thereof, be it enacted by the authority aforesaid, that the several
ministers within the said several places, are hereby required to read
this Act or a copy thereof, in the presence of their several
congregations, upon the next Lords-day after the same shall be
60 delivered unto them, and to exhort the people to a cheerful and
liberal contribution. . . .

C. H. Firth and R. S. Rait (eds), *Acts and Ordinances of the
Interregnum* (3 vols, 1911), II, pp 197–9

(b) An Act repealing several clauses in Statutes imposing Penalties for not coming to Church, 27 September 1650

The Parliament of England taking into consideration several Acts,
made in the times of former Kings and Queens of this nation,
against recusants not coming to church, enjoining the use of
65 Common Prayer, the keeping and observing of holy days, and
some other particulars touching matters of religion; and finding,
that by the said Act divers religious and peaceable people, well-
affected to the prosperity of the Commonwealth, have not only
been molested and imprisoned, but also brought into danger of
70 abjuring their country, or in case of return, to suffer death as felons,
to the great disquiet and utter ruin of such good and godly people,
and to the detriment of the Commonwealth, do enact, and be it
enacted by this present Parliament, and by authority of the same,
that all and every the branches, clauses, articles, and provisoes
75 expressed and contained in the ensuing Acts of Parliament . . . [3
Elizabethan Acts named] . . . and all and every the branches,
clauses, articles, and provisoes expressed and contained in any other
Act or Ordinance of Parliament, whereby or wherein any penalty
or punishment is imposed, or mentioned to be imposed on any
80 person whatsoever, for not repairing to their respective parish
churches, or for not keeping of holy days, or for not hearing

Common Prayer, or for speaking or inveighing against the Book of Common Prayer, shall be, and are by the authority aforesaid, wholly repealed and made void. . . .

85 And to the end that no profane or licentious persons may take occasion by the repealing of the said laws (intended only for relief of pious and peaceably-minded people from the rigour of them) to neglect the performance of religious duties, be it further enacted by the authority aforesaid, that all and every person and persons

90 within this Commonwealth and the territories thereof, shall (having no reasonable excuse for their absence) upon every Lord's day, days of public thanks-giving and humiliation, diligently resort to some public place where the service and worship of God is exercised, or shall be present at some other place in the practice of

95 some religious duty, either of prayer, preaching, reading or expounding the scriptures, or conferring upon the same.

And be it further declared by the authority aforesaid, that every person and persons that shall not diligently perform the duties aforesaid, according to the true meaning hereof (not having

100 reasonable excuse to the contrary) shall be deemed and taken to be offenders against this law, and shall be proceeded against accordingly.

Gardiner, *Constitutional Documents*, op. cit., pp 391–4

Questions

a What does the Propagation Act tell you about (i) the state of religion in New England (ii) the nature of English Puritanism?
b How was the scheme for the propagation of the gospel to have been financed?
c Which Elizabethan statutes were likely to have been repealed by the second Act? How severe were their penalties for non-attendance at church?
d How tolerant was the last Act (document B,c)?

C A Puritan Moral Code

(a) An Act for the better Observation of the Lords-Day, Days of Thanksgiving and Humiliation, 19 April 1650

For the more effectual executing of all such Laws, statutes and ordinances of parliament, for the due observation and sanctification of the Lords-day, days of public humiliation and thanks-giving, and for the further preventing the profanation thereof, it is enacted

5 and declared by this present Parliament, and by the authority of

the same, that all and every High Constable, Petty Constable, Headborough, Churchwarden or Overseer of the poor or other officers, or any of the governors of the company of watermen . . . by warrant . . . are hereby authorized and required to seize and
10 secure all such wares or goods cried, showed forth or put to sale upon the days and times aforesaid, contrary to this present Act . . . no traveller, waggoner, butcher, higler, drover, their or any of their servants, shall travel or come into his or their inn or lodging, after twelve of the clock on any Saturday night; nor shall any
15 person travel from his house, inn or other place, till after one a clock on Monday morning, without good and urgent cause . . . [otherwise a 10s. fine].

And if any writ, warrant or order (except in case of treason, murder, felony, or breach of the peace, profanation of the Lords-
20 day, days of thanksgiving or humiliation, or suspicion of them or either or any of them) shall be . . . served or executed upon any the aforesaid days, every such execution of such writ, warrant or order upon the said days respectively, shall be, and is hereby declared to be of no effect . . . [otherwise a £5 fine]
25 . . . no person or persons shall use, employ or travel upon the Lords-day, or the said days of humiliation or thanksgiving, with any boat, wherry, lighter, barge, horse, coach or sedan, either in the City of London or elsewhere (except it be to or from some place for the service of God, or upon other extraordinary occasion
30 . . .) [10s. fine for the user, 5s. for the tradesman] . . . every person and persons which upon the said Lords-day, days of humiliation or thanksgiving, shall be in any tavern, inn, alehouse, tobacco-house, or shop, or victualling-house (unless he lodge there, or be there upon some lawful or necessary occasion) . . . and every
35 person or persons which upon the said days shall be dancing, profanely singing, drinking or tippling in any tavern, inn, alehouse, victualling-house, or tobacco-house or shop, or shall harbour or entertain any person or persons so offending; or which shall grind or cause to be ground in any mill, any corn or grain upon any the
40 said days, except in case of necessity, to be allowed by a Justice of the Peace, every such offender shall forfeit and pay the sum of ten shillings for every such offence. . . .

Firth and Rait, op. cit., II, pp 383–7

(b) An Act for suppressing the detestable sins of Incest, Adultery and Fornication, 10 May 1650

For the suppressing of the abominable and crying sins of incest, adultery and fornication, wherewith this land is much defiled, and
45 Almighty God highly displeased; be it enacted . . . that if any

person or persons whatsoever, marry, or have the carnal knowledge
of the body of his or her grandfather or grandmother, father or
mother, brother or sister, son or daughter, or grandchild, fathers
brother or sister, mothers brother or sister, fathers wife, mothers
50 husband, sons wife, daughters husband, wives mother or daughter,
husbands father or son; all and every such offences are hereby
adjudged and declared incest; and every such offence shall be, and
is hereby adjudged felony; and every person offending therein, and
confessing the same, or being thereof convicted by verdict upon
55 indictment or presentment, before any judge or justices at the assize
or sessions of the peace, shall suffer death as in case of felony,
without benefit of clergy . . . in case any married woman shall . . .
be carnally known by any man (other then her husband) (except in
case of ravishment) and of such offence or offences shall be
60 convicted as aforesaid by confession or otherwise, every such
offence and offences shall be and is hereby adjudged felony; and
every person, as well the man as the woman, offending therein,
and confessing the same, or being thereof convicted by verdict
upon indictment or presentment as aforesaid, shall suffer death as
65 in case of felony, without benefit of clergy. Provided, that this
shall not extend to any man who at the time of such offence
committed, is not knowing that such woman with whom such
offence is committed, is then married. Provided also, that the said
penalty in the case of adultery aforesaid, shall not extend to any
70 woman whose husband shall be continually remaining beyond the
seas by the space of three years, or shall by common fame be
reputed to be dead; nor to any woman whose husband shall absent
himself from his said wife by the space of three years together. . . .
. . . if any man shall . . . have the carnal knowledge of the body
75 of any virgin, unmarried woman or widow, every such man so
offending, and confessing the same, or being thereof convicted by
verdict upon indictment or presentment, as also every such woman
so offending, and confessing the same, or being thereof convict as
aforesaid, shall for every such offence be committed to the common
80 gaol. . . .
    Provided . . . that no person or persons shall incur any of the
penalties in this Act mentioned, unless the said person or persons
be thereof indicted within twelve months after the offence committed. . . .
        Ibid, pp 387–9

(c) *An Act against several Atheistical, Blasphemous and
    Execrable Opinions, derogatory to the honour of God, and
    destructive to human Society, 9 August 1650*

85 The Parliament holding it to be their duty, by all good ways and

means to propagate the gospel in this Commonwealth, to advance
religion in all sincerity, godliness, and honesty, have made several
ordinances and laws for the good and furtherance of reformation,
in doctrine and manners, and in order to the suppressing of
90 profaneness, wickedness, superstition and formality, that God may
be truly glorified, and all might in well-doing be encouraged. But
notwithstanding this their care, finding to their great grief and
astonishment, that there are divers men and women who have
lately discovered themselves to be most monstrous in their opinions,
95 and loose in all wicked and abominable practices hereafter mentioned, not only to the notorious corrupting and disordering, but
even to the dissolution of all human society, who rejecting the use
of any gospel ordinances, do deny the necessity of civil and moral
righteousness among men. . . . all and every person or persons so
100 avowedly professing, maintaining or publishing as aforesaid, the
aforesaid atheistical, blasphemous or execrable opinions, or any of
them, upon complaint and proof made of the same in any the cases
aforesaid, before any one or more justice or justices of peace, mayor
or other head-officer of any city or town corporate by the oath of
105 two or more witnesses . . . the party so convicted or confessing,
shall by the said justice or justices, or other head-officer be
committed to prison or to the house of correction, for the space of
six months . . . [Banishment for the second offence].
    Provided always, that no person or persons shall be punished,
110 impeached, molested, or troubled for any offence mentioned in
this Act, unless he or she be for the same offence accused, presented,
indicted or convicted within six months after such offence committed.
        Ibid, pp 409–12

Questions

a What do these Acts tell you about Puritan morality?
b What does the Adultery Act tell you about Puritan attitudes to
   women?
c How effectively were these Acts likely to have been enforced?
d How far did the 1650 Act differ from former sabbatarian
   measures?
e Why was the Blasphemy Act considered necessary?

D The Work of the Rump: Some Contemporary Observations

(a)

. . . [Cromwell] loaded the Parliament with the vilest reproaches, charging them not to have a heart to do anything for the public good, to have espoused the corrupt interest of Presbytery and the lawyers, who were the supporters of tyranny and oppression,
5   accusing them of an intention to perpetuate themselves in power, had they not been forced to the passing of this Act, which he affirmed they designed never to observe, and thereupon told them that the Lord had done with them, and had chosen other instruments for the carrying on his work that were more worthy. This he spoke
10 with so much passion and discomposure of mind, as if he had been distracted. . . .

> W. C. Abbott, *Writings and Speeches of Oliver Cromwell* (4 vols, Cambridge, Mass., 1937–47), II, pp 643–4 (from Ludlow's account)

(b)

Again, if it should be granted this parliament at the beginning had a legal constitution from the people (the original and fountain of all just power), yet the faction of a traitorous party of officers of
15 the Army, hath twice rebelled against the Parliament, and broke them to pieces, and by force of arms culled out whom they please, and imprisoned divers of them and laid nothing to their charge, and have left only in a manner a few men, besides eleven of themselves . . ., of their own faction behind them that will like
20 spaniel dogs serve their lusts and wills. Yes some of the chiefest of them . . . styling them a mock Parliament. . . . query, whether in law or justice, especially considering they have fallen from all their many glorious promises, and have not done any one action that tends to the universal good of the people, can those gentlemen
25 sitting at Westminster in the House, called the House of Commons, be any other than a factious company of men traitorously combined together with Cromwell, Ireton, and Harrison, to subdue the laws, liberties, and freedoms of England? . . .

> J. Lilburne, 'Picture of the Council of State' in *The Leveller Tracts, 1647–53*, ed. W. Haller and G. Davies (Gloucester, Mass., 1964 edn) pp 206.

(c)

. . . the dissolution is viewed with admiration rather than surprise
30 and gives general satisfaction. The popular voice and the press show how much the nation disapproved the administration of the parliament, which is principally reproached with having constantly promised law reform but never having done anything, and with

having broken faith with those who advanced considerable loans
35 during the civil wars. While instead of seeking to relieve the people,
as they promised, they always deceived and taxed them more and
more and finally they saddled the country with a troublesome and
expensive war with Holland. . . .

Cal. S. P. Venetian 1653–4, p 68, Paulucci (Venetian ambassador) to Sagredo, 2 May 1653

(d)
And they [the officers of the army] now began to assume to
40 themselves all the honour of the past actions, and of the conquests
by them achieved; scarce owning the parliament and their assistance
and provision for them, but taxing and censuring the members of
parliament for injustice and delay of business, and for seeking to
prolong their power and promote their private interest, and to
45 satisfy their own ambition. With these and many others the like
censures they endeavoured to calumniate the parliament, and judge
them guilty of those crimes whereof themselves were faulty; not
looking into their own actions, nor perceiving their own defaults,
yet censuring the actions and proceedings of the parliament very
50 opprobriously. . . .

Thus it pleased God, that this assembly, famous through the
world for its undertakings, actions, and successes, having subdued
all their enemies, were themselves overthrown and ruined by their
servants; and those whom they had raised now pulled down their
55 masters. . . .

Bulstrode Whitelocke, *Memorials of the English Affairs*, III,
p 477, Feb. 1652; IX, p 6, 20 April 1653 (4 vols, 1853)

(e)
We continued four years before we were put an end to. In which
time, I appeal to all, if the nation that had been blasted and torn
began not exceedingly to flourish. At the end of the four years,
scarce a sight to be seen that we had had a war. Trade flourished;
60 the City of London grew rich; we were the most potent by sea
that ever was known in England. Our navy and armies were never
better. . . . What care did the Parliament then take to furnish their
army from London with all necessaries, by land and in ships; all
provided with the greatest diligence. None but a numerous com-
65 pany of good and honest-hearted men could have done the like. . . .

Diary of Themes Burton (ed. J. T. Rutt, 4 vols, 1828), III,
pp 96, 98, Haselrig's speech, 7 Feb. 1659

(f)
The parliament, on the other side, had now, by the blessing of
God, restored the commonwealth to such a happy, rich, and
plentiful condition, as it was not so flourishing before the war, and

although the taxes that were paid were great, yet the people were
70 rich and able to pay them. They [the parliament] were in a way of
paying all the soldiers' arrears, had some hundred thousand pounds
in their purses, and were free from enemies in arms within and
without, except the Dutch, whom they had beaten and brought to
seek peace upon honourable terms to the English. And now they
75 thought it was time to sweeten the people, and deliver them from
their burthens. . . . [Cromwell then dissolved the parliament].
Meanwhile they and their soldiers could no way palliate their
rebellion but by making false [re]criminations of the parliament-
men, as that they meant to perpetuate themselves in honour and
80 office, that they had gotten vast estates, and perverted justice for
gain, and were imposing upon men for conscience, and a thousand
such like things, which time manifested to be false, and truth
retorted all upon themselves that they had injuriously cast at the
others.

Hutchinson, *Memoirs of Colonel Hutchinson*, op. cit., pp 288

Questions

a How was the Parliament dissolved?
b Explain (i) Lilburne's (ii) Cromwell's hostility towards the
   Rump.
c Why was the unconstitutional dissolution of the Rump apparently so popular with the people (document c)?
d Why did Whitelocke, Haselrig and Hutchinson all consider the
   Rump to have been a successful parliament?
e How do Whitelocke and Hutchinson explain the Rump's
   unpopularity? Is this a sufficient explanation?

2 Godly Rule: Barebone's Parliament, 1653

Although the Rump was never intended as anything more than a
stop-gap government, its early demise some eighteen months
before its term officially expired (shortly after Worcester the Rump
had agreed to dissolve itself by 3 November 1654) put the army
leadership into a difficult position for which they were totally
unprepared. The Rump's dissolution may have been popular but it
was unplanned. The officers' claim that they were 'led by necessity
and Providence . . . even beyond and above our own thoughts and
desires' may be accepted as true, for the dissolution had narrowed
their options rather than widened them. Without Rump sanction,
the proposal of 19 April for a shared interim government of forty
worthies could not possibly have succeeded. The calling of a general

election – which, in any case, the military had no power to authorise – was also out of the question if an even more hostile assembly was to be avoided. Neither – despite what some foreign observers may have thought – the General nor his officers wished to establish an autocratic military government. Nevertheless, whether Cromwell and the officers liked it or not, for the time being power lay in their hands – an interim council of state (including civilians) was set up by Cromwell on 29 April until a new 'supreme authority' was constituted – and it was these men who were to determine the Commonwealth's future development.

The millenial vision that the only body capable of bringing about a godly reformation was an assembly of saints – government by the saints for the saints – had been advanced as early as February 1649 by one of the earliest groups of fifth monarchists. At about the same time that fellow traveller, Colonel Thomas Harrison, had agreed at the Whitehall debates that the time would come when the Spirit of God would 'carry through things in a way extraordinary that the works of men shall be answerable to His works'. By April 1653 Harrison, now one of the key figures in the debate as to the new form of government, clearly believed that that time had arrived. Some officers also shared Harrison's vision, at least in part; others were more sceptical, so the form of government that eventually emerged from the negotiations among the leading army officers – a nominated assembly of 140 godly men recommended and chosen by the Council of Officers and summoned by Cromwell as commander-in-chief – was a compromise between the millenial aspirations of Harrison and the more practical attitudes of men like Lambert, with Cromwell sitting somewhat uncomfortably between the two.

Given the nature of the nominating authority, it is not surprising that the resultant assembly also encompassed a wide spectrum of religious belief from Presbyterians like the Speaker, Francis Rous, and George Monck, through orthodox Congregationalists, to the Baptists and the dozen Fifth Monarchists. Neither was it socially homogeneous. The Venetian ambassador's belief (as well as the Royalists' – see documents A) that it was composed of 'mechanics and ignoramuses in government' was nothing more than a caricature and cannot be substantiated. Professor Woolrych has shown that at least a third of its membership came from good gentry stock (some of whose fortunes were rising) who would have been at home in any other seventeenth-century elected House, although there were a greater number of members drawn from lower down the social scale than would have been the case in other parliaments of the period. The number of tradesmen in the assembly, however, was small, and of lay preachers even smaller. Praise-God Barebone – from whom the assembly gained its nickname – was both, but he was a man of some substance and a warden of the Leathersellers'

Company. Most of Barebone's fellow members, moreover, had had extensive experience in local government.

The new members after having 'somewhat uneasily by reason of the scantness of the room and heat of the weather', sat through Cromwell's famous 'day in the power of Christ' address (document B), heard him read the Instrument whereby they were entrusted with 'supreme authority and government of this Commonwealth' until November 1654 at the latest, after which time they were to have made arrangements for their succession. The assembly then made its supremacy as a parliament apparent by deciding that it would meet in future in St Stephen's Chapel, the traditional home of the Commons, rather than in the Council Chamber at Whitehall where Cromwell had addressed them, and by resolving (on 6, 7 July) that it should have the title of 'parliament of the Commonwealth of England'. On 9 July the council of state, which Cromwell had declared to be at parliament's 'disposal', was reappointed and a committee established to enlarge its membership to thirty-one. Thereafter the new parliament got down to business with great earnestness. The Rump had sat on four days a week. This parliament sat every day of the week from 8 a.m., except, of course, on Sundays, and its members were more conscientious in their attendance. Most of the important work was done in the new standing committees, which – according to our only contemporary pamphlet on the parliament – 'sat daily and took great pains morning and evening almost every day in the week to dispatch business and make things ready for the House'. As a consequence, the Barebone's legislative record was not negligible: over thirty statutes were enacted in five months, quite apart from those in preparation when the parliament broke up in December. By far the most significant of these measures was the celebrated Act instituting civil marriage and requiring the register of births, marriages and burials, regardless of denomination (document C). It was one of only two enactments passed during the parliament that was based on the recommendations of the Hale Commission for law reform, which had been set up under the Rump. The measures that failed, however, could have been even more far reaching. But, as the author of the *Exact Relation* observed, the Bills to abolish Chancery, create a new body or model of law, limit the power of key impropriators and abolish tithes (document D) raised 'great dust' and fatally exposed the divisions within the assembly. On 12 December 1653, a group of moderates, tired of being 'condemned unto the fourth monarchy' and vilified as 'obstructors of reformation', and perhaps also suspicious that the 'saints' might try to secede from the House and even undermine the army, took the law into their own hands. Coming to the House earlier than usual, they brought the assembly to a precipitate end, abdicating their power to Cromwell. It was a recognition, by these men at least, that God's Kingdom was not of this world.

A Royalist Views of Barebone's Parliament

(a)

There were amongst them some few of the quality and degree of gentlemen, and who had estates, and such a proportion of credit and reputation, as could consist with the guilt they had contracted. But much the major part of them consisted of inferior persons, of
5   no quality or name, artificers of the meanest trades, known only by their gifts in praying and preaching; which was now practised by all degrees of men, but scholars, throughout the kingdom. In which number, that there may be a better judgement made of the rest, it will not be amiss to name one, from whom that parliament
10   itself was afterwards denominated, who was Praise-God (that was his Christian name) Barebone, a leatherseller in Fleet-street, from whom (he being an eminent speaker in it) it was afterwards called Praise-God Barebone's parliament. In a word, they were a pack of weak senseless fellows, fit only to bring the name and reputation
15   of parliaments lower than it was yet.

> *Selections from Clarendon*, ed. Hugh Trevor-Roper (Oxford, 1978), pp 347–8

(b)

. . . A Parliament is resolved upon with the method of its proceeding, which I cannot find to amount to much more than the administration of country affairs, for taxes, raising of men, quartering of soldiers, ordering committees and such public offices
20   which are attended with trouble and odium which they must free the supreme cabinet from. Their number, as I remember, is 130 or 140, most of them named by the General without consulting the respective counties, but some officious counties (or rather particular factions in those counties) as Kent and some few others have
25   returned the names of 5 or 6 qualified persons out of which his Excellency hath chosen 2 or 3. For the generality of them they are the most unknown (and without doubt unknowing in public affairs) in the Commonwealth: pettifoggers, inn-keepers, mill-wrights, stocking mongers and such a rabble as never had hopes to be of a
30   Grand Jury, and these are the qualified persons and those that must do the work. . . .

. . . The names of our new members are in print but surreptitiously and imperfectly though, near the truth, Lord Lisle, Fairfax and Evers, with some of the present Council and a very few more
35   are the most eminent among them. Those serve to gild the pill, the rest being of a company of the most obscure persons of the

nation. Their several characters cannot be long unknown, for it must needs tempt some of our pamphleteers to expose them to the world in print. This in short, many of them are strangers in the
40 respective counties they serve for and only known for their late employments. They are generally anabaptistical and esteemed men of blood, and of that mean birth and fortune that half of them were not worth half an hundred pounds at the beginning of the late troubles. Never was there so disproportioned a means designed for
45 so great a purpose, but certainly confusion is the thing intended and then we could not have more proper tools. . . .

> Bodleian Library, Clarendon MS. 45, fos 482*v*, 498*r*, Royalist newsletters, 3, 17 June 1653

Questions

a In what ways are these accounts biased? How consistent are they?
b Explain the Royalist indictments of the Parliament.
c Comment on:
    (i) 'fit only to bring the name and reputation of parliaments lower than it was yet' (lines 14–15).
    (ii) 'Those serve to gild the pill' (line 35).
    (iii) 'They are generally anabaptistical and esteemed men of blood' (lines 41–2).

B Cromwell's Speech, 4 July 1653

. . . Having done that that we have done upon this ground of necessity which we have declared, which was not a feigned necessity but real, to the end that the government might not be at a loss; to the end that we might manifest to the world the singleness of our
5 hearts and our integrity, who did these things, not to grasp after the power ourselves to keep it in military hands, no not for a day; but, as far as God enabled us with strength and ability, to put it into the hands of those that might be called from the several parts of the nation. This necessity, I say, and I hope that we may say for
10 ourselves, this integrity of labouring to divest the sword of the power and authority in the civil administration, hath moved us to conclude this course, and having done this, truly we think we cannot, with the discharge of our own consciences, but offer somewhat to you, as I said before, for our own exoneration. . . .
15 Truly God hath called you to this work by, I think, as wonderful providences as ever passed upon the sons of men in so short a time. And truly I think, taking the argument of necessity, for the

government must not fall; taking the appearance of the hand of God in this thing, I am sure you would have been loath it should
20 have been resigned into the hands of wicked men and enemies. I am sure God would not have it so. It comes, therefore, to you by the way of necessity, by the way of the wise Providence of God, though through weak hands. . . .

I confess I never looked to see such a day as this – it may be nor
25 you neither – when Jesus Christ should be so owned as He is, at this day, and in this work. Jesus Christ is owned this day by your call; and you own Him by your willingness to appear for Him; and you manifest this, as far as poor creatures can, to be the day of the power of Christ. . . .
30 I think it may be truly said that never was there a supreme authority consisting of so numerous a body as you are, which I believe are above 140, who were ever in the supreme authority, under such a notion, in such a way of owning God, and being owned by Him. And therefore I may say also, never a people so
35 formed, for such a purpose, so called – if it were a time to compare your standing with those that have been called by the suffrages of the people. Who can tell how soon God may fit the people for such a thing, and none can desire it more than I. . . . I say you are called with a high call. And why should we be afraid to say or
40 think that this may be the door to usher in the things that God has promised; which have been prophesied of; which He has set the hearts of His people to wait for and expect? We know who they are that shall war with the Lamb, against his enemies; they shall be a people called, and chosen and faithful. And God hath, in a military
45 way – we may speak it without flattering ourselves, and I believe you know it – He hath appeared with them and for them; and now in these civil powers and authorities does not he appear? These are not ill prognostications of that good we wait for. Indeed I do think something is at the door: we are at the threshold; and therefore it
50 becomes us to lift up our heads, and encourage ourselves in the Lord. . . .

As I have said elsewhere, if I were to choose any servant, the meanest officer for the Army or the Commonwealth, I would choose a godly man that hath principles, especially where a trust is
55 to be committed, because I know where to have a man that hath principles. I believe if any man of you should choose a servant, you would do so. And I would all our magistrates were so chosen: – this may be done; there may be good effects of this! . . .

Abbott, *Writings and Speeches of Cromwell*, III, pp 53–5, 60–1, 63–5

Questions

a   Pick out the passages that have millenarian overtones. Explain Cromwell's attitude at this time.

b   How sincere was Cromwell when he said that he (i) wished 'to divest the sword of the power and authority in the civil administration' (lines 10–11); (ii) desired to see a parliament 'called by the suffrages of the people'; (iii) would choose 'a godly man that hath principles' (lines 53–4)?

c   By 22 August 1653 Cromwell was writing to his son-in-law: 'Fain would I have my service accepted of the saints . . . but it is not so.' Why was it that, within less than two months of Cromwell's 4 July speech, his optimism had disappeared?

C   An Act touching Marriages and the Registering thereof; and also touching Births and Burials, 24 August 1653

Be it enacted by the authority of this present Parliament, that whosoever shall agree to be married within the Commonwealth of England, after the nine and twentieth day of September, in the year one thousand six hundred fifty three, shall (one and twenty
5   days at least before such intended marriage) deliver in writing, or cause to be so delivered unto the register (hereafter appointed by this Act) for the respective parish where each party to be married liveth, the names, surnames, additions, and places of abode of the parties so to be married, and of their parents, guardians or overseers.
10 All which the said register shall publish or cause to be published, three several Lords days then next following, at the close of the morning exercise, in the public meeting place commonly called the church or chapel; or (if the parties so to be married shall desire it) in the market-place next to the said church or chapel, on three
15 market-days in three several weeks next following, between the hours of eleven and two; which being so performed, the register shall (upon the request of the parties concerned) make a true certificate of the due performance thereof, without which certificate, the persons herein after authorized shall not proceed in such
20 marriage. And if any exception shall be made against the said intended marriage, the register shall also insert the same, with the name of the person making such exception, and their place of abode in the said certificate of publication. . . . That all such persons so intending to be married, shall come before some justice of peace
25 within and of the same county, city or town corporate where publication shall be made as aforesaid; and shall bring a certificate of the said publication, and shall make sufficient proof of the consent of their parents or guardians, if either of the said parties shall be under the age of one and twenty years. . . . And (if there

30   appear no reasonable cause to the contrary) the marriage shall proceed in this manner:

The man to be married, taking the woman to be married by the hand, shall plainly and distinctly pronounce these words:

35   I A.B. do here in the presence of God the searcher of all hearts, take thee C.D. for my wedded wife; and do also in the presence of God, and before these witnesses, promise to be unto thee a loving and faithful husband . . . [the woman similarly]

     . . . the man and woman having made sufficient proof of the consent of their parents or guardians as aforesaid, and expressed
40   their consent unto marriage, in the manner and by the words aforesaid, before such justice of peace in the presence of two or more credible witnesses; the said justice of peace may and shall declare the said man and woman to be from thenceforth husband and wife; and from and after such consent so expressed, and such
45   declaration made, the same (as to the form of marriage) shall be good and effectual in law. . . .

And that a true and just account may be always kept, as well of publications, as of all such marriages, and also of the births of children, and deaths of all sorts of persons within this Com-
50   monwealth, be it further enacted, that a book of good vellum or parchment shall be provided by every parish, for the registering of all such marriages, and of all births of children and burials of all sorts of people within every parish. . . . And for such publications and certificate thereof twelve pence and no more may be taken;
55   and for the entry of every marriage, twelve pence and no more; and for every birth of child four pence and no more; and for every death, four pence and no more. And for publications, marriages, births or burials of poor people who live upon alms nothing shall be taken. And the said justice of peace (if it be desired) shall give
60   unto the parties so married, a certificate in parchment under his hand and seal, of such marriage. . . .

     . . . the age for a man to consent unto marriage shall be sixteen years and the age of a woman fourteen years, and not before. . . .

     . . . the hearing and determining of all matters and controversies
65   touching contracts and marriages, and the lawfulness and unlawfulness thereof . . . shall be in the power, and referred to the determination of the justices of peace in each county, city or town corporate, at the general quarter sessions; or of such other persons to hear and determine the same, as the parliament shall hereafter
70   appoint. . . .

     Firth and Rait, op. cit., II, pp 715–18

Questions

a   Dr Woolrych suggests that 'the act reflects something of
    the radical Puritans' distrust of both the clerical and legal
    professions'. Discuss this statement.
b   In what other ways was this Act important?

D   A Contemporary Pamphlet

. . . There were four great votes that passed in the time of the
sitting of the House, which some interests were much displeased
at, and they passed not without great debate.

   First, for the Chancery. It was looked on as a great grievance,
5   one of the greatest in the nation, so many horrible things were
affirmed of it by members of the House, as those that were, or had
a mind to be advocates for it, had little to say on the behalf of it;
and so at the end of one days debate, the question being put, it
was voted down. . . . How sad a thing is it, that after such
10   appearances of God in the land, such a court, in such a way of
practice, should be continued, to greaten the retainers to it, and
practisers in it, by the ruin of others, eating the fat and sweat of
other men's labours and estates. . . .

   The second vote, which was for a new body of the law, passed
15   not without a large debate. . . . The reasons, or some of them,
that were alleged in the debate producing this vote, was the
intricacy, uncertainty, and incongruity in many things with the
word of God and right reason, in the laws as now they are. Whereas
the laws ought to be easy, plain, and short, so as they that were to
20   be subject to them, and have benefit by them, might be able to
know and understand them in some measure. . . .

   The way the committee took in order to their work, which must
needs be elaborate, was by reducing the several laws to their proper
heads to which they did belong, and so modelizing or embodying
25   of them, taking knowledge of the nature of them, and what the
law of God said in the case, and how agreeable to right reason they
were; likewise how proportionable the punishment was to the
offence or crime, and wherein there seemed anything either deficient
or excessive, to offer a supply and remedy, in order to rectifying
30   the whole. . . . By which means the great volumes of law would
come to be reduced into the bigness of a pocket book, as it is
proportionable in New England and elsewhere; a thing of so great
worth and benefit as England is not yet worthy of, nor likely in a
short time to be so blessed as to enjoy. And this being the true end
35   and endeavour of those members that laboured in that committee,
it is submitted to every godly and rational man in the nation,
whether (as is most falsely and wickedly reported and charged

upon persons acting in so much love to their country) their endeavours tended to destroying the whole laws, and pulling them up by the roots.

40

The third vote was the taking away of patrons' presentations, which thing is one of the strong-holds of Satan. At the passing of this vote some gentlemen were greatly offended, pretending it was a destroying and taking away property. The gentleman that moved to have the House dissolved made this one of his great reasons why he could sit no longer with his fellows, being very conscious, like those that stumble at a straw, and yet leap over a block, tithe mint and cummin, and neglect the great things of the law. This vote, after a sharp debate, was carried in, in which very sober gentlemen concurred, such as are not blemished as secretaries or levellers, though they had of this kind of property themselves some two or three apiece, that out of conscience, for the better advance of the knowledge of the gospel and interest of the Lord Christ, they were willing to part with their right herein. . . .

45

50

The fourth vote, whereupon followed the dissolution of the parliament, was that harmless negative, of not complying with the report of the committee, touching what they offered as the best way to eject ignorant, profane, and scandalous ministers, and encouraging them that are good, &c . . . the report was laid aside, for that the first part of it, whereon the other part depended, was rejected; to wit, that the best way to eject ignorant, profane, and scandalous ministers, and to encourage them that are good, was by sending certain commissioners empowered to do it. . . . There was at the passing this vote 115 members, whereof 54 were for the affirmative, and 56 for the negative. . . .

55

60

65

To go about to tell of the arguments insisted on, from the scriptures and from experience, and other reasons of a prudential consideration, would be too tedious; that this vote, that hurt no body, should occasion such wonderful displeasure and outcry every where, is at least wonderful. If men were asked (as Micah was) what aileth them, they would hardly be able to tell so well as he did. Is it not much, when as godly sober men, in discharge of their duty and trust, for the glory of God, and good of their country, should leave their habitations, relations, and enjoyments, spend their time and means to serve their country, and be so rewarded with scandalous and false reports, and to have judgment of high condemnation passed on them upon hearsay, without the least show of proof? . . .

70

75

L.D. [Samuel Highland], *An Exact Relation of the Proceedings and Transactions of the late Parliament* (1654), as reprinted in *Somers Tracts*, ed. W. Scott (1809–15) VI, pp 275–81

Questions

a Identify the bias of the writer. Substantiate your claim.
b Comment on:
   (i) 'the Chancery . . . was looked on as a great grievance' (line
        4).
   (ii) 'the intricacy, uncertainty and incongruity in many things
         with the word of God and right reason, in the laws as now
         they are' (lines 17–18).
   (iii) 'patrons' presentations . . . one of the strongholds of Satan'
          (lines 41–2).
   (iv) 'that harmless negative, of not complying with the report
         of the committee' (lines 56–7).
c What does the passage tell you about divisions in the Parliament?

VI   The Search for a Perfect Society

1   Conflicting Political Ideas

The spread of diverse religious ideas in revolutionary England was stimulated by the effective end of censorship during the military crisis. This breakdown also assisted the dissemination of visionary political ideas during the civil war and Interregnum. In any period of conflict 'such as the 1640s it is natural for participants and observers to give some attention to the divisive issues of the day and to suggest possible modes of resolution and reconciliation. Thus the English civil war is an immensely fruitful period in political thought – not only the epoch of Hobbes and Harrington but also a time of dramatically divergent emphases in proposals for social and political reform. Nevertheless, it should not be assumed that all political philosophy written during the 1640s was uniformly progressive or necessarily ahead of its time. Some of the most interesting if neglected political ideas of the English revolution were Royalist in origin. Before the 1640s supporters of the Crown such as Robert Filmer, John Spelman and Henry Ferne employed two broad arguments to prove the legitimacy of absolutist government. Firstly, arguing by correspondence, kingship was compared to the role of a partriarchal father or to the head of a body – a contention used by James I among others. The analogy suggested that kings would inevitably act in the best interests of their subjects, but also held that monarchs possessed greater knowledge and understanding of matters of government than subordinate members of the community. The prince was solely answerable to God for his actions, and it followed that political authority resided in the person of the monarch alone. This 'descending theory of government' could incorporate more familiar divine right arguments, emphasising the unique attributes of the king and denying any formal role to the representatives of the community in the process of government (document A,a).

Other Royalists came to distrust this approach, arguing in favour of a mixed and balanced version of the constitution. They contended that the historical development of English government revealed a gradual symbiosis of monarchical and parliamentary authority – a process much to the advantage of all sections of the community. The constitution depended, therefore, not upon divine right alone but rather allocated power within a balanced and structurally differentiated hierarchy comprising the king, the Lords spiritual and temporal, and the representatives of the Commons (in practice sections of the gentry). This was potentially a more conciliatory approach as advocates of this 'ascending theory' did not locate sovereignty exclusively in the person of the king, but rather attributed the monarch's right to rule to his pre-eminent position in mixed government. They remained ardent Royalists, however. Blame for the outbreak of civil war still lay with those who tried to elevate Parliament into an unprecedented position of power thereby subverting the ancient constitution. While Royalists could concede the possibility that misgovernment might emanate from policy errors on the part of Charles' I, monarchical fallibility was not of itself sufficient reason for parliamentary attempts to reapportion the balance of authority in English government.

For Royalists, the search for a perfect society naturally entailed a return to monarchical government, whether absolutist or defined in terms of ultimate sovereignty over a harmonious combination of the three estates. They felt obliged to justify kingly power in the course of the civil war, and employed traditional and novel ways of doing so. Royalist authors, including Dudley Digges, Peter Heylyn and Henry Ferne, flocked to the king's side at Oxford, producing many pamphlets supporting the constitutional position of the monarch: some emphasised divine right as the basis of legitimate royal authority; others stressed patriarchal arguments, the law of conquest, or the logical fallibility of Parker's defence of parliamentary sovereignty. Prominent among these pamphlets were Bishop Bramhall's work *The Serpent-Valve*; Heylyn's *Rebells Catechism, The Resolving of Conscience* by Henry Ferne, Filmer's *Patriarcha*, John Maxwell's tract *Sacro-Sancta Regum Majestas* (document A,b) and *The Unlawfulness of Subjects taking up Armes against their Soveraigne* by Dudley Digges.

As the war proceeded, moderate parliamentarians also began to tire of the protracted conflict and particularly of the growing militant enthusiasm of Levellers, apprentices and the New Model soldiery. Parliamentarians such as Henry Parker found the rebellion becoming altogether too radical with the spread of novel political ideas, religious separatism and military hererodoxy, as recorded in alarm by Richard Baxter. Parker produced *A Plea for the Lords* in 1648, recommending the virtues of a bicameral legislature including a hereditary chamber and requesting the return of 'the ancient, regular ways of proceeding in all parliamentary affairs'. For many Parliamentarians, the decline of Presbyterianism and the antipathy towards a national church organised in traditional lines proved the primary source of disillusion. But others were alarmed at the plethora of innovative political proposals emanating from Levellers, republicans, Diggers and millenarians – it seemed that the civil war had opened a Pandora's box of political opinions, making the desired restoration of order in government much more remote and problematic. With some difficulty, a moderate parliamentary majority retained control over legislation in the House of Commons, but 'Pride's Purge' of December 1648 and the subsequent trial and execution of Charles I gave credence to the popular fear that the ultimate conclusion of civil strife would be the irrevocable breakdown of government and dissolution into anarchy and social chaos.

What were the new political and social ideas which so distressed conservative Parliamentarians? In Chapter IV, Leveller constitutional proposals were outlined: regular parliaments, redistribution of seats, extension of the franchise and political accountability. But the Leveller programme, while indisputably radical in its political ramifications, also included not only religious toleration but new demands for secular social reform. For Levellers, the perfect society required the removal of popular grievances – especially the poverty and hardship endured by many of the lower sort in the city of London. Initially, Levellers blamed monopolists exclusively for the problem of social deprivation, but gradually their criticism extended to incorporate all those who enjoyed favourable social circumstances. John Lilburne described the combined effects of a succession of poor harvests and the disruption of trade (blamed upon monopolists): 'the poore is in great necessity, wanting wherewith to set themselves on worke, their children uneducated, and thereby prepared to wickednesse and beggary'. Demands for attention to the dilemma of the poor took on a more aggressive tone in the anonymous pamphlet *The Mournfull Cries of Many Thousand Poore Tradesmen* (document B,a). A similar theme recurs in Leveller works such as *The Humble Petition* and Walwyn's *Vanitie of the Present Churches*. Lilburne particularly criticised the Merchant Adventurers Company for monpolising 'the sole trade of all woollen commodities' between England and the Netherlands and reached a pessimistic conclusion: 'the next Monopoly, it is to be feared will be upon Bread and Beere'.

The major question for the Levellers became how to remedy the popular grievances associated with widespread poverty. They did not consider egalitarian property ownership in England, arguing that the constitution should bind 'all future Parliaments from abolishing propriety, levelling mens Estats, or making all things common'. Members of the movement disagreed publicly over provisions necessary for relief of the poor, and no definitive statement of Leveller social policy exists. Levellers universally avoided redistributive economic programmes, although Lilburne was prepared to criticise Pym's excise for its effects on urban craftsmen and to suggest a more equitable system of taxation (document B,b). Overton went even further in his famous *Appeale*, outlining rudimentary proposals for public education and health care available to those without independent means (document B,c). While Leveller statements on social issues concentrated on urban problems to the virtual exclusion of rural poverty, Buckinghamshire radicals associated with the Levellers vehemently attacked recent enclosures of common land: 'For a man to inclose all Lands . . . from this kind, is utterly unnatural, wicked and treacherous; for if a man shall eat bread by his sweat, then he must needs have ground to sow corn; therefore to inclose . . . is theft in the highest degree.' Agrarian reform was also promoted by Richard Overton who held that 'all grounds which anciently lay in common . . . may forthwith (in whose hands soever they are) be cast out, and laid open again to free and common use and benefit of the poor'. Despite these Leveller statements on rural issues, it is worth remembering that most Levellers gave no consideration to land tenure and so Overton's enthusiasm should not be regarded as programmatic. The perfect society for Leveller leaders involved the end of poverty and destitution through tax reform; abolition of monopolies, provision of limited public services for the very needy, use of confiscated Royalist estates to finance military arrears, and some restrictions on enclosures. This constitutes a crude social policy based on the demands of the urban poor which expressly avoided redistribution of wealth or property – the intention was summarised by Buckinghamshire Levellers as 'a just portion for each man to live, that so none need to begge or steale for want, but every one may live comfortably'.

The Levellers were by no means the only individuals to develop socio-economic strategies as a solution to the grievances of the community in the 1640s. Henry Robinson was an old acquaintance of the Levellers from the early days of the civil war and the campaign for toleration; his tract *Liberty of Conscience* (1643) attacked Presbyterian uniformity, and William Prynne claimed that Robinson's printing press had published some of Lilburne's work. But if Robinson was initially a fellow-traveller his later concerns bear little resemblance to those of the Levellers. Robinson descended from a line of successful merchants and his perfect society entailed full economic freedom for the commercial aristocracy. In two important works, *England's Safety, in Trades Encrease* and *Brief Considerations, concerning the Advancement of Trade and Navigation* (1649), Robinson rejected mercantile protection through restrictive tariffs. Over a century before Adam Smith, Robinson grasped the basic principles of the modern commercial state whereby national prosperity is deemed to depend upon imperial domination of trade, backed by naval force if necessary.

Robinson's social proposals contained specific remedies as well as general principles dealing with the decay of trade. For example, he believed that extensive legal reforms were vital to achieve social perfectibility (document B,d). Following the Parisian Renaudot, Robinson and Samuel Hartlib suggested a paternalistic system of self-help for the urban unemployed – a project outlined in *The Office of Adresses and Encounters* (1650). The intention was to establish an 'Office of Adresses' to act as a rudimentary form of labour exchange for collection of information on employment opportunities. Those out of work could register and would receive details of suitable openings, thus permitting greater employment to the mutual benefit of workers and employers. While Robinson's Office was also designed to provide distress loans at reasonable rates, it is clear that his fundamental concern was *not* for the lower orders. Robinson conceded that the primary objective of his scheme was to maintain low wage rates, thereby assisting merchants to enjoy greater profits (document B,e).

The civil war and Interregnum produced a host of visionary political and social proposals from various groups on the fringes of conventional society. The development of printing and the accessibility of comparatively cheap pamphlets in London and the home counties ensured that many of the radical solutions to the issue of social reconstruction have been transmitted to modern historians. For contemporaries, the execution of the king on 30 January 1649 confirmed that fundamental alterations in English government were occurring, encouraging radicals to publicise their own suggestions for the remodelling of society. For a brief period, access to the political universe was open to virtually anyone – in this fluid situation many groups emerged which rapidly faded into obscurity following persecution in the 1650s, such as the Ranters, Diggers and Fifth Monarchists. Others, initially viewed as equally unconventional, survived by maturing into predominantly religious sects and practising political quietism – such as Baptists, Quakers and Muggletonians. Many of these groups were basically millenarian, believing with Milton that the turbulent events of the 1640s prefigured the 'wars and rumours of wars' prophesied in St Matthew 24:6 and, therefore, that the end of the world was at hand. The corrupt reign of Charles Stuart was to be replaced by an anticipated thousand years ruled by Christ and the saints. Chiliastic suppositions were clearly responsible for the urgency prevalent in most sectarian publications between 1649 and 1650 – it appeared vital that the stewards of God's kingdom should prepare the Commonwealth for the imminent return of divine-majesty.

Of all the visionary economic and social groups of the Interregnum the Diggers – led by the mystic Gerrard Winstanley – were the most politically advanced. Winstanley's origins are obscure, although he was probably a failed tradesman from Lancashire, struggling to make ends meet in the harsh circumstances of the

1640s. By 1649 he believed himself inspired by God to promote cooperative cultivation of common lands for the benefit of the poor. Accordingly, in April 1649 a small Digger colony was established by Winstanley and William Everard on St George's Hill in Surrey – having symbolically defied conventional pieties by commandeering the local church and commencing to dig the waste ground on a Sunday. There were never more than 100 Diggers during the year that the colony survived; they called themselves 'True Levellers' but did not exercise any real political influence. The Digger movement collapsed through the hostility of local landowners and the indifference of other radicals – few Levellers approved of Winstanley's scheme and Lilburne explicitly condemned the Diggers. Modern historians tend to exaggerate the significance of the Digger movement. Officers sent to investigate the colony after local complaints had no doubts concerning the importance of Winstanley's experiment (document C, a). Yet the Diggers' contribution to politics during the Interregnum should not be ignored; Winstanley's chief contribution lies in the mysticism and genuine social radicalism of his rustic political philosophy as contained in several pamphlets, particularly *The True Levellers' Standard Advanced* (April 1650) and *The Law of Freedom in a Platform* (November 1651). These writings contain a profound critique of contemporary social relations couched in terms of primitive egalitarianism (documents C, b–d).

Throughout the later 1640s, groups of wandering 'seekers' became significant components of the religious fabric in England – individuals who attended various churches searching for doctrinal inspiration. Such persons often moved from Anglicanism, Presbyterianism or the independent congregations towards radical separatists including Baptists and Quakers. The latter group, gathered around George Fox, were stigmatised by the orthodox Richard Baxter in *The Quakers' Catechisme*, but his criticism was ridiculed by James Naylor who provided an insider's account of this sect in the early 1650s (document C, e). While Quakers affirmed the basic equality of all men, the religious extremists of the Interregnum were the Ranters – disaffected seekers and former Baptists who attained brief notoriety between 1649 and 1651. Theologically, Ranters were Antinomians, contending that divine grace was freely available and that the indwelling of the Holy Spirit rendered the elect free from conventional moral standards. Many Ranters repudiated predestinarian doctrine in favour of universal redemption. Pamphlets written by Thomas Webbe, Lawrence Clarkson, Abiezer Coppe, Jacob Bauthumley, Joseph Salmon and Andrew Wyke elaborated on Ranter beliefs, but Ranters in general were vilified by contemporaries for their intemperate and licentious living. Even Gerrard Winstanley attacked the Ranters, in *England's Spirit Unfoulded*. Ranters were often pantheistic, rejecting formal religious practice and treating the scriptures as allegorical rather than literal. Heaven and hell, for instance, become states of mind in Ranter writings, whereas contemporary fundamentalists decreed their tangible physical existence as eternal locations for the soul. Celebration of the residence of God within man led Ranters towards *adamitism* – the practice of worship while naked. When allied to the Ranters' repudiation of traditional notions of sinful behaviour, it is not surprising that Ranting became associated with orgiastic debauchery. Ranters regarded the moral law as inapplicable to true believers, following the Antinomian insight that no actions could be sinful to those purged of sin by Christ. Consequently Ranters openly smoked, drank, cursed and advocated promiscuity. Tobias Crisp praised libertinism: 'you may esteem all the curses of the law as no more concerning you than the laws of England concern Spain'. Many Ranters affirmed their calling by indulging personal fondness for activities proscribed by law and conventional morality in the seventeenth century. In *A Fiery Flying Roll* Abiezer Coppe advocates swearing (document C,f), which Christopher Hill describes as 'an act of defiance, both of God and of middle class society, of the Puritan ethic'; while Lawrence Clarkson's *Lost Sheep Found* is not only a chronicle of the author's religious development but a vindication of fornication (document C,g). Clarkson was associated with a bawdy Antinomian group in London known as 'My One Flesh', and Thomas Webbe allegedly claimed 'there's no heaven but women, nor no hell save marriage'. Ranter activity was largely responsible for the passage of an Adultery Act (May 1650) and a Blasphemy Act (August 1650, see pp 112–14) – at various times Webbe, Coppe, Salmon and Wyke were imprisoned under these statutes. Most good citizens of the 1650s despised Ranter beliefs, although many were disturbed by the social implications of Ranting practice. John Reading exposed the veneration of swearing and adultery in *The Ranters' Ranting* (1650), George Fox attempted to dissuade Ranters from immoral conduct, and John Bunyan believed Ranters were motivated by wanton lust and lacked any conviction of sin. For all their hedonistic activity, however, Ranter beliefs were consciously designed to overthrow contemporary mores and symbolically turn the world upside down, being founded on a firm perception of class divisions within society (document C,h).

Prescriptions for the perfect society varied enormously in the aftermath of the second civil war and were evidently irreconcilable. Defeated Royalists clung tenaciously to traditional patterns of government, although arguments favouring absolutism – especially based on *jus conquestus* – were no longer practically relevant. Agitators and Levellers urged Parliament to redress the grievances of soldiers and the urban poor, producing demands not simply for political improvements but for novel social reform based upon an equitable taxation system, abolition of monopolies and provision of crude education and health services to allow elimination of poverty and want. Robinson and Hartlib desired a society of extensive commercial liberty, with low wage conditions and free trade to encourage importers and exporters; whereas the numerically insignificant Diggers looked to reclaiming common lands and the destruction of enclosures as the means of alleviating agrarian distress. Millenarians hoped to create the basic framework of Christ's anticipated kingdom on earth – in the case of Ranters interpreting this as licence to repudiate conventional behavioural mores. In a series of ways, therefore, the discontinuities produced by the civil war and execution of Charles Stuart led to creative responses. It was, however, equally evident that the disparate goals of reformers could not be reconciled within any one political universe – the military victory over absolutism led to propagation of an array of mutually exclusive proposals. The existing constitutional machinery under the Rump Parliament proved incapable of dealing with the discrete objectives of opponents of the Crown, leading to the realisation that far more effective coordination of government and administration was required.

A   Filmer's View of Royal Authority

I have nothing to do to meddle with mysteries of the present state. Such arcana imperii, or cabinet councils, the vulgar may not pry into. An implicit faith is given to the meanest artificer in his own craft; how much more is it, then, due to a Prince in the profound
5   secrets of government: the causes and ends of the greatest politic actions and motions of state dazzle the eyes and exceed the capacities of all men, save only those that are hourly versed in managing public affairs: yet since the rule for each man to know in what to obey his Prince cannot be learnt without a relative knowledge of
10   those points wherein a sovereign may command, it is necessary when the commands and pleasures of superiors come abroad and call for an obedience that every man inform himself how to regulate his actions or his sufferings, for according to the quality of the thing commanded an active or passive obedience is to be yielded,
15   and this is not to limit the Prince's power, but the extent of the subject's obedience, by giving to Caesar the things that are Caesar's, etc. . . . as Adam was lord of his children, so his children under him had a command over their own children, but still with subordination to the first parent, who is lord paramount over his
20   children's children to all generations, as being the grandfather of his people.
I see not then how the children of Adam, or of any man else, can be free from subjection to their parents. And this subordination

of children is the fountain of all regal authority, by the ordination
25   of God himself. From whence it follows, that civil power, not only
in general is by Divine institution, but even the assigning of it
specifically to the eldest parent. Which quite takes away that new
and common distinction which refers only power universal or
absolute to God, but power respective in regard of the special form
30   of government to the choice of the people. Nor leaves it any place
for such imaginary pactions between Kings and their people as
many dream of. . . .

This lordship which Adam by creation had over the whole
world, and by right descending from him the Patriarchs did enjoy,
35   was as large and ample as the absolutest dominion of any monarch
which hath been since the creation. . . .

It may seem absurd to maintain that Kings now are the fathers
of their people, since experience shows the contrary. It is true, all
Kings be not the natural parents of their subjects, yet they all either
40   are, or are to be reputed, as the next heirs of those progenitors
who were at first the natural parents of the whole people, and in
their right succeed to the exercise of supreme jurisdiction. And
such heirs are not only lords of their own children, but also of their
brethren, and all others that were subject to their Fathers. . . .

45   In all kingdoms or commonwealths in the world, whether the
Prince be the supreme Father of the people or but the true heir of
such a Father, or whether he come to the Crown by usurpation,
or by election of the nobles or of the people, or by any other way
whatsoever, or whether some few or a multitude govern the
50   commonwealth, yet still the authority that is in any one, or in
many, or in all of these, is the only right and natural authority of a
supreme Father. There is, and always shall be continued to the end
of the world, a natural right of a supreme Father over every
multitude, although, by the secret will of God, many at first do
55   most unjustly obtain the exercise of it.

To confirm this natural right of regal power, we find in the
Decalogue that the law which enjoins obedience to Kings is
delivered in the terms of 'Honour thy Father', as if all power were
originally in the Father. If obedience to parents be immediately due
60   by a natural law, and subjection to Princes but by the mediation of
a human ordinance, what reason is there that the law of nature give
place to the laws of men, as we see the power of the Father over
his child gives place and is subordinate to the power of the
magistrate? . . .

65   If we compare the natural duties of a Father with those of a
King, we find them to be all one, without any difference at all but
only in the latitude or extent of them. As the Father over one
family, so the King, as Father over many families, extends his
care to preserve, feed, clothe, instruct and defend the whole
70   commonwealth. His wars, his peace, his courts of justice, and all

his acts of sovereignty, tend only to preserve and distribute to every subordinate and inferior Father, and to their children, their rights and privileges, so that all the duties of a King are summed up in an universal fatherly care of his people.

Sir Robert Filmer, *Patriarcha*, in Peter Laslett (ed.) *Filmer: Patriarcha and other Political Works* (Oxford, 1949) pp 54–63

(b) Divine ordination of monarchical authority

75   Do we not see all the creatures established in a subordination one to another? See we not in the lifeless and senseless creatures that the inferior gives a tacit reverence and silent obedience to the superior? See we not, upon the other part, that the superior creature has a powerful and effectual influence upon the inferior for its good
80   and wellbeing, without which it could neither subsist nor act as is fitting and convenient to its nature? In this subordination, do we not see that from the lowest we ascend to a superior, from one superior to another, until at last we come to One Supreme which receives nothing . . . only due reverence and obedience, and
85   notwithstanding has a powerful and benign influence upon all beneath it. From whence, I pray you, is this but from the sacred and inviolable God of nature? The impartial may judge how much this pleads for the excellence of monarchy; and how alike it is to the order God has established in the universe. Look up to Heaven,
90   consider those happy and blessed angels in the Heavens: is there not there this established order with this subordination, and it is probably consummated at last in an excellent one – supereminent above all. . . . How can it then be conceived that God has left it to the simple consent and composition of man, to establish a heraldry
95   of sub and supra, of one above another, which neither the Gospel or nature warrants? To leave it in this arbitrary way . . . mankind may be without government at all, a paradox which cannot be maintained since without order (which naturally and intrinsically includes a priority and a posteriority, superiority and inferiority)
100   neither being nor happy being can be preserved.

I humbly entreat those who are contrary minded to consider seriously how Almighty God in the creation of man, before the woman was made of him and for him, and before he had any child or subject to govern, fixed authority and power for government
105   in the person of Adam. This to aver, that government was fixed in a governor before he had over whom he was to bear rule, is no paradox in philosophy . . . nor a more strange thing to consider than when a *posthumus* (one born after the death of his father) by right inherits his father's honour and revenues. Is it not very
110   considerable that God did not make Eve of the earth, as He did

Adam, but made her of the man and declareth too, made her for
the man? Is it more than probable then God in his wisdom did not
think it fit (that he was able to do it I hope none dare to deny) to
make two independents; and liked best of all governments of
115 mankind the sovereignty of one, and that to the extent that
both wife and posterity should submit and subject themselves to
him. . . .

And by this we may be led on to consider how *Monarchia fundatur
in paterno jure*, how monarchy is founded in paternal sovereignty,
120 and the best way to find out *jura majestatis*, the sovereign's
prerogative, is to consider well what in scripture, what in nature,
we find to be the true and natural right of a father – only probably,
because of man's corruption and untowardness by reason of sin, it
is likely God has allowed more to sovereign power to enable and
125 secure it.

John Maxwell, *Sacro-Sancta Regum Majestas* (1644), pp 83–5

Questions

a Using document (a), explain how royal absolutism could be
defended employing patriarchal theories.
b Evaluate John Maxwell's attempt to vindicate monarchical
powers.
c What arguments were employed by Parliamentarians to criticise
absolutism in the 1640s?

B   The Problem of Poverty

(*a*)
*The mournfull Cryes of many thousand poor Tradesmen, who are ready
to famish through decay of Trade.*

Or, The warning Tears of the Oppressed.

Oh that the cravings of our Stomacks could be heard by the
5 Parliament and City! Oh that the Tears of our poor famishing
Babes were bottled! Oh that their tender Mothers Cryes for bread
to feed them were ingraven in Brasse! Oh that our pined Carkasses
were open to every pitifull Eye! Oh that it were known that we
sell our Beds and Clothes for Bread! Oh our Hearts faint, and we
10 are ready to swoon in the top of every Street!

O you Members of Parliament, and rich men in the City, that
are at ease, and drink Wine in Bowls, and stretch your selves upon
Beds of Down, you that grind our faces, and flay off our skins,

Will no man amongst you regard, will no man behold our faces
15 black with Sorrow and Famine? Is there none to pity? The Sea
Monster drawes out the brest, and gives suck to their young ones,
and are our Rulers become cruell like the Ostrich in the Wildernesse?
Lament. 4.3.

Oh ye great men of *England*, will not (think you) the righteous
20 God behold our Affliction, doth not he take notice that you devour
us as if our Flesh were Bread? are not most of you either Parliament-
men, Committee-men, Customers, Excise-men, Treasurers, Governors of Towns and Castles, or Commanders in the Army, Officers
in those Dens of Robbery, the Courts of Law? and are not your
25 Kinsmen and Allies, Colectors of the Kings Revenue, or the
Bishops Rents, or Sequestratours? What then are your rustling Silks
and Velvets, and your glittering Gold and Silver Laces? are they
not the sweat of our brows, & the wants of our backs & bellies?

Its your Taxes, Customs, and Excize, that compells the Country
30 to raise the price of food, and to buy nothing from us but meer
absolute necessaries; and then you of the City that buy our Work,
must have your Tables furnished, and your Cups overflow; and
therefore will give us little or nothing for our Work, even what
you please, because you know we must sell for moneys to set our
35 Families on work, or else we famish: Thus our Flesh is that
whereupon you Rich men live, and wherewith you deck and adorn
your selves.

And O ye Souldiers who refused to disband, because you would
have Justice and Freedom, who cryed till the Earth ecchoed, *Justice,*
40 *Justice*; forget not that cry, but cry speedily for Peace and Justice,
louder than ever. There is a large Petition of some pittifull men,
that is now abroad, which contains all our desires, and were that
granted in all things, we should have Trading again, and should
not need to beg our Bread, though those men have so much mercy,
45 as they would have none to cry in the Streets for Bread.

Oh though you be Souldiers, shew bowels of Mercy and Pity to
a hunger-starved People; Go down to the Parliament, desire them
to consume and trifle away no more time, but offer your desires
for Us in that large Petition, and cry *Justice, Justice; Save, save,*
50 *save the perishing People*; O cry thus till your importunity make
them hear you.

O Parliament men, and Souldiers! *Necessity dissolves all Laws and
Government*, and *Hunger will break through stone Walls*; Tender
Mothers will sooner devour You, then the Fruit of their own
55 womb, and Hunger regards no Swords nor Canons. It may be so
great oppressours intend tumults, that they may escape in a croud,
but your food may then be wanting as well as ours, and your Arms
will be hard dyet. O heark, heark at our doors, how our children
cry *Bread, Bread, Bread*; and we now with bleeding hearts, cry,
60 once more to you, *pity, pity an oppressed, inslaved People*: carry

our cries in the large Petition to the Parliament, and tell them, if they be still deaf, the Teares of the oppressed will wash away the foundations of their houses. Amen, Amen, so be it.

Anon in Wolfe, *Leveller Manifestoes . . .*, pp 275–8

(b)

Innumerable instances there are throughout these three mourning
65 and bleeding Kingdomes, to prove all these businesses, but I will onely chuse a Citie instance, and let every man who is in his profession after that manner grieved and wronged, turne the simile home to himself, according to his smart; Though the poore Hatmakers, who earne their living with heavy and hot labour, both
70 early and late, doe pay Excise both for all the materialls, and fire which they use, for the bread they eate, for the liquor they drinke, and clothes they weare, yet when they have made their Hatts, and done all they can with great trouble and toyle, day and night, they are forced to pay Excise over againe out of their very labour,
75 notwithstanding it was both so deare and heavy in buying all the necessaries before. . . .

When this Kingdom was in any way or possibility of subsistance, the ancient custome was, that Taxations should be raised by way of Subsidie, which is the most just, equitable, and reasonable way
80 of all, for it sets every tub on its owne bottome, it layes the burthen upon the strong shoulders of the rich, who onely are able to beare it, but spareth and freeth the weake shoulders of the poore, because they are scarcely able to subsist, pay rent, and maintain their families.
85 But our new invented pay, layes the burden heavily upon the poore, and men of middle quality or condition, without all discretion, and scarcely maketh the rich touch it with one of their fingers: yea, many of them are more and more advanced in their prosperous estate, by their great salleries they have for executing
90 their places, . . . besides all the bribes they get, and the false Accounts they make; So that in this life, the rich have their pleasure, but poore Lazarus paines.

John Lilburne, *England's Birth-Right Justified* in Aylmer (ed.), *The Levellers in the English Revolution*, p 61

(c) Leveller Proposals for Rudimentary Welfare

Concerning Schooles.

That all ancient Donations for the maintenance and continuance
95 of Free-Schooles which are impropriate or converted to any private use, and all such Free-Schooles which are destroyed or purloyned

of any freedome for propriety may be restored and erected againe, and that in all parts or Counties of the Realme of England, and Dominion of Wales destitute of Free-Schooles (for the due nurture
100 and education of children) may have a competent number of Such Schooles, founded, erected, and indowed at the publique charges of those respective Counties and places so destitute, that few or none of the free men of England may for the future be ignorant of reading and writing.

105 *Concerning Hospitalls.*

That all ancient charitable Donations towards the constant reliefe of the poor, impropriate, and converted to other use, and all Hospitalls that are either impropriate, corrupted or vitiated from their primitive constitution and end, or be deprived of any of their
110 franchise, profits or emoluments, may be restored, relieved, and rectified, and safely preserved to the reliefs and maintenance of poore Orphans, Widowes, aged and impotent persons, &c. And that there be a convenient number of Hospitalls, founded, erected, and constituted in all the Counties of England and Wales, at the
115 publique charge of the respective Counties, for the good education and nurture of poore fatherlesse or helplesse children, maintenance and reliefe of poore widowes, aged, sick, and lame persons. And to that end, that all the Gleabe-Lands in the Kingdome, may be converted to the maintenance and use of those charitable houses.

120 *Concerning Commons inclosed.*

That all grounds which anciently lay in Common for the poore, and are now impropriate, inclosed, and fenced in, may forthwith (in whose hands soever they are) be cast out, and laid open againe to the free and common use and benefit of the poore.

125 *Concerning Petitions.*

That strong provision be made that neither the Parliament, nor any inferior Court, Officer, or Minister of the Law whatsoever, may in any wise let, disturb, or molest any person or persons, from contriving, promoting or presenting any Petition or Petitions
130 concerning their grievances, liberties, to the High Court of Parliament.

> Richard Overton, Certain Articles Appended to '*An Appeale from the Degenerate Representative Body . . . to . . . the Free People . . . of England*' (July 1647) in Aylmer, *The Levellers in the English Revolution* (London, 1975) pp 86–7

(d) The need for legal reform

May you then please to let it be enquired into; whether the

multiplicity of courts of justice does not cause a more mischievous confusion in the world, than the Babylonian confusion of languages?
135 . . . The variety of courts of justice in any land or nation, perplexes and confounds the people thereof among themselves; the proceedings in them are so various, as that it is above any one man's ability and strength to be experienced in more than one of them. . . . From hence proceeds it in part, that lawsuits become
140 more lasting and chargeable. Particularly, to what purpose served the king's prerogative Court of Exchequer, one of the most eminent badges of conquest and tyranny? Surely all courts should be the Commonwealth's in general, and every man's in particular. Justice should not know any distinction of persons, but be still one and
145 the same in all courts alike, whether touching the letter of the law, or equity. . . .

Besides, our laws of themselves are so numerous and intricate, as that it is not possible to know them all, much less keep them in memory, or avoid being entangled by them, and injured by law.
150 Nay, I am afraid it may be found, that never such juggling, if not very cheating, was consistent with the rules of any Faculty, as of this I speak, and is at present practised in England. . . . How comes it else to pass that an executor may be forced to pay as long as he has assets, and yet afterwards be forced to pay the same sums
155 over again, because he could not keep himself from being forced to pay them away before? In brief, how comes it else to pass that a Debitor may keep his Creditor in prison until he be compelled to give him a discharge, or yield to whatsoever he desires? I only wish that some honest public-spirited lawyer who thoroughly
160 understands the various meanders, quirks and subtlties of this overpowering Faculty, would anatomise, and lay open unto the nation, how easily it is for the very best laws we have to be evaded and frustrated, and the whole formality and proceedings to be avoided and deluded by legal fallacies and tricks. . . .
165 The keeping the Jury without fire, light, bread or drink, as the law requires, may possibly make the major part of them, if not all, agree upon a verdict contrary to their consciences to be freed from any of these exigencies, at least, some of them to strike up with the rest in a joint verdict, since it is well near impossible for 12
170 men, all circumstances considered, much more in a doubtful case, to be of one opinion: and though the case were never so clear, yet one peremptory man of a strong constitution, whether his judgement be right or wrong, may starve all the rest unless they will give verdict as he will have them.

Henry Robinson, *Certain Considerations in order to a more Speedy, Cheap and Equal distribution of Justice throughout the Nation* (London, 1651), Intro, p 3

(e) Robinson's 'Office of Adresses and Encounters'

175 We find by experience that multitudes of people of all sorts, both
handicrafts, artificers, manufactors and others are brought to
poverty and beggary, because they do not timely meet with any
one to set and continue them at work. And yet at the very same
time we likewise meet with multitudes of others, both merchants
180 and shopkeepers of all callings, that cannot furnish their customers
so cheap and speedily as were to be desired, because either they
cannot presently get work-folk, or else not at such cheap rates as
to make a benefit thereof.

Now if such as have occasion to desire to set poor people on
185 work, and poor people that desire continually to be kept at work,
knew where to find one another at all times, they should never be
necessitated to be idle. And being all the week long set at work,
they would earn more at a low rate than in working 3 or 4 or 5
days in a week only, at a high rate; and so might afford their
190 workmanship cheaper unto the merchants and shopkeepers, and
they unto their customers consequently, which would be the life
of trade.

And the great relief unto the poor, and advantage to the increase
of trade, is infallibly secured by this register of addresses, this
195 common centre of intelligence, from whence all persons may
forthwith be directed, and receive satisfaction. . . .

Now that mankind might not be longer thought constituted in
a more unhappy condition than the irrational and brutish creatures
after a revolution of so many ages and thousands of years; it has
200 pleased God in these latter times, to make some men instruments
of very great discoveries, whereby the state of man has already and
may be much more meliorated – amongst which the invention of
an Office or register of addresses and encounters will not be found
one of the least. . . .

205 The only way to prevent the multiplying of poor people is
forthwith to give all opportunities, and improve all advantages,
that may be unto all manner of people, to relieve themselves by
their own labour and industry without loss of time or expense of
money . . . they have hitherto had no means to come to the speedy
210 knowledge of such persons as stand as much in need of poor mens
labours, as the poor people do of rich mens monies. . . .

Whereas at present poor people, and others, spend much time in
running up and down, from one place to another to seek employment and sell their work, if they repair unto this office, they shall
215 either be directed forthwith to one that wants such artificers,
manufactors, labourers and others, or their workmanship; if they
but leave their names, with the place of their abode, what employment they desire, and upon what terms, in a ticket at this office.
So soon as their turn comes they will have notice of it. . . .

220   The poor shall have all these services done for them in charity, and all others for six pence a time. . . .

> Henry Robinson, *The Office of Adresses and Encounters . . . the only course for poor people to get speedy employment, and to keep others from approaching poverty for want of employment. To the multiplying of trade . . .* (London, 1650), pp 1–6

Questions

a   How does the author of *The Mournfull Cries* attribute the spread of poverty and distress to the failure of the nobility and of parliament?

b   Assess the remedy proposed by Lilburne in document (b). Can this be reconciled with Overton's desire for public funding of rudimentary education and health care? (document c)

c   Why did many Parliamentarians demand legal reform during the civil war?

d   Can Robinson's proposals in his *Office of Adresses* (document e) be described as genuinely philanthropic?

C   The 'Digger' Experiment (1649–50)

(*a*)

According to your order I marched towards St George's Hill and sent four men before to bring certain intelligence to me; as they went they met with Mr. Winstanley and Mr. Everard (which are the chief men that have persuaded these people to do what they
5   have done). And when I had enquired of them and of the officers that lie at Kingston, I saw there was no need to march any further. I cannot hear that there has been above twenty of them together since they first undertook the business. Mr. Winstanley and Mr. Everard have engaged both to be with you this day: I believe you
10 will be glad to be rid of them again, especially Everard who is no other than a mad man. Sir, I intend to go with two or three men to St George's Hill this day, and persuade these people to leave this employment if I can, and if then I see no more danger than now I do, I shall march back again to London tomorrow. . . . Indeed the
15 business is not worth the writing nor yet taking notice of: I wonder the Council of State should be so abused with informations.

> *Captain John Gladman* to Lord Fairfax 19 April 1649, in L. H. Firth (ed.) *The Clarke Papers* (Camden Soc. and Royal Historical Soc., Camden Series, 4 vols, 1891–1901, Reprinted 1965), II, pp 211–12

(b)

In the beginning of time, the great creator Reason made the earth to be a common treasury, to preserve beasts, birds, fishes and man, the lord that was to govern this creation; for man had domination given to him, over the beasts, birds and fishes; but not one word was spoken in the beginning, that one branch of mankind should rule over another.

And the reason is this, every single man, male and female, is a perfect creature of himself; and the same spirit that made the globe dwells in man to govern the globe; so that the flesh of man being subject to reason, his maker, hath him to be his teacher and ruler within himself, therefore needs not run abroad after any teacher and ruler without him; for he needs not that any man should teach him, for the same anointing that ruled in the Son of Man teacheth him all things.

But since human flesh (that king of beasts) began to delight himself in the objects of the creation, more than in the spirit reason and righteousness, who manifests himself to be the indweller in the five senses of hearing, seeing, tasting, smelling, feeling; then he fell into blindness of mind and weakness of heart, and runs abroad for a teacher and ruler. And so selfish imagination, taking possession of the five senses and ruling as king in the room of reason therein, and working with covetousness, did set up one man to teach and rule over another; and thereby the spirit was killed and man was brought into bondage, and became a greater slave to such of his own kind, than the beasts of the field were to him.

And hereupon the earth (which was made to be a common treasury of relief for all, both beasts and men) was hedged into enclosures by the teachers and rulers, and the others were made servants and slaves: and that earth, that is within this creation made a common storehouse for all, is bought and sold and kept in the hands of a few, whereby the great creator is mightily dishonoured, as if he were a respecter of persons, delighting in the comfortable livelihood of some, and rejoicing in the miserable poverty and straits of others. From the beginning it was not so. . . .

But for the present state of the old world that is running up like parchment in the fire, and wearing away, we see proud imaginary flesh, which is the wise serpent, rises up in flesh and gets dominion in some to rule over others, and so forces one part of the creation, man, to be a slave to another; and thereby the spirit is killed in both. The one looks upon himself as a teacher and ruler, and so is lifted up in pride over his fellow-creatures. The other looks upon himself as imperfect, and so is dejected in his spirit, and looks upon his fellow-creature of his own image as a lord above him.

> G. Winstanley, *The True Levellers' Standard Advanced* (20 April 1649) in Christopher Hill (ed.) *Winstanley: The Law of Freedom and other Writings* (Cambridge 1983) pp 77–9

(c)
60 When mankind began to buy and sell, then did he fall from his
innocence; for then they began to oppress and cozen one another
of their creation birthright. As for example: if the land belong to
three persons, and two of them buy and sell the earth and the third
give no consent, his right is taken from him, and his posterity is
65 engaged in a war.

When the earth was first bought and sold, many gave no consent:
as when our crown lands and bishops' lands were sold, some
foolish soldiers yielded, and covetous officers were active in it, to
advance themselves above their brethren; but many who paid taxes
70 and free-quarter for the purchase of it gave no consent but declared
against it as an unrighteous thing, depriving posterity of their
birthrights and freedoms.

Therefore this buying and selling did bring in, and still doth
bring in, discontent and wars, which have plagued mankind
75 sufficiently for so doing. And the nations of the world will never
learn to beat their swords into ploughshares, and their spears into
pruning hooks, and leave off warring, until this cheating device of
buying and selling be cast out among the rubbish of kingly power.

'But shall not one man be richer than another?'
80 There is no need of that; for riches make men vain-glorious,
proud, and to oppress their brethren; and are the occasion of wars.

No man can be rich, but he must be rich either by his own
labours, or by the labours of other men helping him. If a man have
no help from his neighbour, he shall never gather an estate of
85 hundreds and thousands a year. If other men help him to work,
then are those riches his neighbours' as well as his; for they may
be the fruit of other men's labours as well as his own.

But all rich men live at ease, feeding and clothing themselves by
the labours of other men, not by their own; which is their shame,
90 and not their nobility; for it is a more blessed thing to give than to
receive. But rich men receive all they have from the labourer's
hand, and what they give, they give away other men's labours,
not their own. Therefore they are not righteous actors in the earth.

G. Winstanley, *The Law of Freedom in a Platform* (1652) in
Hill, op. cit., pp 286–7

(d)
This Adam appears first in every man and woman. But he sits
95 down in the chair of magistracy in some above others. For though
this climbing power of self-love be in all, yet it rises not to its
height in all. But everyone that gets an authority into his hands
tyrannises over others: as many husbands, parents, masters [and]
magistrates . . . do carry themselves like oppressing lords over
100 such as are under them, not knowing that their wives, children,
servants [and] subjects are their fellow creatures and have equal

privilege to share with them in the blessing of liberty. And this first Adam is to be seen and known in a two-fold sense. First, he is the wisdom and power of the flesh in every man . . . and he
105 spreads himself within the creation, man, into divers branches: as into ignorance of the creator of all things, into covetousness after objects, into pride and envy, lifting himself above others, and seeking revenge upon all that crosses his selfish honours, and into hypocrisy, subtlety, lying imagination, self-love. From whence
110 proceeds all unrighteous outward acting. Secondly, the first Adam is the wisdom and power of the flesh broke out and set down in the chair of rule and dominion in one part of mankind over another. And this is the beginner of particular interest, buying and selling the earth from one particular hand to another, saying, 'this is mine',
115 upholding this particular propriety by law of government of his own making, and thereby restraining other fellow-creatures from seeking nourishment from their mother earth (so though a man was bred up in a land yet he must not work for himself where he would sit down, but [for] such a one that had bought part of the
120 land or came to it by inheritance of his deceased parents and called it his own land) . . . He that had no land was to work for those (for small wages) who called the land theirs. And thereby some are lifted up into the chair of tyranny and others trod under the footstool of misery, as if the earth were made for a few, not for all
125 men. For truly the common people by their labours . . . have lifted up their landlords and others to rule in tyranny and oppression over them. And let all men say what they will, so long as such are rulers as call the land theirs, upholding this particular propriety of 'mine' and 'thine', the common people shall never have their
130 liberty nor the land ever [be] free from troubles, oppressions and complainings, by reason whereof the creator of all things is continually provoked. . . . O thou proud, selfish, governing Adam in this land called England! Know that the cries of the poor, whom thou layeth heavy oppressions upon, is heard. . . .

G. Winstanley, *The New Law of Righteousness* (1649) in Andrew Sharp, *Political Ideas of the English Civil Wars 1641–49* (London, 1983) pp 201–2

Questions

a   What were the origins of the Digger movement, and how are these reflected in the Diggers' characteristic social philosophy?
b   Assess the Diggers' view of land tenure.
c   Does the claim that the earth 'was made to be a common treasury . . . for all' (lines 42–3) imply a primitive egalitarian impulse in the Digger perspective?

(e) A Quaker's account of contemporary attacks on minor sects

135 Thou saist, pride is the master sin of the Quakers, and thou proves
it, because that we go out in a poor garb, and cry out against pride,
as if we were sent from Heaven to persuade men to wear no lace,
cuffs or points, and to damn so many Ministers for being called
Master. But saist thou, spiritual pride is the most killing. . . .

140 Thou sets down four particulars, wherein thou wilt prove our
language of Hell, and the Devil speaking by our mouths, and the
first is They affirm themselves perfect without sin. . . . I say, that
we affirm self-perfection is but lying slander; or that we say we
are Christ or God, as thou saist we do, but . . . we witness

145 perfection from sin, so far as we have received Christ, but own it
as God's command and gift, the end of Christ's coming.

The second thing is, that we set ourselves above all the people
of God on earth, that we vilify the most holy and eminent servants
of God, and condemn all the churches of the world. . . . This thou

150 would make people believe with adding lies, saying that we say
the Pope is not Antichrist, that we undermine the Scriptures, decry
the Ministry, unchurch Churches, slight justification by imputed
righteousness . . . set up strength of man's free-will, the exalting of
monastical community and virginity, and alienation from worldly

155 employment. . . .

The third thing . . . may well be a matter of offence to thee, to
deny all thy generation since the Pope to this day: therefore thou
callest it unmatchable pride; but for those whom you have tortured,
martyred and burned, whipped and imprisoned, to this day, who

160 suffered for conscience' sake, following the Lamb; in their measure
them we own, and with them we suffer. . . .

The fourth thing is, that which thou callest our proud, scornful,
railing language . . . the language of Christ we use to thee, who
art found in the work of Satan, therefore thou cannot bear it. . . .

165 Thou saist, that the Papists have begotten this present sect of
Quakers . . . if thou know such among us, and do not produce it,
then thou art deceitful to the trust of the nation; but if thou know
none, then thou art a false accuser, and out of thy mouth art thou
judged, who says we are headed with dissembling Friars; and . . .

170 to which I shall say no more but this, that these are three of thy
lies ranked up together.

James Naylor, *An Answer to a book called The Quaker's
Cathechism* (London, 1655), pp 11–12

(f)
(1)

10 There are Angels (now) come down from Heaven, in the
shapes and formes of men, who are full of the vengeance of the

Lord; and are to poure out the plagues of God upon the Earth, and
175 to torment the Inhabitants thereof.
   Some of these Angels I have been acquainted withall.
   And I have looked upon them as Devils, accounting them Devils
incarnate, and have run from place to place, to hide my self from
them, shunning their company; and have been utterly ashamed
180 when I have been seen with them.
   But for my labour; I have been plagued and tormented beyond
expression. So that now I had rather behold one of these Angels
pouring out the plagues of God, cursing; and teaching others to
curse bitterly.
185   And had rather heare a mighty Angell (in man) swearing a full-
mouthed Oath; and see the spirit of *Nehemiah* (in any form of man,
or woman) running upon an uncleane Jew (a pretended Saint) and
tearing the haire of his head like a mad man, cursing, and
making others fall a swearing, than heare a zealous Presbyterian,
190 Independent, or spirituall Notionist, pray, preach, or exercise.
   11 Well! To the pure all things are pure. God hath so cleared
cursing, swearing, in some, that that which goes for swearing and
cursing in them, is more glorious then praying and preaching in
others.
195   And what God hath cleansed, call not thou uncleane.
   And if Peter prove a great transgressor of the Law, by doing that
which was as odious as killing a man; if he at length (though he be
loath at first) eat that which was common and unclean &c. (I give
but a hint) blame him not, much lesse lift up a finger against, or
200 plant a hellish Ordinance – against him, lest thou be plagued, and
damned too, for thy zeale, blinde Religion, and fleshly holinesse,
which now stinks above ground, though formerly it had a good
favour.
   12 But O thou holy, zealous, devout, righteous, religious one
205 (whoever thou art) that seest evill, or any thing uncleane; do thou
sweare, if thou darest, if it be but (I'faith) I'le throw thee to Hell
for it (saith the Lord) and laugh at thy destruction.
   While Angels (in the forme of men) shall sweare, Heart, Blood,
Wounds, and by the Eternall God, &c. in profound purity, and in
210 high Honour, and Majesty.
   13 Well! one hint more; there's swearing ignorantly, i'th darke,
vainely, and there's swearing i'th light, gloriously.
   Well! man of the earth! Lord Esau! what hast thou to do with
those who sweare upon the former account?
215   Vengeance is mine, Judgement, Hell, Wrath &c. all is mine (saith
the Lord), dare not thou to set thy foot so impudently and
arrogantly upon one step of my Throne: I am Judge myself – Be
wise, give over, have done –
   14 And as for the latter sort of swearing, thou knowest it not
220 when thou hearest it. It's no new thing for thee to call Christ Beel-

zebub, and Beel-zebub Christ; to call a holy Angell a Devill, and a
Devill an Angell.

15 I charge thee (in the name of the Eternall God) meddle not
with neither, let the Tares alone, lest thou pull up the Wheat also,
225 woe be to thee if thou dost.

> Abiezer Coppe, *A Fiery Flying Roll* (1649) in Andrew
> Hopton (ed), *Abiezer Coppe: Selected Writings* (London,
> 1987), pp 27–8

(2)

To this end (saith *Paul*) *I know and am persuaded, by the Lord Jesus,
that there is nothing unclean of it self, but to him that esteemeth any thing
to be unclean, to him it is unclean.* [Rom. 14.14]

So that the extent thereof is in reference to all things, as well as
230 meats and drinks; let it be what act soever. Consider what act
soever, yea though it be the act of Swearing, Drunkenesse, Adultery
and Theft; yet these acts simply, yea nakedly by, as acts nothing
distinct from the act of Prayer and Prayses. Why does thou wonder?
why art thou angry? they are all one in themselves; no more
235 holynesse, no more puritie in one than the other.

But once the Creature esteemeth one act Adultery, the other
honesty, the one pure, the other impure; yet to that man that so
esteemeth one act unclean to him it is unclean, (as saith the History)
there is nothing unclean of it self, to him that esteemeth it unclean;
240 yea again and again it is recorded that to the pure all things, yea all
things are pure, but to the defiled, all things are defiled: Yea the
Prayer and Prayses of the wicked are defiled, as saith the History,
The Prayers of the wicked are abomination to the Lord. [Prov. 15.8]

> Lawrence Clarkson, *A Single Eye* (1650), Bodleian Library,
> Oxford, cf. Donald G. Wing, *Short-title Catalogue of Books
> Printed in England . . . 1641–1700*, 3 vols (New York, 1945–
> 51), C.4584

(g)

So after this we went to *Maidston* and *Town-maulin*, and there I
245 preached up and down, so at last having given me about five
pounds, I went to my wife and promised in two weekes to return
again, which I did, but I found not *Lokier* nor the rest so affectionate
as before, for he had a gift of preaching, & therein did seek honor
so suspicious of my blasting his reputation, slighted and persecuted
250 me, so that I left them, and towards *Maidston* travelled, so
one *Bulfinch* of *Town-maulin* having friends towards *Canterbury*,
persuaded me to go with him, and so again the next Lords-day,
having no steeple free, we had a Gentlemans barn free, where a
great company was assembled: then for *Sandwich* I went, and up
255 and down found friends, so coming to *Canterbury* there was some
six of this way, amongst whom was a maid of pretty knowledge,

who with my Doctrine was affected, and I affected to lye with her,
so that night prevailed, and satisfied my lust, afterwards the mayd
was highly in love with me, and as gladly would I have been shut
260 of her, lest some danger had ensued, so not knowing I had a wife
she was in hopes to marry me, and so would have me lodge with
her again, which fain I would, but durst not, then she was afraid I
would deceive her, and would travel with me, but by subtilty of
reason I perswaded her to have patience, while I went into *Suffolk*,
265 and setled my occasions, then I would come and marry her, so for
the present we parted, and full glad was I that I was from her
delivered, so to *Maidston* I came, and having got some six pounds,
returned to my wife, which a while after I went for *Kent* again,
but found none of the people so zealous as formerly, so that my
270 journey was but a small advantage to me, and then I heard the
maid had been in those parts to seek me, but not hearing of me,
returned home again, and not long after was married to one of that
sect, and so there was an end of any further progress into *Kent*.

I took my progress into the Wilderness, and according to the day
275 appointed, I found Mr. *Brush*, Mr. *Rawlinson*, Mr. *Goldsmith*, with
Mary Lake, and some four more: now *Mary Lake* was the chief
speaker, which in her discourse was something agreeable, but not
so high as was in me experienced, and what I then knew with
boldness declared, in so much that *Mary Lake* being blind, asked
280 who that was that spake? *Brush* said the man that *Giles Calvert* sent
to us, so with many more words I affirmed that there was no sin,
but as man esteemed it sin, and therefore none can be free from
sin, till in purity it be acted as no sin, for I judged that pure to me,
which to a dark understanding was impure, for to the pure all
285 things, yea all acts were pure: thus making the Scripture a writing
of wax, I pleaded the words of *Paul, That I know and am perswaded
by the Lord Jesus, that there was nothing unclean, but as man esteemed it*,
unfolding that was intended all acts, as well as meats and drinks,
and therefore till you can lie with all women as one woman, and
290 not judge it sin, you can do nothing but sin: now in Scripture I
found a perfection spoken of, so that I understood no man could
attain perfection but this way, at which Mr. *Rawlinson* was much
taken, and *Sarah Kullin* being then present, did invite me to make
trial of what I had expressed, so as I take it, after we parted she
295 invited me to Mr. *Wats* in *Rood-lane*, where was one or two more
like herself, and as I take it, lay with me that night: now again
next [S]unday it was noised abroad what a rare man of knowledge
was to speak at Mr. *Brushes*; at which day there was a great
company of men and women, both young and old; and so from
300 day to day increased, that now I had choice of what before I aspired
after, insomuch that it came to our Officers ears; but having got
my pay I left them, and lodged in *Rood-lane*, where I had Clients
many, that I was not able to answer all desires, yet none knew our

actions but our selves; however I was careful with whom I had to
305 do. This lustful principle encreased so much, that the Lord Mayor
with his Officers came at midnight to take me, but knowing
thereof, he was prevented. . . .
I was moved to write to the world what my Principle was, so
brought to publick view a Book called *The Single Eye*, so that men
310 and women came from many parts to see my face, and hear my
knowledge in these things, being restless till they were made free,
as then we called it. Now I being as they said, *Captain of the Rant*,
I had most of the principal women came to my lodging for
knowledge, which then was called *The Head-quarters*. Now in the
315 height of this ranting, I was made still careful for moneys for my
Wife, onely my body was given to other women. . . .
But now to return to my progress, I came for *London* again, to
visit my old society; which then *Mary Midleton* of *Chelsford*, and
Mrs. *Star* was deeply in love with me, so having parted with Mrs.
320 *Midleton*, Mrs. *Star* and I went up and down the countries as man
and wife, spending our time in feasting and drinking, so that
Tavernes I called the house of God; and the Drawers, Messengers;
and Sack, Divinity; reading in *Solomons* writings it must be so, in
that it made glad the heart of God; which before, and at that time,
325 we had several meetings of great company, and that some, no
mean ones neither, where then, and at that time, they improved
their liberty, where Doctor *Pagets* maid stripped her self naked,
and skipped among them, but being in a Cooks shop, there was
no hunger, so that I kept my self to Mrs. *Star*, pleading the
330 lawfulness of our doings as aforesaid, concluding with *Solomon* all
was vanity.
Laurence Clarkson, *The Lost Sheep Found* (1660), Bodleian
Library, Oxford, Wing, op. cit., C.4580

(*h*)
. . . you plead that had it not been for oppressions and divisions
you had not chosen a Parliament. . . . Experience with reason can
make it appear that your oppressions and divisions came by those
335 that you have chosen to ease you. . . . Consider how unprofitable
it is for those that oppress you to ease and free you from oppressions.
For who are the oppressors but the nobility and gentry? And who
are oppressed? Is not the yeoman, the farmer, the tradesman, the
labourer? Then consider: have you not chosen oppressors to relieve
340 you from oppression? So that your oppression is just, in not
choosing self-denying men hating covetousness, yea – such as are
your equals . . . in estates, in love and humility, such that were
your companions in oppressions and sufferings. These are the men
worthy that place. Yea, none but these are able to quell the
345 oppressors and ease the oppressed. For reason affirmeth [that] so
long as you choose such as you say are your lords, your patrons

and impropriators, injustice will continue, oppression will reign. For experience may teach you that it is naturally inbred in the major part of the nobility and gentry to oppress the persons of
350 such that are not as rich and honourable as themselves, to judge the poor but fools and themselves wise. And therefore it comes, when you the commonalty calleth a Parliament, they are confident such must be chosen that are the noblest and richest in the county, not questioning but they are the wisest and ablest for that place,
355 when reason affirmeth . . . these are not your equals, neither are these sensible of the burden that lieth upon you (for indeed how can they [be] whereas you, the commonalty, is oppressed?). It is they that oppress you, insomuch as that your slavery is their liberty, your poverty is their prosperity. Yea, in brief, your honouring of
360 them dishonoureth the commonalty; [and it is] no marvel but when you oppose them they oppress you . . . You have armed them with your armour, so that if they destroy you it is by your own weapon. For from whom have they what they have, or by whom are they what they are, but from and by you, the commonalty?
365 Therefore it is your prerogative, if you see cause to unlord those that are lorded by you, to unoffice those that are made officers by you.

> Laurence Clarkson, *A General Charge, or Impeachment of High Treason* (1647) in Sharp, op. cit., pp 187–8

Questions

a What was peculiar about the Quaker sect in terms of social and religious radicalism?
b 'having no steeple free, we had a gentleman's barn free' (line 253). What does this teach us about the decline of clerical authority?
c How did Ranters justify their claim that acts of blasphemy and fornication should be regarded as holy and pure?
d What was the response of Commonwealth authorities to the Ranters?
e Does radical religious belief necessarily entail a radical programme for social reform?

VII   The Puritan State and the World

1   Perceptions of Regicide

The defeat of the Scots in 1648 ensured the ultimate victory of Parliament in the second civil war. The position of the king became increasingly vulnerable after Colonel Pride's purge of Parliament removed remaining conciliatory influences and established the authority of the 'war party'. The New Model had already demanded justice against Charles Stuart 'that man of blood', and few were surprised by the Rump's decision to place the king on trial for his life. Charles was to answer for his conduct during the civil wars; for his treacherous negotiations with the Scots, and for conspiracy against Parliament during the years of conflict. The king had little doubt that his days were numbered.

It is difficult today to grasp the impact of the trial and subsequent execution upon contemporaries in Britain and Europe. The violent death of a monarch was not unusual of itself – many rulers had been killed in battle, murdered in prison or assassinated – and Veronica Wedgwood reminds us that the king's grandmother met a similar fate, being tried for treason and executed in February 1587. But Charles I, unlike Mary Queen of Scots, had not been deposed – he was brought to trial as King of England, Scotland and Ireland by his own subjects in his own country. Defeated Royalists were confounded by this alarming reversal of sovereignty: one (Marchmont Nedham?) marvelled at the constitutional arrogance of subjects who dared to try their king: 'In no history can we find a parallel for this, that ever the rage of rebels extended so far as to bring their sovereign lord to public trial and execution, it being contrary to the law of Nature, the custom of Nations, and the sacred scriptures. . . . What court shall their King be tried in? Who shall be his peers? Who shall give sentence? What eyes dare be so impious to behold the execution?' The implication was that the events of January 1649 were unique because Charles was tried as king for acts committed as monarch. This fact is an indication of the radical progress of the English revolution: in 1644 the Earl of Manchester could restrain junior officers in the Parliamentary army by reminding them that Charles I would always remain king, whereas military defeat for Parliament 'would be an end of their pretences; and they should all be rebels and traitors, and executed and forfeited by the law'. Within five years, the same army was instrumental in bringing the defeated king to the scaffold, being entirely disillusioned of any prospect of successful negotiations to restore the king due to his personal arrogance and political duplicity.

The rapid execution of Charles I caused outrage among European nations, including the protestant United Provinces. Yet the intentions of the New Model towards Charles had been clear from at least November 1648 and the military *Remonstrance*. European rulers were therefore aware of the imminent danger facing Charles, and the Peace of Westphalia (October 1648) seemed to resolve major internal disputes by terminating the Thirty Years War and the protracted conflict between Spain and the Netherlands. Apparently European monarchs were free to act in a concerted manner to assist the king of England – yet the fact remains that they universally failed to do so. English Royalists greeted the end of European hostilities with relief, in the firm expectation of decisive action against the rebels at Westminster – yet such hopes were quickly dashed. The Peace of Westphalia did not settle European affairs and continental governments failed to support Charles I effectively. Many refused to believe that the army faction in the Rump would actually execute the king. Mazarin was dismayed to read demands for the immediate trial of the king in the army *Remonstrance*, and wrote to the French ambassador in London on 6 December 1648: 'I have read with horror the demands of the army, and I trust that God will not allow this unhappy Prince to fall into such great misfortune, nor do I believe that the English will bring themselves to carry out such dire intentions against him.' On the same day the army carried out its purge of moderate members at Westminster, securing a House of Commons which was prepared to bring the king to justice. Mazarin also faced acute domestic problems, and Condé's troops (which Royalists still hoped would spearhead a combined European initiative to reinstate the king) were required to blockade Paris while the court fled to St Germain. Abandoned and comparatively isolated in the deserted Louvre, Henrietta Maria realised that practical French assistance for her beleaguered husband was now out of the question. Fearing the worst, she wrote to Cromwell begging permission to join the king in England. The letter received no reply.

Other European nations were no better placed to offer help. The energies of the Vatican were consumed by coordination of opposition to the religious clauses of the Peace of Westphalia; while Royalists grouped around the Prince of Wales in the United Provinces found it increasingly difficult to obtain financial support. The powerful Spanish court recognised the possibility of damaging French interests through future alliance with the English, and so pursued a policy of cautious pragmatism. The Spanish ambassador in London, Alonso de Cardeñas, received instructions to give tacit support to the Parliamentary government – Spain hoped to secure the future assistance of English rebels and French Huguenots in disrupting Mazarin's regime. Thus Spanish policy remained indifferent to the plight of Charles I. This combination of factors ensured that European powers were unable or unwilling to act on behalf of the English king. Moreover, events in London moved with unprecedented speed – when the Dutch government finally sent two envoys to express concern over the treatment of Charles, they arrived in London on 26 January, too late to alter the course of events.

2 The Trial and Execution of Charles I

Reading contemporary accounts of the trial of Charles I, the historian is conscious of the procedural irregularity and dubious legality of the judicial process employed to convict the king. The residue of the Lords refused to concur with the purged Commons' decision to put the king on trial, and so the established constitutional method of trying defendants before the House of Lords had to be suspended. The Commons adopted supreme authority to deal with Charles I, creating a High Court of Justice which convened in the Painted Chamber at St James's Palace on 20 January 1649. Despite the fact that virtually all records of the trial were Parliamentarian in origin (e.g. Gilbert Mabbott's *Perfect Narrative . . .* and Henry Walker's *Collection of Notes*) nonetheless the king's character and argument seem generally more convincing than his accusers. The charge alleged that Charles had 'maliciously levied war against the present Parliament and the people', solicited foreign invasions, and renewed military conflict by instigating the second civil war. Solicitor-General John Cook indicted 'the said Charles Stuart as a tyrant, traitor and murderer, and a public and implacable enemy to the Commonwealth of England'. When called upon to reply, the king refused to discuss the charge – demanding to know by what authority subjects could exercise judgement over their sovereign. The impasse lasted for three days with the king refusing to answer and denying the jurisdiction of the court. Finally, the king was refused leave to question the legality of judicial proceedings, and business continued on 24 January. The fact that Charles had not officially entered a plea was taken as presumption of guilt, and the court proceeded to sentence. Execution would follow the next Tuesday – 30 January 1649. The memoirs of the republican regicide Edmund Ludlow contain one account of the trial and sentence (document a).

Three days later, the king's speech on the scaffold reflected upon his innocence; forgiveness of his enemies, his regretted acquiescence in the execution of the Earl of Strafford, and ruminations upon government (document b).

On the fringes of the crowd, Philip Henry recorded the expectant silence as the axe fell, followed by 'such a groan as I never heard before, and desire I may never hear again'. The Parliamentary cavalry rapidly dispersed the large crowd.

A Trial and Execution

(*a*)

All things being thus prepared for the trial, the King was conducted from Windsor to St James's. From whence, on the 20th of January, he was brought to the bar of the high court of justice; where the President acquainted the King with the causes of his being brought
5   to that place: for that he, contrary to the trust reposed in him by the people, to see the laws put in execution for their good, had made use of his power to subvert those laws, and to set up his will and pleasure as a law over them: that, in order to effect that design, he had endeavoured the suppression of parliaments, the best defence
10 of the people's liberties: that he had levied war against the parliament and people of England, wherein great numbers of the good people had been slain; of which blood the parliament presuming him guilty, had appointed this high court of justice for the trial of him for the same. Then turning to Mr. Broughton, clerk of the court,
15 he commanded him to read the charge against the King; who, as the clerk was reading the charge, interrupted him, saying, 'I am not intrusted by the people, they are mine by inheritance;' demanding by what authority they brought him thither. The President answered, That they derived their authority from an act made by the
20 Commons of England assembled in parliament. The King said, The Commons could not give an oath; that they were no court, and therefore could make no act for the trial of any man, much less of him their sovereign. . . .

In order to which, the President commanded his answer to be
25 entered; directing Serjeant Dendy, who attended the court, to withdraw the prisoner; which, as he was doing, many persons cried out in the hall, *Justice, Justice*. The King being withdrawn, the court adjourned into the Painted chamber, to consider what farther was fit to be done; and being desirous to prevent all objections tending
30 to accuse them of haste or surprise, they resolved to convene him before them publicly twice more: after which, if he persisted in his demurrer to the jurisdiction of the court then to give judgement against him. And that nothing might be wanting, in case he should resolve to plead, they appointed witnesses to be examined in every
35 article of the charge. At the King's second appearance before the

court, which was on the 22nd of January, he carried himself in the same manner as before. Whereupon his refusal being again entered, and he withdrawn, the court adjourned to the Painted chamber. On the 23d of January, the King was brought a third time before the commissioners; where refusing to plead, as he had done before, his refusal was entered; and witnesses examined publicly, to prove the charge of his levying war against the parliament. After which, Solicitor-General Coke demanded of the court, that they would proceed to the pronouncing of sentence against the prisoner at the bar. Whereupon the court adjourned into the Painted chamber; and upon serious consideration, declared the King to be a tyrant, traitor, murderer, and a public enemy to the commonwealth: that his condemnation extend unto death, by severing his head from his body; and that a sentence grounded upon those votes be prepared; which being agreed upon, the King should be ordered on the next day following to receive it. The sentence being ingrossed, was read on the 27th of January: and thereupon the court resolved, That the same should be the sentence, which should be read and published in Westminster-hall the same day; that the President should not permit the King to speak after the sentence pronounced; that he should openly declare it to be the sense and judgement of the court; and that the commissioners should signify their consent by standing up. In the afternoon, the King was brought to the bar, and desired that he might be permitted to make one proposition before they proceeded to sentence; which he earnestly pressing, as that which he thought would tend to the reconciling of all parties, and to the peace of the three kingdoms, they permitted him to offer it. The effect of which was, that he might meet the two houses in the Painted chamber, to whom he doubted not to offer that which should satisfy and secure all interests; designing, as I have been since informed, to propose his own resignation, and the admission of his son to the throne, upon such terms as should have been agreed upon. This motion being new and unexpected to the court, who were not willing to deny or grant any thing without serious deliberation, they withdrew to consider of it into the inner court of wards: and being satisfied, upon debate, that nothing but loss of time would be the consequence of it, they returned into the court with a negative to his demand; telling him, That they met there as a court of justice, commissionated by the parliament, of whose authority they were fully satisfied: that, by their commission, they were not authorised to receive any proposals from him, but to proceed to the trial of him: that, in order thereto, his charge had been read to him; to which, if he would have pleaded, the counsel for the commonwealth were ready to have proved it against him: that he had thrice demurred to the jurisdiction of the court; which demurrer the court had over-ruled, and registered; ordering to proceed against him, as if he had confessed the charge: and that if he had any proposition to make, it was proper for him

to address it to the parliament, and not to them. Then the President
enlarged upon the horrid nature of those crimes of which he had
85 been accused, and was now convicted; declaring, That the only just
power of Kings was derived from the consent of the people: that
whereas the people had intrusted him to see their laws put in
execution, he had endeavoured, throughout the whole course of his
reign, to subvert those good laws, and to introduce an arbitrary and
90 tyrannical government in the room of them. . . .

Whereupon the President, being moved by Mr. Solicitor Coke,
in the name, and on the behalf of the good people of England,
commanded the clerk of the court to proceed in the reading of the
charge against him. Which being done, the King was required to
95 give his answer to it, and to plead Guilty or Not guilty. The King
demurred to the jurisdiction of the court; affirming that no man,
nor body of men, had power to call him to an account, being not
intrusted by man, and therefore accountable only to God for his
actions. . . .

100 He had levied war against them, that he might not only dissolve
them, but, by the terror of his power, for ever discourage such
assemblies from doing their duty: that in this war many thousands
of the good people of England had lost their lives: that, in obedience
to what God commanded, and the nation expected, the parliament
105 had appointed this court to make inquisition for this blood, and to
try him for the same: that his charge had been read to him, and he
required to give an answer to it; which he having thrice refused to
do, he acquainted him, that the court had resolved to pronounce
sentence against him; and thereupon commanded the clerk to read
110 it; which he did, being to this effect: THAT THE KING, FOR THE
CRIMES CONTAINED IN THE CHARGE, SHOULD BE CARRIED BACK TO THE
PLACE FROM WHENCE HE CAME, AND THENCE TO THE PLACE OF
EXECUTION, WHERE HIS HEAD SHOULD BE SEVERED FROM HIS BODY.
Which sentence being read, the commissioners testified their
115 unanimous asset by their standing up. The King would have spoken
something before he was withdrawn; but being accounted dead in
law immediately after sentence pronounced, it was not permitted.
The court withdrew also; and agreed, that the sentence should be
put in execution on the Tuesday following, which would be the
120 30th of January 1648.

Memoirs of Edward Ludlow, ed. C. H. Firth (London, 1894),
I, pp 214–19

(*b*)
The King being come upon the Scaffold, look'd very earnestly on
the Block, and asked Col. *Hacker* if there were no higher: and then
spake thus (directing his Speech chiefly to Colonel *Thomlinson*)

King.   I Shall be very little heard of any body here, I shall therefore

125 speak a word unto you here: Indeed I could hold my peace very
well, if I did not think that holding my peace would make some
men think, that I did submit to the guilt, as well as to the
punishment: but I think it is my duty to God first, and to my
Countrey, for to clear my self both as an honest man, and a good
130 King, and a good Christian. I shall begin first with my Innocency,
In troth I think it not very needful for me to insist upon this, for
all the world knows that I never did begin a War with the two
Houses of Parliament, and I call God to witness, to whom I must
shortly make an account, That I never did intend for to incroach
135 upon their Privileges, they began upon me, it is the Militia they
began upon, they confess that the Militia was mine, but they
thought it fit for to have it from me. . . .
    God forbid that I should be so ill a Christian, as not to say that
Gods judgements are just upon me: Many times he does pay Justice
140 by an unjust Sentence, that is ordinary: I will onely say this, That
an unjust Sentence that I suffered for to take effect, is punished
now by an unjust Sentence upon me, that is, so far I have said, to
shew you that I am an innocent man.
    Now for to show you that I am a good Christian: I hope there
145 is a good man that will bear me witness, That I have forgiven all
the world, and even those in particular that have been the chief
causers of my death: who they are, God knows, I do not desire to
know, I pray God forgive them. But this is not all, my Charity
must go farther, I wish that they may repent, for indeed they have
150 committed a great sin in that particular: I pray God with St Stephen,
That this be not laid to their charge, nay, not only so, but that
they may take the right way to the Peace of the Kingdom, for my
charity commands me not onely to forgive particular men, but my
Charity commands me to endeavour to the last gasp the Peace of
155 the kingdom. . . .
    For the King, indeed I will not (then turning to a Gentleman
that touched the Axe, said, Hurt not the Axe, that may hurt me).
For the King the Laws of the Land will clearly instruct you for that;
therefore because it concerns my own particular, I onely give you
160 a touch of it.
    For the people: And truly I desire their Liberty and Freedom as
much as any body whomsoever, but I must tell you, That their
Liberty and their Freedom consists in having of Government; those
Laws, by which their Life and their Goods may be most their own.
165 It is not for having share in Government (Sir) that is nothing
pertaining to them; A Subject and a Soveraign are clean different
things, and therefore until they do that, I mean, That you do put
the People in that Liberty as I say, certainly they will never enjoy
themselves.
170   Sirs, It was for this that now I am come here: If I would have
given way to an Arbitrary way, for to have all Laws changed

according to the power of the Sword, I needed not to have come here, and therefore I tell you (and I pray God it be not laid to your charge) That I am the Martyr of the People.

175 Introth Sirs, I shall not hold you much longer, for I will onely say this to you, That intruth I could have desired some little time longer, because that I would have put this that I have said in a little more order, and a little better digested than I have done, and therefore I hope you will excuse me.

180 I have delivered my Conscience, I pray God that you do take those courses that are best for the good of the kingdom, and your own salvations.

Doctor Juxon. Will your Majesty (though it may be very well known your Majesties affections to Religion, yet it may be expected

185 that you should) say somewhat for the worlds satisfaction?

King. I thank you very heartily (my Lord) for that I had almost forgotten it. Introth Sirs, My Conscience in Religion I think is very well known to all the world, and therefore I declare before you all, That I dye a Christian, according to the profession of the

190 Church of England, as I found it left me by my Father, and this honest man I think will witness it. . . .

Then the King speaking to the Executioner, said, I shall say but very short prayers, and when I thrust out my hands——. Then the King called to Dr *Juxon* for his Night-cap, and having put it on,

195 he said to the Executioner, Does my hair trouble you? who desired him to put it all under his Cap, which the King did accordingly, by the help of the Executioner and the Bishop: Then the King turning to Dr *Juxon*, said, I have a good Cause, and a gracious God on my side.

200 *Doctor Juxon.* There is but one Stage more. This Stage is turbulent and troublesome; it is a short one: But you may consider, it will soon carry you a very great way: it will carry you from Earth to Heaven; and there you shall finde a great deal of cordial joy and comfort.

205 *King.* I go from a corruptible to an incorruptible Crown; where no disturbance can be, no disturbance in the world.

Doctor Juxon. You are exchanged from a temporal to an eternal Crown, a good exchange.

The King then said to the Executioner, is my hair well: Then

210 the King took off his Cloak and his George, giving his George to Doctor *Juxon*, saying, Remember——. Then the King put off his Dublet, and being in his Waistcoat, put his Cloak on again, then looking upon the Block, said to the Executioner, You must set it fast.

215 *Executioner.* It is fast Sir.

King. It might have been a little higher.

Executioner. It can be no higher Sir.

King. When I put out my hands this way, then——.

After that having said two or three words as he stood to Himself
220 with hands and eyes lift up; Immediately stooping down, laid his
neck upon the Block: And then the Executioner again putting his
Hair under his Cap, the King said Stay for the sign.
Executioner. Yes, I will and it please your Majesty.
And after a very little pause, the King stretching forth his hands,
225 The Executioner at one blow severed his head from his body.
That when the Kings head was cut off, the executioner held it
up, and shewed it to the Spectators.

> Anon. *King Charles his Speech, Made upon the Scaffold at
> Whitehall-Gate* (London, 1649) pp 1–8 (not published). For
> source see Donald G. Wing, *Short-title Catalog of Books
> Printed . . . 1641–1700* 3 vols (New York, 1945–51) c. 2792

Questions

a Assess the arguments used by the king's opponents during his
  trial (document a). How convincing was the legal procedure
  employed?
b Why did the king make the following statement on the scaffold:
  'An unjust sentence that I suffered for to take effect is punished
  now by an unjust sentence upon me' (lines 141–2)?

3 Reactions to the Execution

News of the death of Charles I horrified the European powers to
an unprecedented degree, but failed to induce a united, active
response. Popular revulsion in France was signified by assaults on
Cavalier exiles, in the apparent belief that all Englishmen were
stigmatised by regicide. Heads of European states had good reason
to react indignantly, for the execution was more than a personal
affront to monarchs in that it established a potentially disastrous
precedent. Vitriolic protest, however, became a substitute for
practical action to punish the regime which had perpetrated this
heinous crime. Cardinal Mazarin did not break off diplomatic
relations with London, and most states found it expedient to
tolerate the *de facto* government of England. This placed many
governments in an embarrassing predicament over diplomatic
courtesies. In expressing condolences to the former Prince of Wales,
how should the younger Charles Stuart be addressed? While *de iure*
king of England by hereditary succession, only the Virginians and
Portuguese adopted a wholly unequivocal approach in proclaiming
him 'your Majesty' – other rulers prudently dissociated themselves
from close identification with the cause of monarchy in England.

de Cardenas obtained eighteen wagons of royal artistic treasures from Stuart palaces to console the pragmatic king of Spain, who became the first monarch to grant official recognition to the Commonwealth in December 1650.

Despite the execution and the lukewarm response from European powers, Parliamentarians came off worse in the propaganda *coup* which immediately followed the regicide. Within hours of the execution, an apparently autobiographical account of the king's fortitude in the face of death and oppression was available on the streets of London. In fact the *Eikon Basilike* (subtitled 'A Portrait of His Sacred Majesty in His solitude and suffering') was probably the work of the Royalist divine John Gauden, rewarded for his service with the bishopric of Exeter at the Restoration. In political terms, the 'King's Book' was an unqualified success; it ran to 46 English editions in 1649 alone and was also published in Latin, Dutch, French and German. *Eikon Basilike* was consciously pitched at an emotive level, being designed to convince the world that the king died a regal martyr at the hands of dangerous and deluded men (document a).

Most Parliamentarians were convinced that the King's Book was an imposture, but they were nonetheless startled by the popularity of the deception, allied to improbable rumours of miraculous cures attributable to rags dipped in royal blood around the scaffold. Moreover, Europeans began to take up cudgels against regicide, a demonstrable crime against God and man. Declarations of indignation gave way to logical and legalistic condemnations of the trial procedure and the execution, including *Defensio Regia*, published on 11 May 1649 by Salmasius, a celebrated contemporary scholar at the University of Leiden. In John Milton the English Commonwealth found a firm supporter of regicide and a Latin scholar of equivalent stature, who could be entrusted with the task of justifying the actions of Parliament before a hostile European audience. Accordingly, Milton was employed by the Council of State, initially to refute *Eikon Basilike* in two works: *Eikonoklastes* ('the image broken') and *The Life and Reign of King Charls; or the Pseudo-Martyr Discovered* (both 1651). In these ripostes, Milton approved the execution on the basis of the king's duplicity; repudiated the suggestion that the trial was legally unsound, and attacked *Eikon Basilike* which 'principally induced me to take (in brief) the true dimensions of this sainted king and innocent martyr, and to pull off that false vizzard wherewith his juggling party had decked his effigy and presented him to the public view, for the most pious prince of this age' (document b).

Royalists, on the other hand, attested to the importance of the King's Book and attacked Milton's apologetics in such works as *The Image Unbroken* by Joseph Jane (1651). Jane vilified the new government, appealed to sympathetic Europeans for support, and suggested to Parliamentarians that ultimate victory might be elusive: 'Though armies have been defeated, a good cause can never. . . . Tyrants cannot sleep while lawful heirs survive' (document c).

The European debate upon the legitimacy of regicide, conducted primarily between Milton and Salmasius, continued until the Restoration. Milton's *Pro Populo Anglicano Defensio* (1651) was the most effective response to European criticism containing a rigorous justification of Parliamentary actions (document d).

A Royalist Propaganda and Parliamentary Apologetics

(*a*)

I am not so old, as to be weary of life; nor (I hope) so bad, as to be either afraid to die, or ashamed to live: true, I am so afflicted, as might make Me sometime even desire to die; if I did not consider, That it is the greatest glory of a Christians life to *die daily*, in
5   conquering by a lively faith, and patient hopes of a better life, those partiall and quotidian deaths, which kill us (as it were) by piece-meales, and make us overlive our owne fates; while We are deprived of health, honour, liberty, power, credit, safety, or estate; and those other comforts of dearest relations, which are as the life of
10   our lives.

Though, as a King, I think My self to live in nothing temporall so much, as in the love and goodwill of My People; for which, as I have suffered many deaths, so I hope I am not in that point as yet wholly dead: notwithstanding, My Enemies have used all the
15   poyson of falsity and violence of hostility to destroy, first the love and Loyalty, which is in My Subjects; and then all that content of life in Me, which from these I chiefly enjoyed.

Indeed, they have left Me but little of life, and only the husk and shell (as it were) which their further malice and cruelty can take
20   from Me; having bereaved Me of all those worldly comforts, for which life it self seems desirable to men.

But, O My Soule! think not that life too long, or tedious, wherein God gives thee any opportunities, if not to doe, yet to suffer with such Christian patience and magnanimity in a good
25   Cause, as are the greatest honour of our lives, and the best improvement of our deaths. . . .

That I must die as a Man, is certain; that I may die a King, by the hands of My own Subjects, a violent, sodain, and barbarous death; in the strength of My years; in the midst of My Kingdoms;
30   My Friends and loving Subjects being helplesse Spectators; My Enemies insolent Revilers and Triumphers over Me, living, dying, and dead, is so probable in humane reason, that God hath taught me not to hope otherwise, as to mans cruelty; however, I despaire not of Gods infinite mercy. . . .

35   It is, indeed, a sad fate for any man to have his Enemies to be
Accusers, Parties, and Judges; but most desperate, when this is
acted by the insolence of Subjects against their Soveraigne; wherein
those, who have had the chiefest hand, and are most guilty of
contriving the publique Troubles, must by shedding My bloud
40   seem to wash their own hands of that innocent bloud, whereof
they are now most evidently guilty before God and man; and I
believe in their owne consciences too, while they carried on
unreasonable demands, first by Tumults, after by Armies. Nothing
makes meane spirits more cowardly-cruell in managing their
45   usurped power against their lawfull Superiours, than this, the *Guilt
of their unjust Usurpation*; notwithstanding, those specious and
popular pretensions of Justice against Delinquents, applied onely
to disguise at first the monstrousnesse of their designes, who
despaired, indeed, of possessing the power and profits of the
50   Vineyard, till the Heire, whose right it is, be cast out and slaine. . . .
    My greatest conquest of Death is from the power and love of
Christ, who hath swallow'd up death in the victory of his
Ressurrection, and the glory of his Ascension.
    My next comfort is, that he gives Me not onely the honour to
55   imitate his example in suffering for righteousnesse sake, (though
obscured by the foulest charges of Tyranny and Injustice) but also,
that charity, which is the noblest revenge upon, and victory over
My Destroyers: By which, I thank God, I can both forgive them,
and pray for them, that God would not impute My bloud to them
60   further then to convince them, what need they have of Christs
bloud to wash their soules from the guilt of shedding Mine. . . .
    I blesse God, I pray not so much, that this bitter cup of a violent
death may passe from Me, as that of his wrath may passe from all
those, whose hands by deserting Me, are sprinkled, or by acting
65   and consenting to My death are embrued with My bloud.
        Anon., *Eikon Basilike*, or *The King's Book* (1649), reprinted,
        ed. by Edward Almack (London, 1907) pp 265–72

(b) *Milton's support for regicide*

After to the year 1645, when the King's cabinet letters were taken
at Naseby, I began to bethink myself . . . that the Parliament had
then to deal with a King . . . who was not to seek without the
help and influence of a malicious council, to play his own part, I
70   shall not say better, but more dextrous and cunningly for his own
ends, and to the reducing of the Kingdom under his absolute
power, than any of those could direct him, whom he most trusted
with the managery of his designes and secrets; truly Sir, on that
discovery [the publishing of his letters] let me tell you there were

75   many thousands which fell off, and from the opinion they held of his integrity and the justice of his cause, it being in the next degree to a miracle that after so full a disclosure of the King's jugglings and dissemblings there should any remain to take his part. . . .

    As to the late purging of the Houses, it is acknowledged that in
80   the midst of such a confusion as was both raised, cherished and formented by the King himself and the Malignant party, it was done by the power of the army, and as I take it on this ground, that the major part of both Houses voted for the readmittance of the King on such condition which himself refused, which the lesser
85   and more foreseeing part well understood would in the end come to no other issue than the setting him up into his own power to enable him anew to embroil the kingdoms, having so long before engaged the Prince in his quarrel and disciplined him in his designs, in so much as no other hopes were then left the Parliament but
90   either a perpetuating of the war and more bloodshed, or the invassalage of the nation which necessarily would be the consequence on the admittance either of the father or the son. Upon these grounds 'tis confessed, that the soldiery ended the controversy, in assisting the weaker party in Parliament, though doubtless the
95   more able in judgement and foresight of the future evils and calamities which in all probability might and would befall the nation; which to prevent, on the evidence of the King's obstinacy, it was resolved to remove the effects by taking away the cause, in calling the principal author of all the former bloodshed to his public
100   trial, to stop which issue it was further resolved to cut him off, and to cast that pilot overboard that not more out of ignorance than wilfulness, would obstinately have sunk the ship of the public in the vast ocean of his prerogative.

             John Milton, *The Life and Reign of King Charls, or the Pseudo-Martyr Discovered* (1651), pp 55–6, 222–3

(c) Royalist attacks on Milton and regicide

    The present age must needs have a deep sense of his loss and
105   posterity as well as strangers will wonder, when they read his story and find such groundless slanders and barbarous cruelties acted against so eminent virtue, and the confidence in obtruding such gross absurdities for reasons, as are used by this author and others, will be the infamy of the present age, when such evident folly and
110   wickedness find credit. Can any man be so stupid to think that such wretches, as boast of their destroying the innocent, will cease to defame their memory? And that such as had no mercy on their lives, will have a tenderness of their sufferings? That they which suborned detractors and raised lewd reports to give colour to their

115 cruelty, would have a tenderness to him they had tormented, and
express no tenderness for their own villanies? It had been contrary
to his Majesty's wisdom to have expected tenderness to himself
from such monsters, and contrary to the nature of such savage
beasts to have their bloodthirstiness slaked or their cruelty calmed
120 with any successes. . . .

Doth Iconoclastes think any Parliament infallible, or that all men
condemned by Parliament had justice done them? He will then find
that they condemn one another, and for this last misnamed
Parliament, their bloody executions have such apparent marks of
125 injustice and cruelty as themselves cannot deny it. . . . There are
in his Majesty's book many particulars that the Parliament neither
could nor did deny, and through the whole book the author hath
produced few or none of their denials. There hath been much use
made of the name of Parliament, but the author must think he hath
130 an enchanting pen, if after the murder of the King, abolishing the
Lords' house, plucking out the members of the lower house,
prostituting the very constitution of Parliament to the lawless
multitude, and packing the room with a few mean persons, either
terrified by power or flattered by promises, he can persuade any
135 . . . He may as well give the name of Parliament to a parish
vestry. . . .

Its no new thing for persons of most eminent virtue to fall into
obloquy and suffer by the rage of a misled people, and therefore
no wonder if innocence find an orator to accuse it, and treason an
140 advocate to defend it. Rebellion never wanted a trumpet and though
the contrivance of it be in caves and vaults, yet success makes it
outface the light. His Majesty's book hath passed the censure of
the greatest part of the learned world, being translated into the
most spread languages, and strangers honour his memory and
145 abhor his murderers but such as regard not the all-seeing eye of
God beholding their wickedness, despite the judgement of the
whole world.

> Joseph Jane, *The Image Unbroken: A perspective of the Impu-
> dence, Falshood, Vanitie and Prophannes, published in a libell
> entitled Eikonoklastes against Eikon Basilike* (1651), pp 4, 18,
> 71

(d) Milton defends Parliament before a European audience

Though Salmasius is a foreigner and . . . a grammarian, yet he is
not content with the rewards of his trade and would prefer to be a
150 great busybody. . . . If his present writings, composed in a kind
of Latin, had been published in England in our language, I believe
they would hardly have seemed to anyone worth the trouble of

answering. . . . Now, however, when he makes his turgid pages
current among foreigners who know nothing of our affairs, it is
155 necessary that those who misunderstand our situation should be
instructed. . . .

My discourse, indeed, will be of matters neither small nor mean:
a king in all his power, ruling according to his lust after he
had overthrown our laws and oppressed our religion, at length
160 overcome in battle by his own people which had served under a
long term of slavery; and after that put under guard: and, when
neither in word or deed had he given the slightest ground for hope
of his improvement, condemned to capital punishment by the
highest court of the realm and beheaded before the very gates of
165 the palace. . . .

When in times past kings refused their assent to acts of Parliament
such as Magna Carta and the like, our fathers in many cases secured
assent by force of arms. Our jurists hold that these laws are no less
valid or legitimate on this account. . . . If Parliament, against the
170 king's will and desire, can revoke his acts and recall such privileges
as he granted to anyone, limit the prerogatives of the king himself
as they see fit, control his yearly income and court expenditures,
his very household servants and all his domestic affairs, remove
his closest councillors and friends or take them for punishment
175 from his very arms; if, finally, any of the populace is assured by
law of an appeal from the king to Parliament in any matter, though
not in turn from Parliament to the king, if, as our public records
and legal scholars testify, all these things both can take place and
have often done so I do not believe that anyone in his right mind
180 would fail to admit that Parliament is above the king! Even between
reigns, Parliament is in power, and it is clearly evidenced by our
history that often by its free vote it chose whom it wished as king
and took no account of rights of inheritance. To sum up the
situation, Parliament is the supreme council of the nation, estab-
185 lished and endowed with full powers by an absolutely free people
for the purpose of consulting together on the most vital issues; the
king was created to carry out all the decrees of the House according
to their advice and intentions.

John Milton, *A Defence of the People of England* (1651)
reprinted in Don Wolfe (ed.), *The Complete Prose Works of
John Milton*, IV, pp 302–3, 306, 497–8

Questions

a Use document (a) to account for the propaganda value of *Eikon
   Basilike*.
b Most Parliamentarians (correctly) believed *Eikon Basilike* to

be fraudulent, but why did some additionally regard it as blasphemous?

c How compelling were Milton's arguments for regicide (document b)? Do they represent an effective riposte to *Eikon Basilike*?

d What evidence exists in document (c) to show that Royalists were convinced by the imposture of 'the King's book'?

e For what reason was Milton employed by the Council of State?

f Milton's political activities ensured his contemporary notoriety. What happened to the defender of regicide at the Restoration, and why?

4 Cromwellian Policy in Ireland and Scotland

Following the execution of Charles I, Cromwell's attention turned to consider sources of potential Stuart rebellion against the new Republic. With Argyle's Covenanters temporarily secure in Scotland, the most pressing threat arose in Ireland where Ormonde – the Lord Lieutenant – had openly declared for the king, inviting Charles II to Ireland and encouraging Royalists to assemble and attack Parliamentary garrisons. In March 1649 Cromwell was appointed Lord Lieutenant by the Commonwealth, a post he accepted with some reluctance, yet knowing that the New Model were unwilling to embark for Ireland without him. Various explanations can be adduced for the campaign in Ireland, among these the possibility of using Irish land confiscated from Royalists finally to end the dispute over military arrears; the need to remedy the neglect of the 1640s including revenge for the massacres of Protestants in 1641, and the fact that a popular campaign against Catholicism would unite the army, Parliament and a Protestant nation. Only extreme Levellers disapproved of the venture, and Cromwell's departure for Ireland was briefly delayed by a final phase of military unrest culminating in the Burford mutiny of May 1649. In August, Cromwell reached Dublin with a force of some 12,000 men, to a rapturous reception from the Protestant population.

The campaign turned first to Drogheda, garrisoned by Ormonde's troops under Sir Arthur Aston, a Roman Catholic and former Royalist governor of Oxford. The siege of Drogheda lasted from 3 to 11 September, but once the Royalist defences were breached no quarter was given either to the garrison or to many of the civilian population. This was on Cromwell's express instruction, as he recounts: 'The governor, Sir Arthur Ashton, and divers considerable officers being there, our men getting up to them were ordered by me to put all to the sword; and, indeed being in the heat of action, I forbade them to spare any that were in arms in the town. . . . I am persuaded that this is a righteous judgement of

God upon these barbarous wretches, who have imbrued their hands in so much innocent blood, and that it will tend to prevent the effusion of blood for the future, which are the satisfactory grounds to such actions.' The slaugher in Drogheda continued for two days, and the Parliamentary chaplain Hugh Peters concluded that the royalist dead numbered 3552. From Drogheda, the 'curse of Cromwell' became common parlance in Ireland, giving witness to the strength of contemporary feelings over these events.

Facing this threat, Ormonde arranged a belated alliance with Owen Roe O'Neill, who commanded the Catholic northern Irish and was believed to be implicated in the events of 1641. But Cromwell's campaign proved practically irresistible – Wexford fell to Parliamentary forces on 11 October, with again around 2000 slain after the capitulation of the town. The final blow to Irish hopes came in August 1650, when Charles II (under pressure from Scottish Presbyterians) denounced the campaign and abandoned his supporters in Ireland, declaring against the 'exceeding great sinfulness and unlawfulness of that treaty and peace made with the bloody Irish rebels, who treacherously shed the blood of so many of his faithful and loyal subjects in Ireland'. Disgusted at this betrayal, Ormonde fled Ireland for France. Thus Cromwell's campaign effectively ended the threat of Royalist invasion from Ireland, at the expense of a savage military campaign which produced its own historical legacy. Edmund Ludlow provides a résumé of events in Ireland between 1649 and 1650 (document a).

The political allegiance of the Scots had vacillated wildly during the 1640s – initial support for the Parliamentary cause rested primarily upon religious grounds, and so the Scottish commissioners were dismayed by the growing tide of English Independency in the later 1640s. The invasion of England and the second civil war were the direct results of the 'Engagement' of December 1647: Hamilton's troops hoped to defend the king's authority against Parliamentary encroachment in return for the king's commitment to Presbyterianism and the Solemn League and Covenant. Hamilton's domestic opponents were the kirk faction led by the Marquis of Argyle, who loosely allied themselves with English Independents based upon mutual distrust of the king. Consequently, the defeat of the Earl of Hamilton at the battle of Preston in 1648 helped Argyle's Covenanters to attain supremacy in Scotland, but only with the vital support of Cromwell's troops to keep the 'Engagers' in check.

The execution of Charles I upset his precarious alliance north of the border, producing anger and frustration in Scotland over the judicial death of a Stuart king. The Scots increasingly identified themselves with monarchy and hereditary right, and Argyle's position was seriously weakened by his association with English Independency. The Scottish Parliament conditionally proclaimed Charles II, and Argyle sent a mission to the Hague seeking a compromise with the new king. Initially he was rebuffed – the king favoured a military campaign in Scotland to recover his authority, led by the Earl of Montrose. However, negotiations between the king and the Marquis of Argyle soon reopened following the defeat of Royalist aspirations in Ireland, and the capture and execution of Montrose in May 1650. (Clarendon describes the treatment of Montrose by his captors in the final days of his life, document b.) In this situation, Charles Stuart had little option but to negotiate with Argyle and personally land in Scotland to rally his supporters. Argyle's faction (fearing the king's tenderness to the 'Engagers') imposed strict conditions upon Charles II during preliminary discussions for the Treaty of Breda. Although only recently returned from Ireland, Cromwell responded immediately to news of the king's arrival by invading Scotland with a Parliamentary army on 22 July 1650. The Scots were ill-equipped to deal with Cromwell due to profound internal divisions and particularly the Covenanters' attempts to purify the Scots army of 'Malignants and Engagers'. Accordingly, the English caught the Scots in low morale and secured an easy victory at Dunbar (3 September 1650).

This defeat precipitated the decline of the Covenanters, although opposition to the invasion prompted greater enthusiasm for the national cause, which was increasingly identified with the king. A new army of 'Remonstrants' emerged – an autonomous Covenanter force attempting to protect the western shires from the twin evils of malignant Scots and sectarian English – but this group were soundly defeated by Colonel Lambert's Parliamentary troops, who ensured English domination over south-west Scotland.

Charles gained increasing political authority in Scotland as the influence of Argyle and the covenanters waned in the early months of 1651, but his military position remained hopelessly weak. Occupying the fortress city of Edinburgh, Cromwell prepared his soldiers for a final offensive to eliminate the Stuart threat in Scotland. By routing a Royalist force at Inverkeithing, Cromwell was able to progress north and secure the cities of Fife, Perth and Stirling. Ultimate defeat for Charles II in Scotland now appeared inevitable, and so Royalist commanders devised a strategy for diverting Cromwell's attention from Scotland by mounting a pre-emptive march into England. As anticipated, Cromwell followed Charles across the border, finally catching and destroying the Royalist army at Worcester (3 September 1651). Although Stuart forces were dispersed, the king was able to make his escape to the continent. Cromwell left Scotland secure in the hands of Lieutenant-General George Monck and around 8000 troops – this force completed the conquest of Scotland. From late 1651 Scotland lost virtually all political and military independence, becoming a mere province of England rather than a potential base for rebellion.

A   Military Action in Ireland and Scotland

(*a*)

After our army had refreshed themselves, and were joined by the forces of Col. Jones, they mustered in all between sixteen and seventeen thousand horse and foot. Upon their arrival the enemies withdrew, and put most of their army into their garrisons, having
5   placed three or four thousand of the best of their men, being most English, in the town of Tredah [Drogheda], and made Sir Arthur Ashton governor thereof. A resolution being taken to besiege that place, our army sat down before it, and the Lieutenant-General caused a battery to be erected against an angle of the wall, near to
10 a fort, which was within, called the Windmill-Fort, by which he made a breach in the wall; but the enemy having a half-moon on the outside, which was designed to flank the angle of the wall, he thought fit to endeavour to possess himself of it, which he did by storm, putting most of those that were in it to the sword. The
15 enemy defended the breach against ours from behind an earth-work, which they had cast up within, and where they had drawn up two or three troops of horse which they had within the town, for the encouragement and support of their foot: the fort also was not unserviceable to them in the defence of the breach. The
20 Lieutenant-General well knowing the importance of this action, resolved to put all upon it; and having commanded some guns to be loaded with bullets of half a pound, and fired upon the enemy's horse, who were drawn up somewhat in view; himself with a reserve of foot marched up to the breach, which giving fresh
25 courage to our men, they made a second attack with more vigour than before: whereupon the enemy's foot being abandoned by their horse, whom our shot had forced to retire, began to break and shift for themselves; which ours perceiving, followed them so close, that they overtook them at the bridge that lay cross the river,
30 and separated that part where the action was from the principal part of the town; and preventing them from drawing up the bridge, entered pell-mell with them into the place, where they put all they met with to the sword, having positive orders from the Lieutenant-General to give no quarter to any soldier. Their works and fort
35 were also stormed and taken, and those that defended them put to the sword also, and amongst them Sir Arthur Ashton, governor of the place. A great dispute there was amongst the soldiers for his artificial leg, which was reported to be of gold, but it proved to be but of wood, his girdle being found to be the better booty, wherein
40 two hundred pieces of gold were found quilted. The slaughter was continued all that day and the next; which extraordinary severity I presume was used, to discourage others from making opposition. ˙ After that the army besieged Wexford; and having erected a battery against the castle, which stood near the wall of the town, and fired

45   from it most part of the day, whereby a small breach was made, commissioners were sent in the evening from the enemy to treat about the surrender of it. In the mean time our guns continued firing, there being no cessation agreed, whereby the breach in the castle being made wider, the guard that was appointed to defend it
50   quitted their post, and thereupon some of our men entered the castle, and set up their colours at the top of it, which the enemy having observed, left their stations in all parts: so that ours getting over the walls, possessed themselves of the town without opposition, and opened the gates that the horse might enter, though
55   they could do but little service, all the streets being barred with cables: but our foot pressed the enemy so close, that crowding to escape over the water, they so over–loaded the boats with their numbers, that many of them were drowned. . . .

    Our army in Ireland, though much diminished by sickness and
60   harassed by hard duty, continued their resolution to march into the enemy's quarters, where they reduced Rosse with little opposition: Goran also was surrendered to them, together with the officers of that place, by the soldiers of the garrison, upon promise of quarter for themselves; their officers being delivered at discretion, were
65   shot to death. The next town they besieged was Kilkenny, where there was a strong castle, and the walls of the town were indifferent good. Having erected a battery on the east side of the wall, our artillery fired upon it for a whole day without making any considerable breach; on the other side our men were much annoyed
70   by the enemy's shot from the walls and castle. But the garrison being admonished by the examples made of their friends at Tredah and Wexford, thought fit to surrender the town timely upon such conditions as they could obtain, which was done accordingly. . . .

    Owen Roe O'Neal, who commanded the old Northern Irish in
75   Ulster, that had been principally concerned in the massacre of the Protestants, being dead, the Popish Bishop of Cloghar undertook the conduct of them, and being grown considerably strong, necessitated Sir Charles Coote to draw his forces together to defend his quarters, which they designed to invade, desperately resolving
80   to put it to the issue of a battle. Their foot was more numerous than ours, but Sir Charles exceeded them in horse. The dispute was hot for some time; but at last the Irish were beaten, though not without loss on our side: amongst others Col. Fenwick, a brave and gallant man, was mortally wounded. The enemy's baggage
85   and train of artillery was taken, though not many made prisoners, being for the most part put to the sword, with the Bishop of Cloghar their general, whose head was cut off and set upon one of the gates of London-derry.

        Ludlow, *Memoirs*, op cit, I, pp 229, 232–4, 255

(*b*)

The marquis of Mountrose, and the rest of the prisoners, were the
90 next day, or soon after, delivered to David Lesley; who was come
up with his forces, and had now nothing left to do but to carry
them in triumph to Edinburgh; whither notice was quickly sent of
their great victory; which was received there with wonderful joy
and acclamation. David Lesley treated the marquis with great
95 insolence, and for some days carried him in the same clothes, and
habit, in which he was taken; but at last permitted him to buy
better. His behaviour was, in the whole time, such as became a
great man; his countenance serene and cheerful, as one that was
superior to all those reproaches, which they had prepared the people
100 to pour out upon him in all the places through which he was to
pass.

When he came to one of the gates of Edinburgh, he was met by
some of the magistrates, to whom he was delivered, and by them
presently put into a new cart, purposely made, in which there was
105 a high chair, or bench, upon which he sat, that the people might
have a full view of him, being bound with a cord drawn over his
breast and shoulders, and fastened through holes made in the cart.
When he was in this posture, the hangman took off his hat, and
rode himself before the cart in his livery, and with his bonnet on;
110 the other officers, who were taken prisoners with him, walking
two and two before the cart; the streets and windows being full of
people to behold the triumph over a person whose name had made
them tremble some few years before, and into whose hands the
magistrates of that place had, upon their knees, delivered the keys
115 of that city. In this manner he was carried to the common gaol,
where he was received and treated as a common malefactor.

That he might not enjoy any ease or quiet during the short
remainder of his life, their ministers came presently to insult over
him with all the reproaches imaginable; pronounced his damnation;
120 and assured him, 'that the judgement he was the next day to
undergo, was but an easy prologue to that which he was to undergo
afterwards'. After many such barbarities, they offered to intercede
for him to the kirk upon his repentance, and to pray with him; but
he too well understood the form of their common prayer, in those
125 cases, to be only the most virulent and insolent imprecations against
the persons of those they prayed against, ('Lord, vouchsafe yet to
touch the obdurate heart of this proud incorrigible sinner, this
wicked, perjured, traitorous, and profane person, who refuses to
hearken to the voice of thy kirk', and the like charitable expressions,)
130 and therefore he desired them 'to spare their pains, and to leave
him to his devotions'. He told them, 'that they were a miserable,
deluded, and deluding people; and would shortly bring that poor
nation under the most insupportable servitude ever people had
submitted to'. He told them, 'he was prouder to have his head set

135 upon the place it was appointed to be, than he could have been to
have his picture hang in the king's bedchamber: that he was so far
from being troubled that his four limbs were to be hanged in four
cities of the kingdom, that he heartily wished that he had flesh
enough to be sent to every city in Christendom, as a testimony of
140 the cause for which he suffered'.

The next day, they executed every part and circumstance of that
barbarous sentence, with all the inhumanity imaginable; and he
bore it with all the courage and magnanimity, and the greatest
piety, that a good Christian could manifest. He magnified the virtue,
145 courage, and religion of the last king, exceedingly commended the
justice, and goodness, and understanding of the present king; and
prayed, 'that they might not betray him as they had done his
father.' When he had ended all he meant to say, and was expecting
to expire, they had yet one scene more to act of their tyranny. The
150 hangman brought the book that had been published of his truly
heroic actions, whilst he had commanded in that kingdom, which
book was tied in a small cord that was put about his neck. The
marquis smiled at this new instance of their malice, and thanked
them for it; and said, 'he was pleased that it should be there; and
155 was prouder of wearing it, than ever he had been of the garter';
and so renewing some devout ejaculations, he patiently endured
the last act of the executioner,

> Edward Hyde, *History of the Rebellion* in *Selections.*, ed. H. R.
> Trevor Roper (Oxford, 1978), pp 338–40

Questions

a Why did Cromwell conduct his military campaign in Ireland
with 'extraordinary severity'?
b What evidence exists in document (b) for Clarendon's sympathy
for Montrose?

5 Cromwell and the Continent

Two conflicting components are conventionally identified as potential motives for Cromwellian foreign policy. Firstly, by emphasising
the Dutch war of 1652–4, it is suggested that Cromwell pursued
economic advantage in relation to English trading interests. On the
other hand, the later war with Spain reveals an underlying Protestant
theme in Cromwellian policy. It is significant that Cromwell, who
had little personal knowledge of Europe, was strongly opposed to
the pacific foreign policy of the early Stuarts. His perceptions were
influenced by shame at the failure of Charles I actively to support
the Dutch and Gustavus Adolphus in the Thirty Years War, and

by traditional Protestant fears of Catholic advance in Europe. During the first years of the Commonwealth, Cromwell's energies were directed towards affairs in Ireland and Scotland, and the Council of State controlled foreign policy decisions. These were difficult years for the republic as many European powers remained hostile, and Royalist exiles assassinated Dorislaus and Ascham – the Commonwealth's first envoys to the Hague and Madrid.

The dispute with the Dutch, whom many regarded as Protestant partners in a predominantly Catholic Europe, arose indirectly from the Peace of Westphalia in 1648. The cessation of European hostilities exposed English merchant shipping to efficient Dutch competition, and by 1651 Dutch domination of maritime trade in the Baltic, the Mediterranean and with the colonies had damaged English commercial interests. Initially the Rump resisted growing demands for protection, clinging to the vision of many Republicans (for example Tom Chalenor and Algernon Sydney) of an expanding Protestant confederation in northern Europe. Such an alliance had been suggested in the Nineteen Propositions of 1642, and accordingly Oliver St John's mission to the Hague in 1650 was designed to lay the foundations for a confederation of the English and Dutch republics. However, this proposal was now anachronistic and based on an obsolete perception of common religious objectives. Indeed the eclipse of the pro-Stuart House of Orange did not imply any close association between England and the Netherlands: the Prince of Wales had been welcome in the Hague; there was little enthusiasm for regicide in the Dutch republic, and the English were regarded as economic competitors. Moreover, the plan for union conflicted with the commercial and political interests of the United Provinces – the Dutch feared potential English domination, loss of trading profits and loss of independence. As the negotiations faltered domestic demands for protection became insistent. In 1651 the Rump approved the Navigation Act, designed to restrict Dutch entrepôt trade and improve prospects for English shipping (document a).

This Act alone did not make conflict inevitable, although it increased tension between England and the United Provinces. Parliament was exasperated by Dutch procrastination over St John's embassy and angered by the failure to expel or prosecute Royalists following the murder of Dorislaus. Additionally, undeclared hostilities between Britain and France caused tribulations for Dutch merchants in the Channel – the States-General responded by ordering a huge increase in naval power. When Admiral Tromp's fleet set sail to prevent further interference with Dutch trade, Parliament viewed this as invasion of the seas and the inevitable incidents sparked off formal hostilities in May 1652.

Cromwell recognised the necessity for war, but he also regarded the struggle with the United Provinces as fratricide. Thurloe reminds us that Cromwell deplored 'the lamentable state of the Protestant Cause, whilst this war continues'. The first Anglo-Dutch war was characterised by a series of sea battles as the Dutch vainly attempted to maintain their vital trading routes in the Channel. With a long Channel coastline, the English possessed enormous strategic advantages, and by late 1653 Admiral Blake controlled the major sea lanes; Tromp was dead, and the Dutch had lost around 1000 merchant ships. The conflict was concluded by the Treaty of Westminster in April 1654 and the English victory was complete. But the influence of the Lord Protector was instrumental in producing an extremely conciliatory settlement with the Dutch, whom Cromwell continued to regard as important allies against European Catholicism.

The treaty with the United Provinces was strenuously opposed by both France and Spain, and they ordered agents in England to obstruct negotiations. Traditional enmity between France and Spain implied that a Cromwellian alliance with either state would seriously threaten the excluded nation. The Spanish faction (headed by Lambert in the Council of State) attempted unsuccessfully to promote a reconciliation with Madrid, but the Protector was finally convinced by the existing association between France and Protestant Sweden, plus evidence of Mazarin's increasing respect for Huguenot rights. Spain had good reason to be fearful – in 1651 Blake's millenial proclamation in the square at Cadiz assured Spaniards of the abolition of temporal monarchy within the decade. Moreover, war with Spain opened the possibility of material benefit from disrupting Spanish trade with colonies in the Carribean. Hostilities broke out in 1655 but the Protector's grandiose scheme for conquest of the West Indies and conversion of the inhabitants to Protestantism proved impractical. Even worse, Cromwell unrealistically hoped that conflict could be confined to the Carribean, yet the struggle provoked a European war which helped only the Dutch as trade between England and Spain terminated. English merchants lost heavily, not only through the disruption of commerce and the activities of hostile privateers in the Channel, but also through additional taxation to finance naval improvements and replacements of men-of-war. The war became exceptionally unpopular with the merchant classes, as revealed in contemporary pamphlets (document b).

By March 1657, Cromwell entered a military alliance with the French to produce a collective assault on the Spanish Netherlands. Dunkirk fell to this combined force in June 1658, giving England a temporary foothold on the continent and removing Royalist privateers from the Channel.

The achievements of Cromwell's foreign policy are open to dispute, and there is little doubt that his perception of a fundamental religious basis in European politics became largely outmoded. On several occasions he failed to recognise appropriate long-term advantages for England; certainly in the French alliance he assisted a strong Catholic power to expand further, while weakening an already declining Spain. In so doing, Cromwell contravened the established conventions of Tudor and Stuart foreign policy. Cromwellian intervention, however, enabled England to attain an unprecedented position of power and respect in Europe, although often at the expense of domestic discord. The final years of Cromwell's life were plagued with fears over internal Royalist plots; threats of assassination, rumours of invasion and concern over the succession. Some authoritarian actions as Protector caused many to turn against his version of 'Godly rule', encouraging Royalist resistance at home and abroad. Even former Levellers such as Lilburne and Wildman, who came to regard Cromwell as a traitor, treated with Royalists for a restoration of the monarchy. Another Leveller, Edward Sexby, in exile in Amsterdam, produced a remarkable pamphlet entitled *Killing Noe Murder* (1657) urging the assassination of Cromwell (document c). Sexby returned to England, but was arrested before he could put his words into practice. Despite his later unpopularity, the historian G.M.D. Howat summarises Cromwell's foreign policy as founded on 'Protestants, products and prestige', which seems apposite. While policies were occasionally misdirected and unsuccessful, the increasing respect for England on the European mainland during the Interregnum was a tribute to Cromwell's influence.

A   Cromwellian Foreign Policy

(a) The Navigation Act

[Oct. 9, 1651.]

Goods from Foreign parts by whom to be imported.

For the increase of the shipping and the encouragement of the navigation of this nation, which under the good providence and protection of God is so great a means of the welfare and safety of
5   this Commonwealth: be it enacted by this present Parliament, and the authority thereof, that from and after the first day of December, one thousand six hundred fifty and one, and from thence forwards, no goods or commodities whatsoever of the growth, production or manufacture of Asia, Africa or America, or of any part thereof;
10   or of any islands belonging to them, or which are described or laid down in the usual maps or cards of those places, as well of the English plantations as others, shall be imported or brought into this Commonwealth of England, or into Ireland, or any other lands, islands, plantations, or territories to this Commonwealth
15   belonging, or in their possession, in any other ship or ships, vessel

or vessels whatsoever, but only in such as do truly and without
fraud belong only to the people of this Commonwealth, or the
plantations thereof, as the proprietors or right owners thereof; and
whereof the master and mariners are also for the most part of them
of the people of this Commonwealth, under the penalty of the
forfeiture and loss of all the goods that shall be imported contrary
to this act; as also of the ship (with all her tackle, guns and apparel)
in which the said goods or commodities shall be so brought in and
imported; . . .

And it is further enacted by the authority aforesaid, that no
goods or commodities of the growth, production, or manufacture
of Europe, or of any part thereof, shall after the first day of
December, one thousand six hundred fifty and one, be imported
or brought into this Commonwealth of England, or into Ireland,
or any other lands, islands, plantations or territories to this
Commonwealth belonging, or in their possession, in any ship or
ships, vessel or vessels whatsoever, but in such as do truly and
without fraud belong only to the people of this Commonwealth,
as the true owners and proprietors thereof, and in no other, except
only such foreign ships and vessels as do truly and properly belong
to the people of that country or place, of which the said goods are
the growth, production or manufacture; . . .

And it is further enacted by the authority aforesaid, that no
goods or commodities that are of foreign growth, production or
manufacture, and which are to be brought into this Commonwealth
in shipping belonging to the people thereof, shall be by them
shipped or brought from any other place or places, country or
countries, but only from those of their said growth, production,
or manufacture, or from those ports where the said goods and
commodities can only, or are, or usually have been first shipped
for transportation; and from none other places or countries, under
the same penalty of forfeiture and loss expressed in the first branch
of this Act, the said forfeitures to be recovered and employed as is
therein expressed.

Gardiner, *Constitutional Documents*, pp 468–70

(b) *Domestic criticism of Cromwell's foreign policy*

He neglected all our golden opportunities, misimproved the victory
God had given us over the United Netherlands, making peace . . .
as soon as ever things came into his hand, upon equal terms with
them. And immediately after, contrary to our interest, made an
unjust war with Spain, and an impolitic league with France bringing
the first thereby under, and making the latter too great for
Christendom, and by that means broke the balance between the

two crowns of Spain and France which his predecessors the Long
Parliament had always wisely preserved. . . .

60   In this dishonest war with Spain he pretended and endeavoured
to impose a belief upon the world that he had nothing in his eye
but the advancement of the protestant cause, and the honour of
this nation. But his pretences were either fraudulent or he was
ignorant in foreign affairs (I am apt to think that he was not guilty
of too much knowledge in them). For he that had known any thing
65   of the temper of the Popish prelacy and the French court's policies
could not but see that the way to increase or preserve the reformed
interest in France was by rendering the Protestants of necessary use
to their king; for that longer than they were so, they could not be
free from persecution, and that the way to render them so was by
70   keeping the balance between Spain and France even as that which
would consequently make them useful to their king. But by
overthrowing this balance in his war with Spain and joining with
France, he freed the French king from his fears of Spain, enabled
him to subdue all factions at home, and thereby to bring himself
75   into a condition of not standing in need of any of them, and from
thence, has proceeded the persecution that has since been and still
is in that nation against the reformed there; so that Oliver, instead
of advancing the reformed interest has by an error in his politics,
been the author of destroying it.
      Slingsby Bethel, *The World's Mistake in Oliver Cromwell*
      (1668), pp 4–5

(*c*)

TO

HIS HIGHNESS OLIVER CROMWELL.

80   MAY IT PLEASE YOUR HIGHNESS,
      How I have spent some hours of the leisure your Highness hath
been pleased to give me this following paper will give your
Highness an account. How you will please to interpret it I cannot
tell; but I can with confidence say, my intention in it is to procure
85   your Highness that justice nobody yet does you, and to let the
people see the longer they defer it the greater injury they do both
themselves and you. To your Highness justly belongs the honour
of dying for the people; and it cannot choose but be unspeakable
consolation to you in the last moments of your life to consider
90   with how much benefit to the world you are like to leave it. It is
then only, my Lord, the titles you now usurp will be truly yours;
you will then be indeed the deliverer of your country, and free it
from a bondage little inferior to that from which Moses delivered
his. You will then be that true reformer which you would be
95   thought. Religion shall be then restored, liberty asserted, and
Parliaments have those privileges they have fought for. We shall
then hope that other laws will have place besides those of the

sword, and that justice shall be otherwise defined than the will and
pleasure of the strongest; and we shall then hope men will keep
100 oaths again, and not have the necessity of being false and perfidious
to preserve themselves, and be like their rulers. All this we hope
from your Highness's happy expiration, who are the true father of
your country; for while you live we can call nothing ours, and it is
from your death that we hope for our inheritances. Let this
105 consideration arm and fortify your Highness's mind against the
fears of death, and the terrors of your evil conscience, that the
good you will do by your death will something balance the evils
of your life. And if in the black catalogue of high malefactors few
can be found that have lived more to the affliction and disturbance
110 of mankind than your Highness hath done, yet your greatest
enemies will not deny but there are likewise as few that have
expired more to the universal benefit of mankind than your
Highness is like to do. To hasten this great good is the chief end
of my writing this paper; and if it have the effects I hope it will,
115 your Highness will quickly be out of the reach of men's malice,
and your enemies will only be able to wound you in your memory,
which strokes you will not feel. That your Highness may be
speedily in this security is the universal wish of your grateful
country. This is the desire and prayer of the good and of the bad,
120 and it may be is the only thing wherein all sects and factions do
agree in their devotions, and is our only common prayer. But
amongst all that put in their requests and supplications for your
Highness's speedy deliverance from all earthly troubles, none is
more assiduous nor more fervent than he who, with the rest of the
125 nation, hath the honour to be,
May it please your Highness,
Your Highness's present slave and vassal,

W.A.★

★*i.e.* William Allen – the pseudonym Sexby assumed.
Edward Sexby *Killing Noe Murder* (Amsterdam, 1657),
reprinted in A. F. Pollard (ed.), Political Pamphlets (London,
1897), pp 33–6

Questions

a   Why did Parliament approve the Navigation Act (document c),
and did this statute make war with the United Provinces
virtually unavoidable?
b   Assess Bethel's attack on the Protector's foreign policy (document d).
c   For what reasons were former radicals and allies disillusioned
with the Protectorate?

VIII Towards a New Model of Government: the Protectorate of Oliver Cromwell

Introduction

The dissolution of Barebone's Parliament caused as little unrest as the demise of the Rump a few months earlier. The situation in December 1653, however, was very different from that of April, for an alternative constitution was now waiting. There is little reason to doubt the contemporary belief that this Instrument of Government (document A) was largely the work of John Lambert and that he and other officers of the Council had been behind the walk-out on the final day of Barebone's. It is equally clear that this was not a hurried piece of constitution-making. Lambert had almost certainly been drafting the instrument for several weeks prior to its formal adoption by Cromwell on 16 December, but its origins go back somewhat further. Some elements are derived from the 1641 legislation of the Long Parliament; others from the Nineteen Propositions and the mixed monarchy theories of 1642–3; others from the 1647 Heads of the Proposals; yet others from the Rump's abortive Bill for a new representative. The Instrument was nothing if not eclectic.

Clause XXX of the Instrument, however, also suggests that the constitution was shaped by expediency. Under this provision the Protector issued over eighty ordinances, the vast majority of which were confirmed by the Second Protectorate Parliament. It is not surprising that much of this early legislation should be concerned with the immediate problems of the new regime since that was the intention of the framers of the clause. The ordinance for repealing the Engagement, for example, widened the potential basis of support in that it gave non-republicans the opportunity for state service. Similarly, the ordinance regulating the treason laws of the same date (19 January 1654) was an obvious attempt to secure the Protectorate against those who endeavoured 'to stir up or raise force against the Protector or the present government'. Even those seemingly innocuous ordinances prohibiting cock-matches, duels and horse-racing (document B,a) should be seen primarily as law and order measures rather than (as Firth did) an attempt at a reformation of manners. What is more remarkable than these security ordinances is that Cromwell should have seized this opportunity to institute some long overdue reforms. The ordinance of 21 June 1654, which brought the public revenues into one treasury, and instituted other reforms (document B,b), was the most important of the twenty-odd financial ordinances. The most significant of the six religious ordinances were those establishing 'Triers' and 'Ejectors', thereby implementing clause XXV of the Instrument. Another ordinance attempted to ensure that the church made a better use of its resources through the uniting of parishes (document B,c). A further attempt was also made to reform and reconstruct Chancery 'to the end that all proceedings touching relief in Equity . . . may be [concluded] with less trouble, expense and delay than heretofore'. Such were some of the important reforming ordinances of Cromwell's first Protectorate. Many of these reforms were unoriginal – the church settlement, for example, was based on Owen's 1652 scheme for ecclesiastical reform, and chancery reform, as we have seen (pp 125–6 above), had been in the offing ever since the Hale Commission; a number, such as the security and financial measures, were determined by expediency rather than any lofty blue-print for social and administrative action; most were successful only in the short term. But, as Professor Woolrych has observed, 'the question is not whether these measures were brilliantly original or effective; the point is that they were attempted'.

The Instrument of Government not only gave constitutional authority for Cromwell's ordinances but also provided for the meeting of a parliament by stipulating when, how often and for how long it should meet, as well as how it was to be composed, elected and summoned. Indeed, it is possible that the original instrument provided for a parliament to meet in February and that it was Cromwell's own decision to defer its meeting until 3 September. The franchise provisions of the Instrument, which included a 50 per cent reduction in borough seats and a similar increase in county seats, produced an even more intractable parliament than Barebone's. Within little more than a week of Cromwell's optimistic opening address of 4 September (document C,a), he was forced to speak to the assembly again in uncompromising terms (document C,b). This made little difference to the obstructionist temper of its members, who soon devised a new constitution with Parliament as its lynch-pin. Cromwell's dissolution of the parliament on the earliest day possible under the Instrument (the 140th), having interpreted clause VIII as five lunar rather than calendar months, is not to be wondered at.

The Protector's dissolution of his first parliament also marked a shift in policy towards the localities. Hitherto, Cromwell had attempted, through a conservative appeal to the moderate gentry, to implement a policy of settlement whereby the Protectorate was

to be peacefully reconciled with the old order. The apparent
irreconcilability of his moderate critics in Parliament, together with
the outbreak of Penruddock's rebellion in March and the opposition
to his taxation ordinances by one George Coney (a latter day
Hampden), determined Cromwell to abandon conciliation and
adopt Lambert's and Desborough's policy of coercion. The policy
was finally implemented in October 1655 through the Major-
Generals' scheme, whereby England and Wales were divided into
eleven military districts, each under a major-general armed with
explicit instructions and extensive powers (document D,a). The
rule by major-generals (October 1655–January 1657) was the only
real innovation of the Protectorate. It was neither new to have
military commanders in charge of particular areas, nor novel to
have penal levies imposed on political enemies or revenue levied
on a county assigned to that area for its military uses. The
combination of responsibilities exercised by the major-generals,
however, together with their co-option onto the commissions of
the peace in each of their respective counties represented a radical
new departure in the history of local government. The Protectorate's aims of achieving local uniformity, revitalising local
government and pushing through godly reform were understand-
able and laudable. As we can see, moreover, from these two sample
letters (documents D,b, and c), the major-generals were a far cry
from the tyrannical 'bashaws' and 'satraps' of folk-legend. In the
early months, at least, they gained some support from the local
gentry and achieved a modicum of reform, although their precise
influence is difficult to measure in that it is impossible to distinguish
their impact from the efforts of godly magistrates active throughout
the 1650s. But what no one can deny is that the major-generals
became unpopular, not only in regions like Wales and the Marches
where there was a relatively high proportion of Royalists per head
of population, but throughout the country. For they represented a
foreign system forcibly grafted on to a voluntary system of local
government, and this made them the natural enemies of the country
gentry, who in any case were usually their social superiors. Their
unpopularity is illustrated in the attitudes of the country gentry at
Westminster during the second Protectorate parliament.
Cromwell's defence of them in his opening speech to that parliament
fell on many deaf ears, and on Christmas Day 1656, numerous
country gentlemen roundly condemned Desborough's attempt to
renew the decimation tax. Little more than a month later the new
Decimation Bill was rejected by thirty-one votes. The Lord
Protector abandoned the experiment and returned to his former
policy of appeasing the traditional rulers of the countryside.

   Cromwell had bowed to political necessity, but it had certainly
not been his intention to dispense with the services of the major-
generals. Indeed, it was the major-generals' confidence that they

could decisively influence the composition of the new assembly that persuaded the Protector to call another parliament, a year before it was necessary to do so under the terms of the Instrument, rather than resort to dubious extra-parliamentary means (as in the 1630s) to raise money to prosecute the war with Spain. The major-generals, however, overestimated their ability to secure a compliant assembly, and many enemies of the Protectorate (crypto-Royalists as well as out-and-out republicans) were returned. Nevertheless, a number of these MPs were forcibly excluded by the Council and some voluntarily withdrew in protest against this executive action, so at least a quarter of the House consisted of government supporters. The prospects for the government, therefore, as Cromwell exhorted the new Parliamentarians to 'quit themselves like men' in both establishing a reformation and providing security against Spain, were by no means intolerable. Indeed the war concentrated minds wonderfully and relations between the Protec-tor and this parliament were initially much better than with the previous one. The persecution of the Quaker, James Naylor, directly contradicted Cromwell's opening pleas for religious toler-ation and prompted him to ask the Speaker 'the grounds and reasons' for the Commons proceedings against him, but Cromwell refused to veto a hostile measure which reintroduced the penal laws. By mid-November 1656 the Protector was congratulating the House for its 'many good laws' and the very day after the decimation tax was rejected the parliament voted £400,000 for 'a just and necessary war with Spain'. Cromwell realised that the sacrifice of the major-generals was the price that had to be paid for maintaining Parliamentary support.

In any case Cromwell was not averse to civilianising the Protecto-rate: it had become clear to him that the Instrument had served its usefulness and was preventing a general recognition of the new regime from the rest of the political nation. To an increasing number of country gentlemen, lawyers, civilian officials, merchants and financiers, a monarchical settlement was the only means of stabilising the country – a need which became ever more apparent as the Protector's health deteriorated and the plots against him increased. Cromwell himself was not philosophically opposed to kingship. As early as (November ?) 1652 he had asked Bulstrode Whitelocke whether 'if a man should take upon him to be king' a satisfactory settlement could be arrived at. Whitelocke had then argued that the 'remedy would be worse than the disease', but by the time of the second Protectorate parliament he had changed his mind, and it was Whitelocke who headed the committee which, after the title had been approved by a large Commons majority (123 to 62 votes) urged Cromwell to take the Crown. On 30 March Cromwell asked Parliament for time to find 'counsel of God and of my own heart' to consider 'the greatest weight of anything that was ever laid upon a man', and for the next six weeks he pondered the offer. Some indication of the agonised state of his mind may be gathered from his tortuous, cryptic and evasive speeches (two of which are produced here : documents E, a, 1–2) to the parliamentary committee. His categorical 'No' on 8 May (document E, a, 3) put an end 'to this great weighty business'.

It did not, however, put an end to the demand for a new form of government for the title was but one part – albeit the most contentious one – of an elaborate constitutional package that had found favour with all but the most intransigent of the military officers and godly elite. The Humble Petition and Advice (document E, b), the fourth and last of the Interregnum settlements, was adopted on 25 May in place of the discredited Instrument of Government. By 21 June some minor alterations, all of which had been suggested by the Protector himself some two months earlier, had been embodied in an Additional Petition and Advice. His Highness, Oliver Cromwell, was then installed as Protector for the second time. This ceremony, however, was rather different from the first one. Cromwell, gorgeously attired in a 'costly mantle . . . lined with ermines', and seated on an elevated throne under a 'prince-like canopy of state' received from Sir Thomas Widdington, the Speaker, in the name of Parliament, a purple robe, a Bible, a sword and a sceptre 'of massy gold' – everything in fact that was symbolic of the authority of kingship except the Crown. As Cromwell took the oath of office for the last time, he was a sovereign prince in all but name.

A The Instrument of Government, 1653

The government of the Commonwealth of England, Scotland and Ireland, and the dominions thereunto belonging [16 December 1653]

I. That the supreme legislative authority of the Commonwealth of England . . . [etc.] shall be and reside in one person, and the people
5 assembled in parliament; the style of which person shall be, 'The Lord Protector of the Commonwealth of England, Scotland and Ireland.'
II. That the exercise of the chief magistracy, and the administration of the government over the said countries and dominions, and the
10 people thereof, shall be in the Lord Protector, assisted with a Council, the number whereof shall not exceed twenty-one nor be less than thirteen.
III. That all writs, process[es], commissions, patents, grants and other things, which now run in the name and style of the Keepers
15 of the Liberties of England by Authority of Parliament, shall run in the name and style of the Lord Protector, from whom for the

future shall be derived all magistracy and honours in these three nations; and [he] shall have the power of pardons (except in case of murders and treason) and benefit of all forfeitures for the public
20 use; and shall govern the said countries and dominions in all things by the advice of the Council, and according to these presents, and the laws.

IV. That the Lord Protector, the parliament sitting, shall dispose and order the militia and forces, both by sea and land, for the peace
25 and good of the three nations, by consent of parliament; and that the Lord Protector, with the advice and consent of the major part of the Council, shall dispose and order the militia for the ends aforesaid in the intervals of parliament.

V. That the Lord Protector, by the advice aforesaid, shall direct
30 in all things concerning the keeping and holding of a good correspondency with foreign kings, princes and states; and also, with the consent of the major part of the Council, have the power of war and peace.

VI. That the laws shall not be altered, suspended, abrogated, or
35 repealed, nor any new law made, nor any tax, charge or imposition laid upon the people, but by common consent in parliament (save only as is expressed in the 30th article).

VII. That there shall be a parliament summoned to meet at Westminster upon the third day of September, 1654, and that
40 successively a parliament shall be summoned once in every third year, to be accounted from the dissolution of the present parliament [of 1654].

VIII. That neither the parliament to be next summoned, nor any successive parliaments, shall during the time of five months, to be
45 accounted from the day of their first meeting, be adjourned, prorogued or dissolved, without their own consent. . . .

XXIII. That the Lord Protector, with the advice of the major part of the Council, shall at any other time than is before expressed, when the necessities of the state shall require it, summon parliaments
50 in manner before expressed, which shall not be adjourned, prorogued, or dissolved without their own consent during the first three months of their sitting; and in case of future war with any foreign state a parliament shall be forthwith summoned for their advice concerning the same.

55 XXIV. That all bills agreed unto by the parliament shall be presented to the Lord Protector for his consent, and in case he shall not give his consent thereto within twenty days after they shall be presented to him, or give satisfaction to the parliament within the time limited, that then upon declaration of the parliament that the
60 Lord Protector hath not consented nor given satisfaction, such bills shall pass into and become law, although he shall not give his consent thereunto; provided such bills contain nothing in them contrary to the matters contained in these presents.

XXV. That [14 persons named] or any seven of them, shall be a
65 Council for the purposes expressed in this writing and upon the
death or other removal of any of them the parliament shall nominate
six persons of ability, integrity, and fearing God, for every one
that is dead or removed; out of which the major part of the Council
shall elect two and present them to the Lord Protector, of which
70 he shall elect one. And in case the parliament shall not nominate
within twenty days after notice given unto them thereof, the major
part of the Council shall nominate three as aforesaid to the Lord
Protector, who out of them shall supply the vacancy. . . .
XX. That the raising of money for defraying the charge of the
75 present extraordinary forces, both at sea and land in respect of the
present wars, shall be by consent of parliament and not otherwise;
save only that the Lord Protector, with the consent of the major
part of the Council, for preventing the disorders and dangers which
might otherwise fall out both by sea and land, shall have power,
80 until the meeting of the first parliament, to raise money for the
purposes aforesaid; and also to make laws and ordinances for the
peace and welfare of these nations, where it shall be necessary,
which shall be binding and in force until order shall be taken in
parliament concerning the same.
85 XXXI. That the lands, tenements, rents, royalties, jurisdictions
and hereditaments which remain yet unsold or undisposed of by
act or ordinance of parliament, belonging to the Commonwealth
. . . shall be vested in the Lord Protector to hold, to him and his
successors Lords Protectors of these nations, and shall not be
90 alienated but by consent in parliament. . . .
XXXIII. That Oliver Cromwell, Captain General, . . . shall be,
and is hereby declared to be, Lord Protector. . . .
XXXIV. That the chancellor, keeper or commissioners of the
Great Seal, the treasurer, admiral, chief governors of Ireland and
95 Scotland, and the chief justices of both the Benches, shall be chosen
by the approbation of parliament, and in the intervals of parliament
by the approbation of the major part of the Council, to be afterwards
approved by the Parliament.

> J. P. Kenyon (ed.), *The Stuart Constitution* (Cambridge,
> 1986), pp 308–11

Questions

a How original was this Instrument? (Refer to particular clauses
of the constitution.)
b Examine the respective powers under this Instrument of the
executive and legislature.
c How far did this constitution signify 'a conservative reaction'?

d What was the importance of clause XXX?

e Why, in practice, did it not provide (as Nedham, one of its defenders, hoped it might) 'a seasonable means . . . of peace and settlement to this distracted nation'?

B Cromwell's Ordinances, 1654

(*a*) *Ordinances prohibiting cock-fighting, duels and horse-racing*

(**1**)

Whereas the public meetings and assemblies of people together in divers parts of this nation, under pretence of matches for cock-fighting, are by experience found to tend many times to the disturbance of the public peace, and are commonly accompanied

5   with gaming, drinking, swearing, quarreling, and other dissolute practices, to the dishonour of God, and do often produce the ruin of persons and their families. For prevention thereof, be it ordained by his Highness the Lord Protector, by and with the advice and consent of his Council, that from henceforth there shall be no

10   public or set meetings or assemblies of any persons within England or Wales, upon matches made for cock-fighting; and that every such meeting and assembly of people for the end and purposes aforesaid, is hereby declared to be an unlawful assembly, and shall be so adjudged, deemed and taken to be, and punished; and all

15   sheriffs, justices of the peace, mayors, bayliffs, constables and headboroughs within their several counties, cities, limits and jurisdictions, are hereby required to suppress, hinder and disperse all such meetings and assemblies.

Firth and Rait, op cit, II, pp 861, 31 March 1654

(**2**)

Whereas the fighting of duels upon private quarrels is a thing in it self displeasing to God, unbecoming Christians, and contrary to

20   all good order and government. And forasmuch as the same is a growing evil in this nation, for preventing whereof there is a present necessity of some more severe law than hitherto hath been made in that behalf, be it therefore ordained by His Highness the

25   Lord Protector of the Commonwealth of England, Scotland and Ireland, etc. by and with the advice and consent of his Council, that if any person or persons of what degree or quality soever within this Commonwealth, shall from and after the first day of July next ensuing, by message, word, writing, or any other way,

30   either challenge or cause to be challenged any other person to fight any combat or duel, or shall accept any such challenge; every such person who shall make, send or accept any such challenge, and every person who shall knowingly carry the same, shall be

committed to prison, without bail or mainprize, there to remain
35 for the space of six months next after his commitment, and from
thence until the next general quarter sessions of the peace, or
general assize and gaol-delivery to be held for that county, city or
town corporate, where before his enlargement out of prison, he
shall enter into recognizance with two or more sufficient sureties,
40 such as the court shall approve, to be of good behaviour during
the space of one whole year then next ensuing. . . . And it is
further ordained by the authority aforesaid, that if any person or
persons shall from and after the publication hereof, actually fight
any duel or combat, whereupon death shall ensue, the same shall
45 be deemed, adjudged and taken to be murder . . . [otherwise
banishment for life, for fighting or assisting in a duel].

Ibid, pp 937–8, 29 June 1654

(3)
Whereas it hath pleased the Lord to discover and bring to light
divers mischievous plots and designs which have been lately
contrived by the enemies of the peace and welfare of this Com-
50 monwealth, who are ready to lay hold of all opportunities for
instilling such their purposes into the minds of others who are
peaceably affected, and to take advantage of public meetings, and
concourse of people at horse-races, and other sports, to carry on
such their pernicious designs, to the disturbance of the public peace,
55 and endangering new troubles. For prevention thereof, it is thought
fit at this time to ordain, and be it ordained by his Highness the
Lord Protector by and with the consent of his council, that from
and after the sixth day of July, one thousand, six hundred fifty and
four, for and during the space of six months from thence next
60 ensuing, there shall be no horse-races, nor meetings of any persons
whatsoever upon pretence or colour of any such horse-races in any
place within England or Wales. And that all and every person and
persons who shall, from and after the said sixth day of July for and
during the time aforesaid, appoint any horse-race, or shall assemble
65 and meet together, upon or by colour of any appointment of an
horse-race, or shall be present at any such horse-race shall forfeit
and lose all and every the horse and horses which they shall bring
with them, or send unto such place or meeting. . . .

Ibid, pp 941–2, 4 July 1654

Questions

a   What evidence is there that the primary object for the passing
of these ordinances was not a 'reformation of manners'?

b What sanctions were to be imposed against those who broke them?

c Why were they likely to have been enforced ineffectively?

(b) Financial reform: ordinance of 21 June 1654

Whereas upon consideration had, it is found necessary that the
70 moneys and other payments arising by the public revenues of this
Commonwealth, or which shall be raised for the uses thereof,
should be paid into one treasury, to the end the same may from
time to time the more readily be employed and disposed as the
occasions of the Commonwealth shall require, that the charges
75 arising by the multiplicity of treasuries and receipts may be reduced,
and the persons who shall be employed in receiving the same, be
brought to a due account. And whereas also the receipt of the
public exchequer at Westminster is judged most fit and convenient
for that purpose.
80   Be it ordained by his Highness the Lord Protector, by and with
the advice and consent of his Council, that from and after the four
and twentieth day of June, one thousand six hundred fifty and
four, the said receipt shall be, and shall be called, the Receipt of
the Exchequer of his Highness the Lord Protector, and shall be
85 kept and executed in the usual and accustomed places, method,
manner and way of Receipt of Exchequer as formerly. And that
all and every sum and sums of money, and other payments which
upon and after the said [date] . . . shall be received or taken, or
shall become due or payable to, or for the use of his Highness the
90 Lord Protector and the Commonwealth . . . shall be paid unto the
said Receipt of the Exchequer. . . .For the payment of which
moneys, and every of them, tallies levied and allowed according
to the usual and accustomed course of the Exchequer, with the
alteration of the words upon the tally from Latin, to English, shall
95 be to every person and persons, bodies politic and corporate,
so paying, and their successors . . . sufficient acquittance and
discharge.
    And be it further ordained and declared . . . that . . . the moneys
. . . shall be received and kept, and charged and accounted for, and
100 also issued and paid out . . . by such person and persons . . . as
his Highness the Lord Protector shall from time to time, by letters
patent under the Great Seal, constitute and appoint. . . . And shall
have and receive for and in respect of his and their execution of,
and attendance in and upon his and their said offices and places
105 respectively, such moderate fees, wages, rewards and allowances
only, as his Highness the Lord Protector, with the advice and
consent of his Council, by the said letters patents, shall think fit to
limit and appoint.

And be it further ordained by the authority aforesaid, that if any
110 person . . . shall at any time directly or indirectly upon any pretence
whatsoever, by colour of such his or their office or employment,
take or receive any other or greater fee or fees, sum or sums of
money, or other gift, reward or gratuity whatsoever, that then all
and every such person and persons, officer and officers shall upon
115 proof or confession thereof before his Highness' Council, forfeit
and lose his and their place and places, office and offices; and the
letters patents in that behalf shall from thenceforth become void.
And all and every person . . . so offending, shall also forfeit and
pay treble the value of such fee or fees, sum or sums of money,
120 gift, reward or gratuity unto such person and persons, as shall sue
for the same by bill, plaint or information in any court of
record. . . .

But as to the issuing of the money mentioned in the nine and
twentieth article of the government of the Commonwealth . . . the
125 same shall not be granted but by consent of Parliament, or of the
Lord Protector and major part of the Council, in the intervals of
Parliaments. . . .

Ibid, pp 918–21, 21 June 1654

(c) *The Church Settlement*

(1)

The Religious Provisions of the Instrument of Government

XXXV. That the Christian religion, as contained in the Scriptures,
130 be held forth and recommended as the public profession of these
nations; and that as soon as may be a provision, less subject to
scruple and contention, and more certain than the present, be made
for the encouragement and maintenance of able and painful teachers,
for instructing the people, and for discovery and confutation of
135 error, heresy and whatever is contrary to sound doctrine. And that
until such provision be made the present maintenance shall not be
taken away nor impeached.

XXXVI. That to the Public Profession held forth none shall be
compelled by penalties or otherwise; but that endeavours be used
140 to win them by sound doctrine and the example of a good
conversation.

XXXVII. That such as profess faith in God by Jesus Christ (though
differing in judgment from the doctrine, worship or discipline
publicly held forth) shall not be restrained from, but shall be
145 protected in, the profession of the Faith, and exercise of their
religion; so as they abuse not this liberty to the civil injury of
others, and to the actual disturbance of the public peace on their

parts. Provided this liberty be not extended to popery nor Prelacy,
nor to such as, under the profession of Christ, hold forth and
150 practice licentiousness.

    Kenyon (ed), *Stuart Constitution* (1986), pp 312–13

(2)
*An Ordinance for the better maintenance and encouragement of Preaching
Ministers, and for uniting of Parishes,* [2 September, 1654].

Whereas many parishes in this nation are without the constant and
powerful preaching of the gospel, through want of competent
155 maintenance and encouragement unto able and godly ministers in
such places; some parishes in regard of their smallness, and of their
propinquity and neighbourhood, and the situation of their churches
or places of meeting, being very convenient to be united and other
parishes are so populous, and of so great an extent, that all
160 the inhabitants thereof cannot with conveniency resort to their
respective parish churches. To the end some provision may be
made herein, and the public maintenance set apart for ministers,
and other pious uses, may be managed, improved and distributed
for the future, so as may be most for the advancement of the
165 gospel, and encouragement of public preachers in all the places of
this Commonwealth; and that the augmentations granted or which
shall be granted out of the same, may be more orderly issued and
certainly paid, and the revenue not overcharged . . . [trustees are
to be appointed] to make any unions of two parishes or more into
170 one; and the whole ecclesiastical revenues, tithes and profits
belonging to the said parishes so united, to be supplied for a
provision for one godly and painful minister to preach in such of
the said parish churches, where such union shall be made, as they
the said trustees shall so judge most convenient as aforesaid. . . .

    Firth and Rait, op cit, II, pp 1000–3

Questions

a How was clause XXXV of the Instrument implemented?
b How tolerant were the religious clauses of the instrument?
c Comment on: 'such as, under the profession Christ, hold forth
   and practice licentiousness' (lines 149–50).
d Examine the religious bias of the authors of these documents.
e What do they suggest was wrong with the state of 'Christian
   religion'?

C Cromwell's Addresses to the First Protectorate Parliament; 4, 12 September 1654

(1)

A remedy hath been applied [to the ills of the nation] . . . this government. . . . hath desired to reform the laws . . . and for that end, it hath called together persons (without reflection) of as great ability and as great integrity as are in these nations, to consider
5   how the laws might be made plain and short, and less chargeable to the people, how to lessen expense for the good of the nation. . . . The Chancery hath been reformed, and I hope to the just satisfaction of all good men. . . . It hath endeavoured to put a stop to that heady way . . . of every man making himself a minister and a
10   preacher. It hath endeavoured to settle a way for the approbation of men of piety and ability for the discharge of that work. . . . It hath taken care, we hope, for the expulsion of all those who may be judged any way unfit for this work, who are scandalous, and who are the common scorn and contempt of that administration.
15   One thing more this government hath done. It hath been instrumental to call a free Parliament, which, blessed be God, we see here this day. . . .

    You have now (though it be not the first in time) peace with Sweden, an honourable peace. . . . You have a peace with the
20   Dane, a state that lay contiguous to that part of this island which hath given us the most trouble. . . . You have a peace with the Dutch. . . . And I think it was as desirable and as acceptable to the spirit of this nation as any one thing that lay before us. . . . As a peace with the Protestant states hath much security in it, so it
25   hath as much of honour and of assurance to the Protestant interest abroad, without which no assistance can be given thereunto. . . . You have a peace likewise with . . . Portugal . . . a peace that your merchants make us believe is of good concernment to their trade. . . . We are upon a treaty with France. . . . And I daresay
30   that there is not a nation in Europe, but they are very willing to ask a good understanding with you. . . .

    We are thus far through the mercy of God. We have cause to take notice of it, that we are not brought into misery; but, as I said before, a door of hope [is] open. And I may say this to you; if the
35   Lord's blessing and his presence go along with the management of affairs at this meeting, you will be enabled to put the top-stone to this work, and make the nation happy. . . . And therefore I wish that you may go forward, and not backward, and that you may have the blessings of God upon your endeavours. It's one of
40   the great ends of calling this Parliament, that this ship of the Commonwealth may be brought into a safe harbour, which I assure you it will not well be without your counsel and advice. . . .

    Abbott, *Writings and Speeches of Cromwell*, III, pp 434–42

(2)

. . . It is true, there are some things in the Establishment that are fundamental, and some things are not so, but are circumstantial.
45 Of such, no question but I shall easily agree to vary or leave out, as I shall be convinced by reason. Some things are fundamentals, about which I shall deal plainly with you; they may not be parted with, but will (I trust) be delivered over to posterity, as being the fruits of our blood and travail.
50 The government by a single person and parliament is a fundamental; it is the *esse*, it is constitutive. And for the person, though I may seem to plead for myself, yet I do not . . . I plead for this nation, and all honest men therein who have borne their testimony as aforesaid, and not for myself. . . . That parliaments should not
55 make themselves perpetual is a fundamental. Of what assurance is a law to prevent so great an evil, if it lie in one or the same legislator to unlaw it again? . . . Is not liberty of conscience in religion a fundamental? So long as there is liberty of conscience for the supreme magistrate to exercise his conscience in erecting what form
60 of church government he is satisfied he should set up, why should not he give it to others? . . .

Another, which I had forgotten, is the militia. That's judged a fundamental, if anything be so. That it should be well and equally placed, is very necessary. For put the absolute power of the militia
65 into one without a check, what doth it? I pray you, what doth your check upon your perpetual parliaments, if it be wholly stripped of this? . . .

Give me leave to say that there is very little power, none but what is co-ordinate, in the supreme officer, and yet enough in him
70 that hath the chief government. In that particular he is bound in strictness by the parliament, out of parliament by the Council, that do as absolutely bind him as the parliament, when parliament is sitting.

For that of money, I told you some things are circumstantials.
75 To have two hundred thousand pounds, to defray civil officers, to pay the judges, and other officers, defraying the charges of the Council in sending their embassies, in keeping intelligence, and doing that that's necessary, and for supporting the Governor-in-Chief – all this is by the Instrument supposed and intended, but it
80 is not of the *esse* so much, and so limited. As to so many soldiers, 30,000 – twenty thousand foot and ten thousand horse – if the spirits of men be composed, five thousand horse and ten thousand foot may serve. These are things between the Chief Officer and the parliament, to be moderated as occasion shall offer.
85 So there are many other circumstantial things, which are not like the laws of the Medes and Persians. But the things which shall be necessary to deliver over to posterity, these should be unalterable, else every succeeding parliament will be disputing to change and

alter the government, and we shall be as often brought into
90 confusion as we have parliaments, and so make our remedy our
disease. The Lord's providence . . . and [our] better judgment will
give occasion for the ordering of things for the best interest of the
people; and those things are the matter of consideration between
you and me. . . .
        Ibid, pp 458–60

Questions

a How convincing do you find Cromwell's vindication of (i) his
   domestic policy (ii) his foreign policy?
b Account for the change in tone between the first and second
   speeches.
c Discuss Cromwell's distinction between things 'fundamental'
   and 'circumstantial'.
d Comment on:
   (i) And for the person, though I may seem to plead for myself,
        yet I do not' (lines 51–2)
   (ii) there is very little power, none but what is co-ordinate, in
        the supreme officer' (lines 68–9).
e Why was the first Protectorate Parliament unable to steer the
   'ship of the Commonwealth . . . into a safe harbour' (lines 40–
   1)?

D The Rule of the Major-Generals, October 1655–January 1657

(*a*)
Whereas the old malignant and popish enemies of this Commonwealth, after an Act of Oblivion, and many other graces and
favours granted to them, have entered into a design and combination
to involve this nation in a new and bloody war, and had by their
5   correspondencies with one another, and with other discontented
parties and humours amongst ourselves, brought their wicked
intentions to such maturity that a general insurrection and rebellion
was by them resolved upon through the whole land, and in many
places thereof executed; which if it had not pleased God in mercy
10 to this poor nation timely to suppress might have proved a
long and bloody war to the destruction and desolation of the
Commonwealth, especially considering that they had invited and
engaged foreigners to invade us at the same time, contracting with
them upon their success to deliver some of our sea towns and forts
15 into their hands and possession. . . . And whereas we have upon

these grounds been necessitated in this time of imminent danger for the safety of the Commonwealth as well against foreign invasions as home-bred insurrections and rebellions to raise a militia of horse of the well-affected in the several counties of England and
20 Wales . . . And there being a necessity to appoint a Commander-in-Chief over the forces aforesaid and such others as shall be raised or assigned to be in those counties, who may lead, discipline, and conduct them as there shall be occasion for the good and safety of the nation. And we, reposing entire trust and confidence in your
25 approved fidelity, wisdom and circumspection, have by and with the advice of our Council assigned, made, constituted, and ordained, and by these presents do assign, make, constitute and ordain you to be Major General and Commander-in-Chief within the said counties of Northampton, Huntington, Rutland and Bedford. . . .

Abbot, *Writings and Speeches of Cromwell*, III, pp 849–50, Col. William Boterler's commission, October 1655

(**b**)
30 I have nothing to plead as excuse, that I wrote not to you since the 8th instant, save that I was constantly attending the commissioners in Norfolk, who have sat *de die in diem* for the carrying on the service desired of them; and I am confident none in England will appear to be more forward. As also was I desirous to see such
35 progress in the work, especially in the tax, as that the whole might be perfected in time. Indeed, such acceptance had this affair in the hearts of all, that it carried its conviction with it, honest men encouraging one another in the action, and the delinquent not one word to say why aught should be remitted him that every tongue
40 must confess it was of the Lord, who is a righteous God in the execution of his judgements; and when his hand is lifted up, he shall not only make them, though most unwilling, to see, but also make them ashamed for their envy to his people. The commissioners did the most of them meet every day for ten days together till
45 Friday last. . . . They have given summons to almost all [who] will be qualified to bear any part of the charge; and the greatest part of them have they assessed, and that with the greatest care they could possibly, exceeding in their assessing the books of sequestration. That which remains there to be done will not be
50 found to be much; so that I fear in that county there will not be enough by a great deal raised to pay the three troops therein. . . . They have [also] considered and acted upon the second head of his Highness' and Council's orders in the apprehending and securing of Mr. Cleveland, a most desperate enemy to God and good men,
55 and one Mr. Sherman, a most malignant episcopal minister. . . . As yet we hear nothing of the Registrar's office at London, to which so much of our work relates. . . . The lists of sheriffs you sent will by no means hold proportion with those qualifications you

intimate. There is but one of all the four counties I have relation
60 to, who is like to answer expectation. . . . This week I hope to set
the wheels agoing in this county [Suffolk], and the next in
Cambridgeshire. . . .

[Postscript] I most humbly thank your honour for the copies of
the letters of my fellow labourers in this work. I hope you'll
65 not judge me of neglect, because I have not communicated the
instructions to the gentlemen of so many counties as they, rather
judging it most for your service to perfect what possibly may be
as I go.

Birch (ed.), *State Papers of John Thurloe*, IV, pp 216–17,
Haynes to Thurloe, 19 Nov. 1655 (from Bury St Edmunds)

(*c*)
. . . We have had meetings in the several counties, and have
70 proceeded to the extra-ordinary tax upon divers of the delinquents
of greatest estates, and have sent out our orders for the rest to
appear before us to be proceeded against accordingly. I cannot but
observe a visible hand of God going along with us in this work, as
well as in raising up the hearts and spirits of good men to be active
75 therein, as also the unexpected submission and subjection of them
we have to deal with; so much that truly I have not heard of one
man of them, that any way disputes or complains against the
justice of those orders and instructions we act upon. We have in
Staffordshire taxed as many as amounts to about thirteen or fourteen
80 hundred pounds *per annum* and have discovered about one hundred
pounds *per annum* in lands of Penruddock, who was in arms at
Salisbury. . . . In Cheshire we have taxed as many as amounted
to one thousand, five hundred pounds *per annum* and in Lancashire
about one thousand, one hundred pounds *per annum* and hope at
85 our next meetings to go through with the greatest part of the tax;
and in all the three counties we have put in execution the ordinance
for ejecting scandalous ministers and schoolmasters; and the last
Thursday sent orders for divers articles against and witnesses to
appear at our next meeting in this county of Lancaster. Many of
90 the delinquents in this county were papist-delinquents, and their
estates quite sold by the state, which will make us all much short
of what we expected. We have found out a considerable estate,
which we conceive is in John Wildman. We have seized and secured
the same to your Highness' use, and hope to find some more. I
95 am now taking security from disaffected persons in the several
counties. We are now proceeding against some considerable persons, which we conceive will fall under the first particular in your
Highness' orders and instructions. I find as many dangerous persons
in these counties, whose estates fall short of one hundred pounds
100 *per annum* as any of what quality soever. . . . We are about to
make some progress upon the rest of the particulars, especially

upon that of wandering idle persons, some being already apprehended. Our greatest want will be for a convenient place and guard
upon them. By the good help of God I doubt not but to give your
105 Highness a good account of the rest of the particulars you gave me
in charge. The Quakers abound much in these counties, to the
great disturbance of the best people. I have done and shall what I
can; but crave your Highness' further orders and instructions, how
to deal with them. . . .

> Ibid, pp 340–1, Worsley to the Protector, 24 Dec. 1655

Questions

a   Comment on the reasons given in Boteler's commission for the
establishment of the major-generals.
b   How extensive were their powers? Refer specifically to these
statements:
(i) 'they have [also] considered and acted upon the second head
of his Highness' and Council's orders' (lines 52–3);
(ii) 'the Registrar's office at London, to which so much of our
work relates' (lines 56–7);
(iii) 'the first particular in your Highness' orders and instructions' (lines 97–8);
(iv) 'the rest of the particulars, especially . . . that of wandering
idle persons' (lines 101–2).
c   Compare and contrast the progress of Haynes and Worsley in
their respective districts, in fulfilling their instructions. In what
ways are their reports likely to have distorted the truth?
d   What evidence is there of Haynes' and Worsley's religious
persuasions?
e   Comment on:
(i) 'Penruddock, who was in arms at Salisbury' (lines 81–2);
(ii) 'We have put in execution the ordinance for ejecting
scandalous ministers and schoolmasters' (lines 86–7);
(iii) 'Many of the delinquents in this county were papist-
delinquents, and their estates quite sold by the state' (lines
89–91);
(iv) 'A considerable estate which we conceive is in [the name
of] John Wildman' (lines 92–3);
(v) 'I find as many dangerous persons in these counties whose
estates fall short of one hundred pounds *per annum* as any
of what quality soever' (lines 98–100).
f   How do you reconcile the major-generals' own comments on
the levy of the decimation tax (lines 34–51; 69–85) with Edmund
Ludlow's observation that: 'The Major Generals carried things
with unheard of insolence in their several precincts, decimating

to extremity whom they pleased . . . and suffering none to escape their persecution'.

E   The Final Settlement

(a) Cromwell Declines the Crown, April–May 1657

(1)

You do necessitate my answer to be categorical, and you leave me without liberty of choice save as to all. I question not your wisdom of doing it, but think myself obliged to acquiesce in your determination. . . . But I must needs say, that what may be fit for
5   you to offer, may not be fit for me to undertake. . . . I ask of you this addition of the parliament's favour, love and indulgence unto me, that it be taken in tender part if I give such an answer as I find in my heart to give in this business, without urging many reasons for it, save such as are most obvious and most for my advantage
10   in answering, to wit, that I am not able for such a trust and charge. . . . I must say I have been able to attain no farther than this, that seeing that the way is hedged up so as it is for me (I cannot accept the things offered unless I accept all), I have not been able to find it my duty to God and you to undertake this charge
15   under that title. . . .

> Abbott, *Writings and Speeches of Cromwell*, IV, pp 445–6, speech to Lord Whitelocke and the Commons Committee, 3 April 1657

(2)

Truly though kingship be not a title, but a name of office that runs through the law, yet it is not so *ratione nominis*, from the reason of the name, but from what is signified. It is a name of office plainly implying the supreme authority; it is no more, nor can it be
20   stretched to more . . . signification goes to the thing and not to the name. . . . Why then there can be no more said but this. Why, this hath been said, this hath been the name fixed, under which the supreme authority has been known. Happily as it hath been fixed, so it may be unfixed. . . . And if it be so that you may, why then,
25   I say there is nothing of necessity in the argument, but consideration of the expedience of it. . . . I say undoubtedly, let us think what we will, what the parliament settles is that which will run through the law, and will lead the thread of government through the land . . . consent of the whole will, I say, be the needle that will lead
30   the thread through all, and I think no man will pretend right against it or wrong. And if so, then, under favour to me, I think all those arguments from the law are, as I said before, not necessary, but are to be understood upon the account of conveniency. . . .

. . . truly I should have urged one consideration more that I had forgotten; and that is, not only to urge from reason but from experience. . . . the supreme authority going in another name and under another title than king, why it has been complied with twice without it. . . . And truly I may say that almost universal obedience has been given from all ranks and sort of men to both. . . . And therefore I say, (under favour) these two experiences do manifestly show, that it is not a title, though so interwoven with the laws, that makes the law to have its free passage and do its office without interruption (as we think) but that if a parliament shall determine that another name shall run through the laws, I believe it may run with as free a passage as this. . . .

. . . I think from my very heart that in your settling of the peace and liberties of this nation, which cries as loud upon you as ever nation did, [you should labour] for somewhat that may beget a consistency, otherwise the nation will fall to pieces. And in that, as far as I can, I am ready to serve not as a king, but as a constable. . . .

I tell you there are such men in this nation that are godly, men of the same spirit, men that will not be beaten down with a carnal or worldly spirit while they keep their integrity. I deal plainly and faithfully with you, I cannot think that God would bless me in the undertaking of anything that would justly and with cause grieve them. . . . Truly the providence of God has laid this title aside providentially. *De facto* it is laid as aside and this not by sudden humour or passion; but it has been the issue of a great deliberation as ever was in a nation. It has been the issue of ten or twelve years' civil war, wherein much blood has been shed. . . . And God has seemed providentially not only to strike at the family but at the name. And as I said before, *de facto* it is blotted out, it is a thing cast out by Act of Parliament, it's a thing has been kept out to this day. . . . I would not seek to set up that that providence hath destroyed and laid in the dust, and I would not build Jericho again. . . .

Ibid, pp 467–74, speech to the same committee, 13 April 1657

(3)

I have only had the unhappiness – both in my conferences with your committees, and in the best thoughts I could take to myself – not to be convinced of the necessity of that thing, that hath been so often insisted on by you – to wit the title of King – as in itself so necessary, as it seems to be apprehended by yourselves. And yet I do, with all honour and respect to the judgment of a parliament, testify that . . . no private judgment is to lie in the balance with the judgment of parliament. But, in things that respect particular persons, every man that is to give an account to God of

his actions, he must, in some measure, be able to prove his own work, and to have an approbation of his own conscience of that, that he is to do, or to forbear . . . I lying under this consideration,
80 think it my duty to let you know . . . that, although I think the government doth consist of very excellent parts, in all but that one thing, the title, as to me, I should not be an honest man if I should not tell you, that I cannot accept of the government, nor undertake the trouble and charge of it: which I have a little more experimented
85 than everybody, what troubles and difficulties do befall men under such trusts, and in such undertakings. I say, I am persuaded to return this answer to you, that I cannot undertake this government with that title of king. And that is my answer to this great weighty business.

Ibid, pp 513–14, speech to the Commons, 8 May 1657

Questions

a Why did Cromwell regard that 'there is nothing of necessity' (line 25) in these arguments?
b For what *other* reasons did Cromwell decline the Crown?
c One historian has observed 'that neither the arguments of those who urged him to accept the Crown, nor his own replies, touched very closely on the real issues at stake'. What were the 'real issues'?
d Comment on:
   (i) 'You do necessitate my answer to be categorical; and leave me without a liberty of choice save as to all' (lines 1–2);
   (ii) 'the supreme authority going in another name and under another title than king . . . has been complied with twice without it' (lines 36–8);
   (iii) 'I am ready to serve not as a king, but as a constable' (lines 50–1);
   (iv) 'God has seemed providentially not only to strike at the family but at the name' (lines 61–3);
   (v) 'I think the government doth consist of very excellent parts in all but that one thing' (lines 80–2).

(*b*)
   The Humble Petition and Advice, 25 May 1657 To his Highness the Lord Protector. . . .

We, the knights, citizens and burgesses in this present parliament assembled . . . have judged it a duty incumbent upon us to present
5 and declare these our most just and necessary desires to your Highness.

1. That your Highness will be pleased, by and under the name and style of Lord Protector of the Commonwealth of England, Scotland and Ireland, and the dominions and territories thereunto belonging, to hold and exercise the office of chief magistrate of these nations. . . . That your Highness will be pleased during your lifetime to appoint and declare the person who shall immediately after your death succeed you in the government of these nations.

2. That your Highness will for the future be pleased to call parliaments consisting of two Houses . . . once in three years at furthest, or oftener, as the affairs of the nations shall require. . . .

3. That . . . those persons who are legally chosen by a free election of the people to serve in parliament may not be excluded from sitting in parliament to do their duties, but by judgment and consent of that House whereof they are members.

4. [Concerns those debarred from voting and being elected to parliament.]

5. That your Highness will consent that none be called to sit and vote in the Other House but such as are not disabled . . . being such as shall be nominated by your Highness and approved by this House. . . .

6. That in all other particulars which concern the calling and holding of parliaments, your Highness will be pleased that the laws and statutes of the land be observed and kept, and that no laws be altered, suspended, abrogated or repealed, or new law made, but by act of parliament.

7. And to the end that there may be a constant revenue for support of the government, and for the safety and defence of these nations by sea and land, we declare our willingness to settle forthwith a yearly revenue of £1,300,000, whereof £1,000,000 for the navy and army, and £300,000 for the support of the government, and no part thereof to be raised by a land-tax, and this not be altered without the consent of the three estates in parliament . . . and do pray your Highness that it be enacted and declared that no charge be laid, nor person be compelled to contribute to any gift, loan, benevolence, tax, tallage, aid or any other like charge, without common consent by act of parliament, which is a freedom the people of these nations ought by the laws to inherit.

8. That none may be admitted to the Privy Council of your Highness or successors, but such as are of known piety and undoubted affection to the rights of these nations, and a just Christian liberty in matters of religion, nor without consent of the Council to be afterwards approved by both Houses of Parliament, and shall not afterwards be removed but by consent of parliament, but may in the intervals of parliament be suspended from the exercise of his place by your Highness, by your successors and the Council, for just cause. . . . And that the standing forces of this Commonwealth shall be disposed of by the chief magistrate by the

consent of both Houses of Parliament, the parliament sitting, and
55 in the intervals of parliament by the chief magistrate by the advice
of the Council; and also that your Highness and successors will be
pleased to exercise your government over these nations by the
advice of your Council.

9. And that the chancellor, keeper or commissioners of the Great
60 Seal of England, the treasurer, or commissioners of the treasury,
the admiral . . . the chief justices of both the Benches, and the chief
baron . . . [and certain officers in Scotland and Ireland] shall be
approved by both Houses of Parliament.

10. And whereas your Highness, out of your zeal to the glory of
65 God and the propagation of the gospel of the Lord Jesus Christ,
hath been pleased to encourage a godly ministry in these nations,
we earnestly desire that such as do openly revile them or their
assemblies, or disturb them in the worship and service of God, to
the dishonour of God, scandal of good men, or breach of the peace,
70 may be punished according to law, and where the laws are defective,
that your Highness will give consent to such laws as shall be made
in that behalf.

11. That the true Protestant Christian religion, as it is contained
in the holy scriptures of the Old and New Testament, and no
75 other, be held forth and asserted for the public profession of these
nations; and that a confession of faith, to be agreed by your
Highness and the parliament, according to the rule and warrant of
the scriptures, be asserted, held forth and recommended to the
people of these nations, that none may be suffered or permitted by
80 opprobrious words or writing maliciously or contemptuously to
revile or reproach the Confession of Faith to be agreed upon as
aforesaid. And such who profess faith in . . . [the Trinity and
acknowledge the scriptures as the word of God] and shall in other
things differ in doctrine, worship or discipline from the public
85 profession held forth, endeavours shall be used to convince them
by sound doctrine and the example of a good conversation, but
they may not be compelled thereto by penalties, nor restrained
from their profession, but protected from all injury and molestation
in the profession of the faith, and exercise of their religion, whilst
90 they abuse not this liberty to the civil injury of others or the
disturbance of the public peace; so that this liberty be not extended
to popery or prelacy, or to the countenancing such who publish
horrid blasphemies, or practise to hold forth licentiousness or
profaneness under the profession of Christ. . . .

Kenyon (ed.), *Stuart Constitution* (1986), pp 324–9

Questions

a Examine the respective powers of the executive and legislature under this constitution.

b How far do these powers differ from those under the Instrument of Government?

c How tolerant were the religious clauses of the Humble Petition and Advice, compared with the Instrument of Government?

d Compare and contrast Cromwell's powers under this constitution with those monarchical powers theoretically enjoyed by Charles I.

IX The End of the Experiment, 1658–1660

1 The Protectorate of Richard Cromwell, September 1658– April 1659

Richard Cromwell's accession was accomplished with the minimum of disruption and won immediate acceptance from the senior army officers and a large part of the political nation. The calm, however, was to be short-lived. As Monck hinted at in his letter of advice (document A) a lot would depend on how shrewdly Richard handled the army's manifest grievances. The first stirrings of unrest concerned the commissioning of officers and the position of Fleetwood as commander in chief of the army (document B,a). Richard's speech to the army officers of 18 October (document B,b) did something to placate unrest, and by the time of the Venetian envoy's letter of 8 November (document B,c) a compromise settlement was within reach. Discontent was soon to be (in Thurloe's phrase) 'skinned over' but it was to prove an uneasy truce. Time, moreover, was not on Richard's side.

In these circumstances, from the Protector's viewpoint the meeting of Parliament was a necessity. Richard had been anxious in late October to have Parliament recalled but it was not until 3 December that the Council acted. It was probably at this meeting that the Privy Council decided to abandon the electoral reforms embodied in the Instrument of Government and return to the old constituencies of pre-Revolutionary times, although the Scottish and Irish constituencies were retained. If the government thought that by doing this the 'Court' interest would be strengthened it was sadly mistaken, for many seats were keenly contested and opportunities for electoral rigging were limited. The new House of 549 MPs – the largest Commons yet convened – proved troublesome to manage. All the most effective official spokesmen had already been elevated to the Upper House by Oliver Cromwell and those that remained in the new Commons were vastly outnumbered by gentry and urban leaders, many of whom had never sat in Parliament before. More ominous for Richard was the return of prominent republican opponents – the 'Commonwealthsmen' – a coalition of anti-Cromwellians rather than a unified party, intent on asserting their right to redefine the constitution. They, too, were a minority but it was easy for them to filibuster the House and thereby incapacitate the government. Such wrecking tactics were potentially disastrous for the Protectorate: the unpaid soldiery, some 40 weeks in arrears, could not be restrained indefinitely. These procedural devices were well demonstrated in the early February debates over Thurloe's Bill for parliamentary recognition of Richard's 'just right to succeed in the government'. The Bill had collapsed in deadlock by the time of Barwick's letter to Hyde of 16 February (document C,b), although within a few days the House had recognised Richard's control of the armed forces. This vote, together with the failure of both the petition of grievances (which had prompted Oliver to dissolve his second Parliament) and another army remonstrance scotched by Richard personally, suggests that the tide was beginning to turn in the Protector's favour.

The fate of the Protectorate, however, was to be decided outside Parliament. Although the republicans might eventually be outvoted in the House, they could make common cause with both the army officers and the extreme sectaries outside it, a combination which Oliver had rightly feared and prevented but one that his son was unable to resist. The republicans and their allies proceeded to do this in a propaganda offensive in February and early March, when a spate of tracts in favour of the 'Good Old Cause' were published. By the end of March, when there was a lull in the campaign, the fate of the Protectorate hung in the balance. The Protector was still supported by a majority in Parliament and the senior army officers had not risen against him, but the junior officers were beginning to stir and this was to prove decisive in determining the allegiance of Fleetwood, Desborough and other senior commanders, without whose support Richard could not stay in power. The conservative outlook of many MPs, whose anti-militarism was apparent in numerous Commons debates in these weeks, served to inflame the temper of the junior officers. Wrangles over the recognition of the Upper House (denounced for the number of officers it contained), the release of political prisoners and the legality of the Commonwealth, also prevented the Houses from making financial provision for the soldiers' arrears. Richard's stock, moreover, was lowered by his defence of his subordinates, Commissary General Whalley and Colonel Ingoldsby, against 'godly' officers. For in the heady days of March and April many saw the crisis as a fight between God's people and his enemies. In such an atmosphere Fleetwood and Desborough could not resist the pressure on them to desert their kinsman and master, and in late March they made two fatal moves: they made overtures to the republicans, and they persuaded Richard to sanction a General Council of Officers. Unwittingly, by doing this they unleashed forces they were unable to control, as the documents in section D explain. There was to be no accommodation like the previous November, and the senior army advisers could do no other than force Richard, deserted by many of his troops, to dissolve a Parliament which (on 21 April) was showing a strong inclination to follow the vote of the City militia and place the armed forces under the joint control of Protector and Parliament. The Protector, by now bereft of an increasingly favourable Parliament and (in Major Nehemiah Bourne's words) 'having not lost only the heart but the name of an army' was powerless to prevent the General Council of Officers and the Commonwealthsmen taking charge of the nation's affairs. The grandees of Wallingford House had been unable to redeem their pledge to save him.

A   The Accession of Richard Cromwell: The Advice of George Monck

I desire . . . you will acquaint his Highness that it is my humble advice to him that the first beginning of his administration of government be at the service of God; and in order thereunto, that before or at the same instant he summons a parliament he also calls
5   together an assembly of godly divines to agree upon some way of union and accommodation, that we may have unity in things necessary, liberty in things unnecessary, and charity in all; which will put a stop to that progress of blasphemy and profaneness that I fear is too frequent in many places by the great extent of
10   toleration. . . . And for a preparation to this great work, it will be good for his Highness to countenance and favour some of the gravest sort of moderate presbyterian divines. . . .
        The calling a parliament will require much consideration, and the House of Lords, as a great part thereof, will not take up the
15   least care of his Highness. Concerning which, in my opinion, it may be fit to summon the most prudent of the old lords, that have been faithful, and some of the leading gentry in the several counties. . . .
        The great debts upon the nation will oblige his Highness to
20   retrench, as much as may be with safety, the charge of the armies and navy. To which I shall humbly offer that as to Ireland, all the single companies there may be disbanded, which (if I am not misinformed) are officered by persons not of the best affections to his Highness' interests. And as to the armies in England, Scotland,
25   and Ireland, in general a great expense may be saved if they be put two regiments into one, whereby his Highness may be freed from some insolent spirits that may not be very safe to be continued. And this action would be much pleasing to the best men in the nation, who were not so free to a hearty conjunction with his
30   Highness' father because they conceived the army in hands they

could not trust. . . . I am not able at this distance to say so much
as I could of the navy, as when I was more conversant in their
affairs; but I find by inquiry many of those brave men that engaged
their lives in the Dutch war out of employment, which may be of
35 ill consequence to his Highness' service if ever occasion be to make
a naval war. . . .

> A Collection of the State Papers of John Thurloe, (ed.) Thomas
> Birch (7 vols London, 1742), VII, p 387, Monck to Thurloe,
> n.d.

Questions

a Comment on the state of the nation at this time.
b What does the letter reveal about Monck's religious and political
views?
c How good is Monck's advice? To what extent did Richard
follow it?
d Comment on:
(i) 'that progress of blasphemy and profaneness that . . . is too
frequent in many places by the great extent of toleration
(lines 8–10);
(ii) 'the best men in the nation, who were not so free to a hearty
conjunction with his Highness' father' (lines 28–30);
(iii) I find . . . many of those brave men that engaged their
lives in the Dutch war out of employment' (lines 33–4).

B Unrest in the Army, Autumn 1658

(*a*)
In spite of the expressions of the army through Lieutenant-General
Fleetwood and the address presented by a number of officers,
promising complete submission to his Highness and a determination
to defend him against all comers, for some days past ill feeling and
5 disputes seem to have arisen between the Protector and some of
the troops, out of which evil consequences might easily arise,
capable of upsetting the present state of affairs and of bringing
about changes prejudicial to the government. On some colonelcy
falling vacant the Protector, who claims also to have succeeded his
10 father as generalissimo of all the forces, without which his other
office is worth little or nothing, granted it to Mountagu, who
commands the Channel squadron. The officers of the army took
exception to this, especially some who have claims to the post,
saying that it was not proper to give land appointments to naval
15 men. Some of them went to the Protector and expressed their

views in a manner not altogether seemly, intimating their intention to have Fleetwood as their generalissimo, and that his Highness ought not to make any sort of military appointment without a council of war. Recognising that these people were all Anabaptists,
20 that is to say opponents rather than supporters of the present government, and suspecting that they had been put forward by others of the same way of thinking, in whom the army abounds, the Protector tried to answer soberly. But he could not refrain from making his answer very sharp. . . . The leaders subsequently
25 met again and were divided, some being for the Protector and others for Fleetwood, and in two different places they debated whether they should yield or uphold their pretensions. As the majority of them were for the Protector it seems most probable that they will prevail and that everything will be decided in his
30 favour. But it is a very nasty business in which there are some ugly features, especially as on Fleetwood's side there is the disgraced Lambert, who is secretly stirring up those who seem discontented. Nothing, therefore, can be predicted as yet. . . .

> *Calendar of State Papers Venetian*, XXXI, pp 254 ff., letter
> 25 Oct. 1658

(*b*)
. . . If I should trust it to any one person or more to fill up the
35 vacancies of the army, otherwise than it is in the Petition and Advice . . . I should therein break my trust, and do otherwise than the parliament intended. . . . To advise with others, whose experience of men and things hath given them an advantage in this respect, is most necessary; and within a few days after my father's
40 death, I did call some of the chief of the army and told them that in filling up of vacancies from time to time in the army, I intended to advise with them, and this is still my intention. . . . But to give it out of my own hands quite, or to place it in such manner that I shall exercise no more of my own judgement, than if I had parted
45 with it, that I cannot do with a good conscience. . . .

There hath been also some discourse about a commander in chief. You know how that stands in the Petition and Advice, which I must make my rule in my government. . . . And though I am not obliged to have any such person besides myself to command
50 all the forces, yet I have made one; that is, I have made my brother Fleetwood lieutenant-general of all the army, and so by consequence commander in chief. . . . And as for the fears, which are of putting anybody over his head, they are groundless and needless jealousies cast into men's minds. . . .

> *Thurloe*, VII, pp 447 ff., Richard Cromwell's speech to the
> army officers, 18 Oct. 1658

(c)

55   . . . Although the conclusion of the meeting of the army officers
has not yet appeared, it seems probable that no disturbance will
result therefrom, as by procrastinating, the Protector, aided by his
representations and threats, has succeeded in forcing the malcontents
to waive their opinions, and as these were by no means good, they
60   could only generate evil consequences. These meetings, which used
to be daily, are now only held once a week, and since it seems that
they do not now speak with so much passion on the question of
the generalship, there is good reason to suppose that they are not
disinclined to let it lapse, and so, for this time, the industry and
65   vigilance of the Protector will have prevailed over the malice and
insolence of the officers. The payment made to the army recently
may easily have contributed much to this momentous change in
the feelings of the malcontents, aided, no doubt, by a resolution
lately passed in the Council to pay the troops all that is due to
70   them, and to make arrangements that they shall receive in the
future what is due to them without the slightest difficulty or delay.
Since this change became noticeable they do not speak so freely
about the Protector's brother Henry coming from Ireland, and this
may be abandoned altogether. . . .

> *Calendar of State Papers Venetian*, XXXI, p 259, letter 8 Nov.
> 1658

Questions

a   Why was the army so divided at this time?
b   What issues concerned the army officers? How were they
    resolved?
c   What do the passages reveal about Richard's position *vis-à-vis*
    the army?
d   Comment on:
    (i)   'these people were all Anabaptists . . . in whom the army
          abounds' (lines 19–22);
    (ii) 'the disgraced Lambert, who is secretly stirring up those
          who seem discontented' (lines 31–2);
    (iii) 'otherwise than it is in the Petition and Advice' (lines 35–
          6).

C   Proceedings in Parliament, February 1658

The proceedings at Westminster are so full of distraction that it is
probable they will end in confusion. For the one party thinks the
protectorists cannot stand and the other that the commonwealth
cannot rise, and those that are indifferent men hope both may be

5   true and then the conclusion will be easy to foresee and foretell.

Since their first convention, the two Houses have never owned one the other. Those they call Lords meet and adjourn and consult about making a catechism and make speeches against plays and the common prayer book. But all mens eyes are upon the Commons 10 . . . [who] look upon it [the Lords] as a personal privilege of the last Protector. To prevent this mischief, the Protector's party brought in a bill [on] January 31st for a recognition of the Protector, wherein were some comprehensive phrases for the other House, the militia and negative voices; but now that it comes to scanning, 15 it finds no small opposition. From their first meeting the Commons have consisted of two extreme parties (one for the Protector, the other for a Commonwealth) and a moderate party between both which being more or less moderate, as occasion serves are able to cast the scales on which side they please. And this makes the 20 foresight of things very obscure, though most men think it will end in a titular protector without either militia or negative voice, if he be so tame as to submit to it. The republicans are the lesser party but are all speakers, zealous, diligent, and have the better cause, admitting those common principles (which are not yet 25 exploded) by which they destroyed monarchy in the Long Parliament. And yet the other can outvote them when they please. . . .

The great contest hath been, and still is, concerning the recognition, etc. After 7 days debate (all other business set apart) they came to a vote on Monday night at 10 a clock that this protector 30 shall be chief magistrate, with such powers and limitations as they shall agree upon, yet so as this vote shall signify nothing till they come to that agreement. . . . There are 2 or 3 difficult questions to be decided before the previous vote (as they call it) can take effect, concerning the militia, negative voice, and the other House, 35 wherein the moderate party are not so zealous as they were to have the government continue in the same frame they found it. And if some of the most considerable persons of the other House could but get the House established, they would put hard to lodge the militia and negative voice in that House, which perhaps in time 40 they would have consist wholly (as it doth for the most part) of the chief officers of the army.

Since the previous vote on Monday night that bill hath slept, and the protectorists are willing it should do so for some time, that the House may slide on into other business that may require a bill 45 to be passed, on purpose that by signing of it the Protector may take possession of his chief magistracy according to the previous vote. But the difficulty is the Commons will not own the other House, and the Protector cannot well sign anything without passing both Houses, though otherwise the temper of some leading men 50 in the other House begins already to show itself to be such as he could wish he were fairly rid of them, for the republicans reckon

of 12 colonels (now in command) that will be for them, and 6 of
them at least are of that House. If this petition of the army goes
on, the House will not signify much after a while. The Protector
55 already relies upon the great officers of the army, and the republicans
on the under officers more than upon the votes of either party. But
it is thought the Protector will be mistaken in some of those he
relies upon, if the other party appears any whit considerable. Monck
hath given him a caution already to carry fair with the parliament,
60 for he finds some reason to suspect his army will divide upon these
matters. And I am told by one of the House, he verily believes
they will shatter all to pieces when the point of the militia comes
to be debated, for though the last vote was carried 3 to one, yet he
thinks the Protector will never get more as to the militia than to
65 be such a general as must be accountable to the Parliament. . . .

Thurloe, VII, pp 615–16, Barwick to Hyde, 16 Feb. 1658
'late at night'.

Questions

a   How were the parties in the Commons aligned? What was the
temper of the majority of MPs?
b   Why, according to Barwick, was the Bill of Recognition brought
in? What problems did this occasion? Why were the government
supporters eventually content that it should 'sleep'?
c   What had happened to the Upper House since the king's
execution? What was its constitutional position at this time and
how good was its relationship with the Commons?
d   How prescient was Barwick's letter?

D   The Fall of the Protectorate

(*a*)
About noon, Colonel Desborough went to Mr. Richard Cromwell
at Whitehall and told him that if he would dissolve his parliament
the officers would take care of him, but that if he refused so to do,
they would do it without him and leave him to shift for himself.
5   Having taken a little time to consider of it, and finding no other
way left to do better, he consented to what was demanded. This
great alteration was made with so little noise that very few were
alarmed at it. The next morning the House met. Few knew of the
resolution taken to put a period to them, or, if they did, were
10 unwilling to take notice of it, so that when the Usher of the Black
Rod, who attended the other House, came to let the Serjeant-at-
Arms know that it was the pleasure of the Protector that the House

of Commons should attend him at the other House, many of them
were unwilling to admit the Serjeant into the House to deliver the
15   message. But the Commonwealth party demanded and obtained
that he should give the House an account of what the Gentleman
of the Black Rod had said to him. The Assembly, being under this
confusion, adjourned themselves till eight of the clock, the next
[Monday] morning; but care was taken to prevent their meeting
20   again, by publishing a proclamation declaring them to be dissolved,
by setting a padlock on the door of the House, and by placing a
guard in the Court of Requests, with order to refuse admittance to
all those who should demand it.

> *Memoirs of Edmund Ludlow* (Vevay, 1698) vol II, pp 641-2

(*b*)
Thursday night all the regiments here, both horse and foot, were
25   in arms. That of the late Lord Pride marched into Whitehall without
opposition. His Highness gave orders to Colonel Hacker's and
other regiments to march to Whitehall for the preservation of his
person, but having before received other orders from the Lord
Fleetwood, they with all the rest obeyed his Excellency's rather
30   than those from his Highness. All this was done without seizing
any man's person, shedding a drop of blood, or making the least
confusion in the city and suburbs. Yesterday his Highness signed a
commission to dissolve both Houses. The other House sent the
Black Rod three times to the Commons to meet them for that
35   purpose, but because it was not brought by a member of their
own, they refused to admit thereof by the messenger, against
whom they locked their doors, who thereupon by order of the
other House brake his black rod at the door of the House of
Commons in testimony of their dissolution, which the judges say
40   is good in law, though the Commons have adjourned themselves
till Monday morning. The Council officers met this day debating
what government shall be settled, whether by the Petition and
Advice, the Long Parliament to be recalled, or a new government
constituted.

> *Clarke Papers*, ed. Sir Charles Firth (4 vols, Camden Soc.,
> 1891–1901), III, p 193, Newsletter, 23 April 1659

(*c*)
45   . . . And having been deeply sensible of the great danger the Good
Old Cause and interest of the people of God was in . . . we thought
it a duty incumbent upon us . . . after serious searching of heart
and solemn addresses to the Lord, to meet together and advise
what was our duty in such a day as to the security of the cause.
50   And being convinced that it was our duty to appear for the
preservation thereof, we met in general council, which produced a
petition and representation to his Highness. . . . Which said petition

and representation, being presented by his Highness to the Parliament, produced effects much contrary to the hopes and expectations
55   of the army, for instead of considering of ways and means for
applying remedies to our just desires, it brought forth a vote for a
dissolution of our meetings and dispersing of our officers (though
nothing was done effectually for the breaking of the councils of
the common enemies by sending away the cavaliers out of town),
60   as also another vote requiring an engagement from us, as though
we were not to be trusted as friends. The consideration whereof
produced a stable and fixed resolution in us once again to put our
lives into our hands, and to trust this great undertaking in the
hands of our good God. . . . It was thought fit to rendezvous that
65   part of the army in and near the city, whereupon the parliament
was dissolved. And in further prosecution of our duty, we resolved
upon some heads (at a general council of officers), in order to the
better settling of the discipline and continuing the union of the
army . . . which were unanimously agreed on . . . we have no
70   design in our hearts but the reviving and prosperity of that Good
Cause in all its essentials wherein the interest, liberties, peace and
settlement of these 3 nations is naturally founded. . . .

Ibid, pp 4–6, General Council of Officers to Monck, 3 May
1659 (at Wallingford House)

Questions

a   From these passages, reconstruct in a short account (using your
own words) the events of late April 1659.
b   Which one, of these accounts, is likely to have been the most
accurate? (Give reasons and justify your answer.)
c   The 'Good Old Cause' is mentioned several times in extract c.
What do you understand to be the meaning of this phrase?
d   How convincing is the explanation of their actions given by the
general council of officers?
e   Account for Richard Cromwell's downfall.

2   The Rise and Fall of the Republican Alliance, April–October 1659

After Richard's downfall, effective power passed to the junior army
officers, gathered at St James's, who were in favour of recalling
the Rump. Within a few days the pressure of these captains and
subalterns, aided by a vigorous propaganda campaign from the
Commonwealthsmen, many of whom were now restored to their
old commands, had been sufficient to persuade the General Council

to readmit the purged Parliament, which met on 7 May (documents A,a and b). These changes met with an enthusiastic response from some observers but their optimism was premature as is clear from the Commonwealthsmen's hostile reaction to the key constitutional clause (XIII) in the army officers' petition (document B,a). Even within the Rump itself, as Ludlow points out (document B,b), there was little agreement on how the constitution could be set on a more permanent footing. The nature of power within the state was not the only source of disagreement between the partners of the fragile republican alliance. Friction between the army grandees and the Rump arose over such issues as Richard's pension, the act of indemnity for those who had served the Protectorate and the remodelling of the militia. The threat of the common Royalist enemy, however, prevented an open rupture until after the August risings (documents C,a and b). Thereafter, old wounds on the proper foundation of government, together with some new ones, such as the September engagement to 'this Commonwealth', reopened. This was the background to the trial of strength between the Rumpers and the army officers that on 13 October had the predictable outcome: the second expulsion of the Rump (documents D,a and b).

A Contemporary Accounts of the Formation of the New Regime

(*a*)

The old Speaker Lenthall after some pretended conflicts with himself, and not without execrations, the day before resumed the chair in the House of Commons, with some 50 more confederates, such only as were sworn enemies to kingship. They entered the
5 House from the Painted Chamber, as the beasts did the ark, in couples and fell presently to their scale of votes, whereof the first was to establish their own royalties, to declare themselves the supreme power of the nations, etc. That day Sir George Booth, Sir John Clotworthy, Knightly, Prynne etc., were repulsed from
10 the doors. They sat again yesterday as lords of the Sabbath. This day were met in the House by the former Sir William Waller, Browne, etc., that challenged their right for themselves, and a number more considerable of that pack that would usurp the House to themselves, and indeed they were the chief assertors of the old
15 cause and first interrupted by Oliver's army. Of this party was Mr. William Pierrepoint, who never offered to sit in the House (since Pride's forcible exemption) till this time. This was interpreted a disturbance and caused a sudden adjournment of the House to the afternoon. And against that meeting a troop of horse and halberdiers
20 attended to abet the Rump and repel Mr. Prynne who indeed spoke

very boldly, denying any power of sitting there. Some protestations
may justly be expected from the excluded party. Their fears are
great, and their task far greater. Famous Henry Martin that was
preferred immediately from a gaol to the present old Parliament,
25 penned, by order of the House, letters to the absent king-killing
members to appear in the sudden and so unexpected assembly. All
of them say they return to the House by the hand of God; but
Martin was brought hither (in his own blasphemous phrase) by
both hands. His late Highness Richard, is now a very Dick with
30 them. Jamaica at most (since it was his father's purchase) will be
his reward. The present declaration of the House is for the settlement
of the civil and religious rights against a single person, kings, and
peers. . . .

> Sir George F. Warner (ed.), *The Nicholas Papers*, Camden
> Soc. 3rd series, XXXI (1920), IV, pp 134–5, 'Miles' to
> Nicholas, 9 May

(b)
. . . The militia of the City and many considerable honest persons
35 well affected out of several parts made their address to the general
council of officers, then sitting daily at Wallingford House, and
with unanimous consent declared against touching the late made
government, or new strange Instrument and Advice, and were
zealous to lay it wholly aside, and call the old Parliament (as being
40 the only visible way and means of our settlement and safety).
Besides this all the inferior officers of the army, yea whole regiments
of soldiers gave in their petitions for it, and almost all persons well
affected centered therein (though they had their fears, yet this was
the best that could be found). I know this met with much
45 opposition, and yet at length the providence of God brought it
about by means of a committee of the army, who met a number
of the old parliament men, amongst which Sir Henry Vane and Sir
Arthur Haselrig, our two eminent good instruments for the
accommodating things betwixt them. And accordingly on the 7th
50 May they sat, and their old Speaker in the chair, which was to the
rejoicing of the generality of honest hearts, and the confusion
and astonishment of the enemy. Yea, of all strangers, and the
ambassadors and agents in town, who are scarce come to themselves
to this day, but are filled with wonderment to see such a total
55 subversion of a government, and behold all shops open, tradesmen
in their callings, and not a broken pate, as some of them have
expressed. Yea, and let me tell you, this is no less admirable in the
eyes of the most sober and godly, both within and without the
army, considering what means was used to set all in a flame both
60 in city and country. But all proved ineffectual (the Lord preventing
all such attempts). During the consult[ation]s about the government
to be established you will imagine what spirit ran through the

nation. I shall only mind you again that there was labouring and
endeavouring to patch and amend the broken image (especially by
65 the great ones), but the meaner sort of the officers, together with
the honest people that flocked in to them, carried it clear for this
parliament. Immediately after they were sat, divers of the secluded
members of 1647 endeavoured to press into the House, and
challenged their places, and some small contest was betwixt them
70 and others who had that care and charge under their hands. But at
last they withdrew, seeing what was resolved, that none should sit
but such as were in 48, and had gone along with them in change
of government, in taking of the king and House of Peers, unless
they would take the engagement. . . .
        Clarke Papers, vol III, pp 214–15

Questions

a Compare and contrast the attitudes of the writers of these
   accounts to the new regime.
b Give and account, *in your own words*, of how the new regime
   was established.
c Why was there so much trouble from the excluded party?
d Comment on:
   (i) 'they were the chief assertors of the old cause and first
       interrupted by Oliver's army' (lines 14–15);
   (ii) 'Famous Henry Martin . . . penned by order of the House,
       letters to the absent king–killing members to appear' (lines
       23–6);
   (iii) 'His late Highness . . . is now a very Dick with them' (lines
       29–30);
   (iv) 'But at last they withdrew' to 'unless they would take the
       Engagement' (lines 70–4).

B The Search for a New Constitution

(*a*)
The Humble Petition and Address of the Officers of the Army, to
the Parliament of the Commonwealth of England, etc. . . . we
have judged it our duty to represent what was chiefly and unanimously upon our hearts, when we engaged in that which made way
5 for your return, which we humbly, as becomes us, lay before
you. . . .
VI. That all persons who profess faith in God and the Father, and
in Jesus Christ, his eternal son, the true God, and in the Holy Spirit
God co-equal with the Father and the Son, one God blessed for

10 ever, and do acknowledge the Holy Scriptures, of the Old and
New Testament, to be the revealed or written word or will of
God, shall not be restrained from their profession, but have due
encouragement and equal protection in the profession of their faith,
and exercise of religion, whilst they abuse not this liberty to the
15 civil injury of others, or disturbance of others in their way of
worship. So that this liberty be not extended to popery or prelacy,
nor to such as shall practice or hold forth licentiousness or
profaneness, under the profession of religion, and that all laws,
statutes, ordinances, and clauses in any laws, statutes, or ordinances
20 to the contrary, may be declared null and void. . . .
XIII. That in order to the establishing and securing the peace,
welfare, and freedom of the people of these nations, for the ends
before expressed, the legislative power thereof may be in a
representative of the people, consisting of a House, successively
25 chosen by the people, in such way and manner as this parliament
shall judge meet, and of a select senate, co-ordinate in power, of
able and faithful persons eminent for godliness, and such as continue
adhering to this cause.
XIV. That the administration of the executive power of
30 government may be in a council of state, consisting of a convenient
number of persons, qualified in all respects as aforesaid. . . .
        Hansard, III, pp 1553–5, 13 May 1659

(*b*)
At this time the opinions of men were much divided concerning a
form of government to be established amongst us. The great
officers of the army, as I said before, were for a select standing
35 senate to be joined to the representative of the people. Others
laboured to have the supreme authority to consist of an assembly
chosen by the people, and a council of state chosen by that assembly
to be vested with the executive power, and accountable to that
which should next succeed, at which time the power of the
40 said council should determine. Some were desirous to have a
representative of the people constantly sitting, but changed by a
perpetual rotation. Others proposed that there might be joined to
the popular assembly, a select number of men in the nature of the
Lacedemonian Ephori, who should have a negative in things,
45 wherein the essentials of the government should be concerned,
such as the exclusion of a single person, touching liberty of
conscience, alteration of the constitution, and other things of the
last importance to the state. Some were of opinion that it would
be most conducing to the public happiness if there might be two
50 councils chosen by the people, the one to consist of about three
hundred, and to have the power only of debating and proposing
laws; the other to be in number about one thousand, and to have
the power finally to resolve and determine: every year a third part

of each council to go out, and others to be chosen in their places. For my own part, if I may be permitted to declare my opinion, I could willingly have approved either of the two latter propositions, presuming them to be most likely to preserve our just liberties, and to render us a happy people.

> *Memoirs of Edmund Ludlow*, ed. Sir Charles Firth (2 vols, Oxford, 1894), II, pp 98–9

Questions

a How extensive was the toleration proposed by the army officers?
b Examine the relationship between the executive and the legislature in the army proposals.
c Discuss the other constitutional schemes outlined by Ludlow.
d Explain why this regime found it impossible to obtain a stable constitutional settlement.

C The August Risings: Two Letters

(a)
. . . Saturday last Sir Richard Willis finding the council confirmed their first resolution as to the day (which was with our consent told the Knot by Colonel Panton), grew enraged and having got together 4 or 5 of those were ever against the king's trusts, declares himself thus: I were neither Christian nor Englishman, should I encourage or give way to action, the blood and miseries considered will ensue. When he came to the reasons [that] occasioned this pious preamble, the only one of weight was the harvest, which that it might be one, he has these 3 months as we now hear, decried the undertaking as totally Presbyterian, and the persons [that] carried it on, as rash, vain, giddy people. . . . they envy us, for the success of so considerable a conjunction, and would, now the crabbedness and hazards of this union and association is over, drive us out of England and mount the horse we have broke to their hands. This we would willingly yield to them too, but that we have too many unanswerable reasons to the contrary. The first, the surprises of Bristol and Gloucester will fall to the ground, and these are the pillars of the engagement; the second is, Major-general Browne and the Lord Willoughby and that party which truly is the most considerable I believe, if the whole is not already betrayed, it soon will. And these people have reason to suspect it, since they know how constantly the last king was served so, by soldiers of fortune, and how many towns they had on that account. For this Sir Richard Willis has so incensed them that they will not hear him

25 named, and this some think has made him so malicious. The 3rd
is most people being retired with long expectation and preparation.
And having now received orders to act, if deferred we shall lose
the most, since only by what the Knot give out Davy Walter is
gone out of England, several have sold their horses, many buried
30 their arms, and a general dissatisfaction in all of their acquaintance.
'Tis observable, they sent Colonel Panton with reasons for delay,
he went away satisfied, engaged to act, yet at the same time when
the first resolution was confirmed and told them, they give out,
all is laid aside, and that the Chancellor had persuaded the king to
35 stop his journey. . . . Thus you see how we miserably jest away
kingdoms, and, though we are styled fools, where the honesty or
wisdom of these people lies. That 'tis plain they have for some
time resolved to destroy this vast preparation, I can assure you that
yet none of these gentlemen have looked towards providing either
40 of money, arms or horses. . . .

> The Letter Book of John Viscount Mordaunt, ed. M. Coate,
> Camden Soc, LXIX (1945), pp 31–3, Lord Mordaunt to
> Hartgill Baron, 26 July 1659

(*b*)

. . . Most of the old formed army are withdrawn hence for West
Chester under the command of Lambert and to the west under
Desborough. The licensed pamphlets speak Sir George Booth near
5000 strong in Cheshire, Lancashire and North Wales. Sir Thomas
45 Middleton at Wrexham, a town 8 miles off Chester, proclaimed
the king, and Chirk Castle, his chief residence, is now garrisoned
for the king; though the others [are as] declaretory for the freedom
of parliaments as to the settlement of sacred and civil rights,
and are zealously consecrated to the quarrel by the Presbyterian
50 pulpiteers in those parts. . . . Two troops of the militia in Cheshire
and Lancashire under the command of Colonels Ireland and Brookes
are gone in to Booth. Lambert hath undertaken the expedition
against Booth, and with a train of artillery from Windsor Castle,
and near 4000 horse and foot is now upon his advance that way.
55 His expressions against the caves and presbiters are so insolently
and odiously high that I wish they were as public and [*sic*, as] the
Journals; they would be more serviceable than a declaration. He
swears (by his God) that he will perish or not allow life to any
gentleman engaged, or above 200 l. *per annum* to any of that party
60 or persuasion surviving. And the Rump is now upon forming a
law that the tenants relating to any in present arms against the
state, and [who] shall oppose their landlords, shall enjoy their leases
in fee, the chief rents being made payable to the state, a precedent
dangerous to all estated gentlemen. . . .

> The Nicholas Papers, IV, pp 177–9, Hill to Nicholas, 8 Aug
> 1659

Questions

a   What were the sympathies of these letter writers?
b   What do they reveal of the state of royalism at this time?
c   Outline the arguments, set out in the first letter, for and against delaying the rising.
d   (i) What was planned to happen in the August risings?
    (ii) What actually happened?
    (iii) Why did they fail?
e   Comment on:
    (i) 'finding the council confirmed their first resolution as to the day (which was with our consent told the Knot)' (lines 1–3);
    (ii) 'they envy us for the success of so considerable a conjunction' (lines 11–12);
    (iii) 'the Chancellor had persuaded the king to stop his journey' (lines 34–5).
    (iv) 'And the Rump' to 'all estated gentlemen' (lines 60–4).

D   The Bloodless Coup: 12–13 October 1659

(*a*)

. . . We have been just upon the brink of confusion these two or three days and are yet so little removed from it, as I can hardly give any particular account of our present condition. The parliament carried it very high against the army, both in their act that no
5   money should be levied but by their consent. And by their declaration that the soldiers, though as freemen of England they might petition, yet must still submit unto and acquiesce in their resolutions. And yesterday they came to that height as to vote nine of the most eminent officers out of command, viz: Lambert,
10   Desborough, Cobbet, Berry, Packer, Kelsey, Barrow, Ashfield and Creed. And to give the chief government of the army, under themselves, unto Fleetwood, Monck, Haselrig, Morley, Ludlow, Overton and Watson, whereof three to be a quorum. But the string is like to break with screwing too high; for the army hereabouts
15   inclines to Lambert and his party. Last night some of the parliament continued in the House all night to keep possession with a strong guard of horse and foot. But all this day they and their guard are besieged by the other party. The Speaker was turned back as he was going to the House, and the captain of the lifeguard dismounted
20   in the head of his command, and Major Creed put and received into his place. The City militia were sent to by the parliament but will not stir. And I hear the Lieutenant of the Tower is also for the officers, and that two troops of Okey's regiment are come in, so that of all the forces hereabouts, the parliament has not full two

25   regiments, and perhaps not this neither by this time. What interest
      they may have in Ludlow, Monck or Overton, time will discover,
      the last was vexed to go along with Sir Henry Vane, and he is with
      the officers, and Fleetwood as they say is come in also. We are yet
      at a gaze, what government we shall have, or what we may
30   prognostic from this resolution. . . .

> The Letter Book of. . . . Mordaunt, pp 58–61, John Barwick
> to the king, 13 Oct 1659

(b)
Parliament dissolved. . . . I heard Haselrig, Morley, Walton was
all night in the House and got in Morley's regiment and Moss's
and some of Okey's horse and Thomson's regiment coming to
them, they barricaded at the palace yards, back and fore, and the
35   army had drawn out a regiment of horse and lineguard and four
regiments of foot. I moved the dealing with both parties to prevent
blood, and went between them and got a meeting of the Council
and the officers at it, and after much debate the Council agreed to
send an order to both parties to withdraw their forces back to their
40   quarters. It pleased God so to bless it as after noon they both
obeyed the order and drew off their forces; and Haselrig and Morley
came to the Council, so did Walton and Scot who had been blocked
up, and so blessed be the Lord that prevented all blood, which was
so near that they were in our place at puisse of pick within one
45   anothers arms, and at another place Morley gave direction to give
fire if Lambert advanced, but Lambert told him he would turn
another way. Both parties eschewed the taking of the first blood,
and the soldiers were unwilling to yoke one with another; and I
think both were content with the order to withdraw, wherein
50   Salwey and I had greatest hand. At night we met at council and
there got knowledge that Lieutenant-General Fleetwood had sent
two companies to the Hall and to the Parliament's door, which
imported the dissolution of the Parliament, as the stopping of the
Speaker's coach in forenoon did, who cried to the soldiers he was
55   their general. The counsellors spake also of dissolving the council
and gave order in things as their letterwill. Every one blamed
another for bringing it to this pass, and some rejoicing they had
done their duty and kept their station 'til cutted off, and others
that they had endeavoured to prevent breaches.

> Diary of Sir Archibald Johnston of Wariston (3 vols, Scottish
> Historical Society, Edinburgh, 1911–40), III, pp 144–5, entry
> for 13 October

Questions

a Reconstruct, in your own words, a short account of the events of 12–13 October 1659.
b What precipitated the Rump's second expulsion?
c Why was the *coup* bloodless?
d 'We are yet at a gaze what government we shall have' (lines 28–9). What type of government succeeded the dissolution of the republican alliance?

3 The Breaking of the Army, October–December 1659

The Rump's second suspension was less prolonged than the first – just over two months, in fact, from Thursday 13 October to Monday 26 December 1659. Within this period the general council of officers, aided initially by a Council of State, assumed direct control of government. The officers (as they wrote to Monck on 20 October) wanted to 'endeavour such a settlement in the government as that the affair of the Commonwealth may be steadily and prudently managed', but were unable to fulfil this aim. Interim arrangements were made for the carrying on of government – Fleetwood was acknowledged to be commander-in-chief, and a ruling Committee of Safety was established by ten officers and councillors – but this activity concealed deep fissures within the state (documents A). The Committee of Safety of twenty-three members (like the Jewish Sanhedrin although the full number never attended) was bitterly divided between the few Rumpers who consented to serve and the sectarian army officers. The long-term constitutional settlement, moreover, proved as elusive as ever; Vane's model of government, for example, was bitterly opposed by Johnston in the subcommittee on the constitution. Given such hostility to these and other visionary schemes, it is not surprising that there was no effective settlement.

Neither were the officers able to count on Monck's 'best help and service' as army commander in Scotland, as they had hoped. Indeed, Monck's reaction to the October coup was hostile and decisive. When the news of the Parliament's expulsion reached him on 17 October, he immediately – and without advice – opposed the military usurpation. Within days he had publicly declared for the Rump (document A,a), secured the loyalty of most of his army and moved his troops towards the border. At this time and in the coming weeks, he also sent a stream of letters to England explaining and justifying his conduct. Whatever Monck's motives – and we can glimpse something of them from the letters printed here (documents A,a–d) his army colleagues in London were astounded at his stance: the more so because of his previous support for the ejection of parliaments in 1653, 1654 and April 1659. Lambert begged him to consider the 'mischiefs [that] must fall upon this Commonwealth [if] that the armies thereof [be] divided and come to blows amongst themselves', and correctly prophesied that Monck's opposition would play into the hands of 'the king's party' in both kingdoms. Nevertheless, Monck refused to be deflected from his course, and the council of officers in London was compelled to send a force to the north, under Lambert's command, to meet Monck's army. Concurrently, an attempt was made to deflect Monck by negotiation; but the provisional treaty that was drafted proved unacceptable and the delay only served Monck's purposes. For the longer the delay the stronger the country's opposition to the council of officers became, and the greater the chance of paralysis among the members of Lambert's unpaid and ill-equipped force.

This is exactly what happened: England in late 1659 was drifting into anarchy. As early as 3 November a far-sighted news writer gave Monck an account of the chaotic state of the capital, a message which was repeated even more vividly nine days later. These gloomy reports were confirmed in subsequent weeks by Monck's other correspondents and by Royalist letter writers, as well as being privately recorded by diarists such as Thomas Rugg (document C). One of the earliest signs of unrest in London came from the City apprentices, who had been so prominent in the disturbances of the 1640s, and who began to petition in mid November for the restoration of Parliament and the preservation of the national ministry. The hostile republicans, joined by their supporters in the army, were also plotting in secret and mounting an extensive propaganda campaign so that the government was forced to act against their leader, Haselrig, and expel him from London. This move backfired for he and his colleagues were able to persuade sympathetic county leaders to enforce a tax strike to help starve the army into submission. Furthermore, they were instrumental in organising the defection of the Portsmouth garrison. The breaking of this news in the capital on 5 December coincided with the apprentices' riot, after the Committee of Safety had attempted to prevent the presentation of their petition to the Common Council. Thereafter violence in the City escalated – a plot to take the Tower was narrowly foiled – and business came almost to a standstill. And on the very day (13 December) that the council of officers belatedly declared for a free Parliament, the fleet mutinied and then sailed into the Thames and blocked the river. In the next few days the isolation of the government – from the newly elected common council (on 21 December), most of the London citizens and much of the army – was completed. In such circumstances there was no escape for the officers of the council when they finally dispersed to their regiments, for many units had already deserted their cause.

By early January this fate had even befallen Lambert's retreating force. As Johnston confided to his diary on 17 December, the army officers had revealed their 'unfitness to manage such a business as government', a comment repeated with more venom a week later when he railed furiously against them. Even in the eyes of its foremost civilian official, the council of officers had forfeited its right to rule.

A Two Diary Accounts of the New Government

(a)

17 October. I find first by Sir Henry Vane that he was loath that I should continue in the chair, and thereafter Whitelocke was chosen. . . . I was with Sir Henry Vane and Salwey and Sir James Harrington in at Sir Arthur Haselrig in his chamber, where they
5   fell out in mutual challenges and expressions of jealousies. At council Fleetwood proposed that four of the council might speak with four officers of the army. I heard privately Sir Henry Vane had been with Lord Lambert. . . . After this I was chosen one of the five for the council, Sir Henry Vane, Major Salwey, Whitelocke,
10   Sir James Harrington and I to meet and confer with my Lord Fleetwood, Lambert, Desborough, Berry and Sydenham about the sitting of the council and carrying on affairs of this Com- monwealth. . . . We found they would not hear to re-admit the parliament again, would have the council engaging with them and
15   would appoint a new government. . . .
27 October . . . This day they were about their Declaration. . . . Sir Henry Vane and Major Salwey and I had much debate about the present dispensation, Sir Henry Vane looking on it as an introduction to the glorious appearance of the Kingdom of God,
20   and so calling much for faith and expectation of its approach; I, looking to the ordinary rules in the word, apprehending it looked judgementally to the nation for their provocations; and Salwey making use of both and inclining more [nor?] to my mind nor to Sir Henry Vane. . . .
25   28 October. Committee of Safety. . . . Their divisions are like to plunge us all in blood. . . . We met and the powers were delivered to us and we fell in a debate. . . .
1 November . . . I saw Sir Henry Vane's draft of the government and disliked the foundation of it and toleration in it, and had a
30   debate with Salwey, Whitelocke and Ludlow on it; and beyond my expectation I saw my name among that sub-committee appointed about it. . . .
         Diary of . . . Johnston of Wariston, III, pp 145 ff

(b)

17 [October]. They [the council of officers] suspended from their
commands the officers of the army who appeared against them.
35　They nominated a committee of ten of the council of state,
Fleetwood, Lambert, Whitelocke, Vane, Desborough, Harrington,
Sydenham, Berry, Salwey, and Wareston, to consider of fit ways
to carry on the affairs and government. At a general council of
officers, they agreed upon articles of war; they declared Fleetwood
40　to be commander-in-chief of all the forces, and Lambert to be
major general of the forces in England and Scotland and this
discontented Monck. They appointed Fleetwood, Lambert, Vane,
Desborough, Ludlow, and Berry, to be a committee to nominate
officers of the army; and they kept a day of humiliation in Whitehall
45　chapel. . . .
27. The general council of officers agreed to call the new council
the committee of safety; and that letters should be sent to the several
members of it, to undertake the trust. . . . I was in some perplexity
what to do upon this letter, and had much discourse with my
50　friends about it. Desborough and some other great officers of the
army, and actors in this business, came to me, and made it their
earnest request to me to undertake this trust, and told me that some
of this committee, as Vane, Salwey, and others, had a design to
overthrow magistracy, ministry, and the law; and that, to be a
55　balance to them, they had chosen me and some others to oppose
this design, and to support and preserve the laws, magistracy, and
ministry in these nations. That they knew their abilities to do it,
and depended much upon them; and that if I should deny to
undertake this charge, it would much trouble the general council
60　of officers, and be of great prejudice to the intended settlement. . . .
28. The committee of safety were to meet; I had revolved in my
mind the present state of affairs, that there was no visible authority
or power for government at this time but that of the army; that if
some legal authority were not agreed upon and settled, the army
65　would probably take it into their hands, and govern by the sword,
or set up some form prejudicial to the rights and liberties of the
people, and for the particular advantage and interest of the soldiery
more than would be convenient. That I knowing the purpose of
Vane and others to be such, as to the lessening of the power of the
70　laws, and so to change them and the magistracy, ministry, and
government of the nation, as might be of dangerous consequence to
the peace and rights of my country: to prevent which, and to keep
things in a better order and form, I might be instrumental in this
employment. Upon these and the like grounds, as also be the
75　engagement of divers of the committee to join with me therein, I
was persuaded to undertake it, and did meet with them at the place
appointed; where I was received by them with all respect and civility.
1 [November]. The committee of safety appointed Fleetwood,

Vane, Ludlow, Salwey, and Tichburn a committee, to consider of
80   a form of government for the three nations, as a commonwealth,
and to present it to the committee of safety. . . .
        Whitelocke's Memorials, IV, pp 365–9

Questions

a   Compare and contrast these diary entries.
b   What are their respective strengths and weaknesses as sources
     for the historian?
c   What do they reveal about the two diarists?
d   What do they tell you about the formation of the new
     government?

B Monck's Reaction in Scotland

(*a*)
That understanding that the Parliament is broken up by some
officers, who . . . his Lordship cannot conceive otherwise but their
attempting an action of so great concernment against the privileges
85   of the nation can be to no other end than setting up themselves;
and therefore the officers here have considered of it, and his lordship
hath thought fit to write to my Lord Fleetwood and my Lord
Lambert to desire them that the parliament may be called to sit
again, that the country may not lose their privileges, and to keep
90   us from running into confusion. What effect those letters will have
we know not, but we are resolved, all on this side the water, to
stand for the government by the parliament without a king,
kingship, single person, or House of Lords, and for the liberties of
the people and a godly ministry. . . .
        Clarke Papers, vol iv, p 66, letter to Capt. Coulson, n.d.
        c.20 Oct 1659

(*b*)
95   . . . we say and unanimously declare that the armies of these
nations, whereof we are a part, were raised by authority of the
present parliament for the defence of our religion, the laws and
liberties of our nation, and privileges of parliament. From the
authority [of Parliament] we received our commissions; to the
100   defence thereof we are by sundry vows and engagements obliged,
some of them of a very late date. Your late petition to them,
and solemn acceptance of commissions from them, are sufficient
acknowledgement that to them belongeth the right of making a
commander-in-chief and other subordinate officers, and therefore
105   for us to usurp it were a manifest breach of their acknowledged

privilege, and a direct way to subject the nation under an arbitrary and tyrannous government, which is the abhorring of our soldiers, and against which we have hitherto with so happy success borne arms. . . . And although the tie of conscience and duty obliges us
110 to dissent from you . . . as the state of affairs now stands, yet we solemnly profess that such our dissent doth not proceed from any disrespect we bear to the persons mentioned in your agreement. We bear great honour and affection to most of them as persons that have eminently affected the rights of their country, countenanced
115 godliness, and been blessed of God in so doing. . . .

Ibid, pp 75–6, Monck to the officers at Whitehall, n.d., c. 24 Oct 1659

(c)
. . . I bless God the same impression hath been upon the hearts of God's people here, with ours, wholly to pray and labour for a peaceable accommodation; and all that I have yet done or shall do shall be directed to that end, as you have seen by our printed
120 papers. But. . . . I beseech you put your souls in my soul's stead, and then judge. Should I sit still in such a day as this is? Am I not to give an account to the nation – nay, to the great God? What shall I answer for all vows and engagement[s], nay, for all the blood of all the saints that hath been in the prosecution of this
125 cause? You cannot but remember our late address; and should we desert the parliament, when they have done nothing this 2nd session but what will recommend them to posterity, asserting our rights as men and Christians? And I beseech, what can be the issue of this contempt of authority but an arbitrary government by the sword,
130 to enslave the consciences, laws, and estates of the people of these nations to the lusts of a few ambitious persons? What danger are [the] churches of Jesus Christ in, when protected by those who, by breach of promises and engagements, manifest no conscience of God, what ever their profession be! How frequently and very
135 lately I have urged my dismission the parliament can witness, to avoid the falling of this ruin in my hand. But since it hath pleased God to call me to this work, I will not repine, being ready to do and to suffer, if it be his pleasure. . . .

Ibid, pp 90–1, Monck's letter, Edinburgh, 3 Nov 1659

(d)
Having a call from God and his people to march into England, to
140 assert and maintain the liberty and being of parliaments, our ancient constitution, and therein the freedom and rights of the people of these three nations from arbitrary and tyrannical usurpations upon their consciences, persons, and estates, and for a godly ministry, I do therefore expect from you the nobility, gentlemen, sheriff, and
145 the rest of the justices of peace, and each one of you, that you do

preserve the peace of the Commonwealth in the shire. And I do hereby authorize you to suppress all tumults, stirrings, and unlawful assemblies, and that you hold no correspondency with any of Charles Stuart's party or adherents, but apprehend any such as shall make any disturbance, and send them into the next garrison. And [I] do further desire you to countenance and encourage the godly ministry, and all that truly fear God in the land. And that you continue faithful to own and assert the interest of parliamentary government in the several places and stations. . . .

150

Ibid, p 115, Monck's speech, Edinburgh, 15 Nov 1659

Questions

a Why did Monck support the Rump this time after having acquiesced in the dissolution of parliaments in 1653, 1654 and April 1659?
b Examine Monck's attitude towards his former colleagues.
c Explain Monck's religious views.
d How do you reconcile Monck's vehement anti–Royalist statements with his subsequent conduct in 1660?
e How sincere were Monck's motives?

C The Collapse of Order in London: The Journal of Thomas Rugg

. . . although the apprentices did go under the name of discontenters, they were very much unquiet for that their trading began daily to decay and that many young men that were newly out of their times, these met and were often discoursing of these times that they had now lived to see. These young men began, with the help of better head pieces to frame a petition, and in a very little time they had got about three or four thousand hands to this petition, which they always intended to present to the Lord Mayor and the Court of Aldermen and Common Council [of] London at Guild Hall; and this was the intention of these discontented young men of London. There was at this time a fast kept and observed in the City of London, which was very strictly kept and observed; but the night following the apprentices and others that were weary of the soldiers and their laws and manners and also their company in the City, which was then indifferent full of them, and these now little regarding the Committee of Safety, which was then called shifty, these persons gave the soldiery many affronts, although the army had several guards in London. . . .

The 16th day of this month [November] there came forth a very

5

10

15

20   large remonstrance, called The Remonstrance and Protestation of
the well-affected people of the cities of London and Westminster,
and other the cities and places within the Commonwealth of
England, against those officers of the army who put force upon
and interrupted the parliament the 13 October, and against all
25   pretended power or authority that they have or shall set up to
rule or govern this Commonwealth that [was] established by
parliament. . . . It was signed by above four hundred and fifty
hands, by men of quality. . . .
Then on the fifth day of December the apprentices and other
30   discontented young men did, as well as [they] could, gather
themselves together, for that over night they had contrived a rising
in the morning, if possible; for they were now quite weary of the
soldiery, which they knew well enough. In the morning the
apprentices began to appear in a disorderly manner, but with a
35   foot-ball, thinking that there would appear a party in arms for
them; for they knew where to have arms, but still they wanted a
head to lead them on [and had] but here and there a pocket pistol.
Now the Committee of Safety, having intelligence that in London
they had a great mind to be rid of the soldiery, they ordered that
40   some regiments of horse and foot should forthwith march into
the City, which accordingly they did, of horse and foot three
thousand. . . . Now in their march into the City there was many
affronts offered and a great many of uncivil actions offered to them
in their march into the City, but especially to Colonel Hewson['s]
45   regiment of foot; they were more abused then any other. He was a
cobbler by his trade, but a very stout man and a very good
commander of foot; but in regard of his former employment and
[what] the apprentices once got into their mouths, they very well
employed their mouths. He had but one eye, but they called him
50   blind cobbler, blind Hewson, and did throw old shoes and old
slippers and turnips tops, brickbats and stones and tiles at him and
his soldiers. He marched through the City to the Royal Exchange,
where he stayed a little space. Then he marched to Guildhall, where
he met with many affronts by the way, so that among the rude
55   multitude there were some [that] did fire a pistol at the soldiers
and some that threw great stones at the soldiers, that did very
much kindle wrath [so] that at last they fired in earnest, and four
or five of the apprentices and others, whereof one was a cobbler,
were killed and others wounded, and some likewise of the army
60   very dangerously wounded. But this action was done contrary to
the orders of the Lord Mayor and Court of Aldermen. Then the
Lord Mayor appeared in this tumultious multitude and made a
short speech, and desired them that they would desist from that
headstrong action acted by them, and told them that this was not
65   the way, but the ready way to destroy the City; and at the last, by
his much entreating, they left and resorted home, although not

well pleased in their minds, for their intention was, if they had had
strength enough, to have beat them quite out of the City. . . .

Now upon better considerations, and finding that there were
70 some of the citizens killed and wounded and such affronts should
be thus acted in the City, the next morning there went divers of
the master citizens to the Lord Mayor and Court of Aldermen,
who were sitting in the Guildhall, in reference to the abuses that
they had so lately received by the soldiery. The Lord Mayor told
75 them that at that time it did not lie in his power to help them, but
that with all speed in a fair way he would, for that a violent way at
this time would but only destroy the City; and that he was very
sensible of the abuse of their just laws, rights and privileges, and
ancient customs that the soldiers had violated so lately. But for all
80 this the promise of the Lord Mayor and Court of Aldermen, the
young men apprentices, their hearts, were so extremely bent with
anger against the soldiers that still they were contriving a way for
to clear the City of these lobsters, as they called the horsemen. . . .

The Diurnal of Thomas Rugg, 1659–61, ed. William L. Sachse
(Camden Soc., vol 91, 1961), pp 9 ff

Questions

a   How good is this source for the historian?
b   Describe and explain the actions of the following groups: (i)
City fathers and officers; (ii) apprentices; (iii) army officers and
soldiers in London.
c   How near to anarchy do you judge London to have been at this
time?